Fighting for Human Rights

In a world that is increasingly disillusioned with formal politics, people are no longer prepared to wait for governments and international institutions to act on human rights concerns. This book identifies civil society activism as a key means of realising human rights and as a new form of politics.

Fighting for Human Rights documents and compares high-profile campaigns to cancel debt in the developing world, ban landmines and set up the International Criminal Court as well as campaigns that focus on democratisation, environmental justice, HIV/AIDS and blood diamonds.

These campaigns aim to establish national and international agreements that will become the basis for processes of monitoring and enforcement. This book asks how this can be done, examines the strategies used, and discusses the crucial issue of how formalisation of agreements can be made a stepping-stone to implementation rather than an end in itself.

This important work is an essential read for everyone interested in the pressing issue of upholding human rights and the assistance that civil society can provide.

Paul Gready is a lecturer at the Institute of Commonwealth Studies, University of London. He has worked for the research department of Amnesty International, a number of human rights organisations in South Africa, and as a human rights consultant.

Fighting for Human Rights

Edited by Paul Gready

Routledge
Taylor & Francis Group

LONDON AND NEW YORK

First published 2004
by Routledge
11 New Fetter Lane, London EC4P 4EE

Simultaneously published in the USA and Canada
by Routledge
29 West 35th Street, New York, NY 10001

Routledge is an imprint of the Taylor & Francis Group

Typeset in Sabon by Exe Valley Dataset Ltd, Exeter, Devon
Printed and bound in Great Britain by The Cromwell Press, Trowbridge, Wiltshire

British Library Cataloguing in Publication Data
A catalogue record for this book is available from the British Library

Library of Congress Cataloging in Publication Data
Fighting for human rights / edited by Paul Gready.
     p. cm.
   Includes bibliographical references and index.
   1. Human rights–Case studies. 2. Civil society–Case studies.
3. Non-governmental organizations–Case studies. 4. Political participation–
Case studies. I. Gready, Paul.

JC571.F497 2004
323—dc22   2003026489

ISBN 0–415–31291–4 (hbk)
ISBN 0–415–31292–2 (pbk)

Contents

Illustrations

Table

Boxes

Contributors

Simon Bullock works for Friends of the Earth England, Wales and Northern Ireland on sustainable development issues.

Nick Buxton has been a campaigner and activist on development and human rights issues for a number of years. As Communications Manager for Jubilee 2000, he was responsible for helping to build up and assist communications between national, regional and international networks supporting the worldwide campaign for debt cancellation. He is the author of "Dial up networking for debt cancellation and development" in S. Hick and J. McNutt (eds) *Advocacy, Activism and the Internet: community organisation and social policy* (2002). Nick Buxton is currently Online Communications Manager for the Catholic development agency, CAFOD.

Richard Falk is Albert G. Milbank Professor Emeritus of International Law at Princeton University where he was a member of the faculty for 40 years. Since 2001 he has been Visiting Professor, Global Studies, University of California at Santa Barbara. He is also Chair of the Nuclear Age Peace Foundation and a member of the Editorial Board of *The Nation*. His most recent books are *Human Rights Horizons* (2000), *Religion and Humane Governance (2001)* and *The Great Terror War* (2003).

Paul Gready is a Lecturer in Human Rights at the Institute of Commonwealth Studies, University of London. He has worked for a number of human rights organizations over a 15-year period, including Amnesty International. His academic publications include *Writing as Resistance: life stories of imprisonment, exile and homecoming from apartheid South Africa* (2003) and the edited volume *Political Transition: politics and cultures* (2003). Among his research interests are South Africa, human rights, political transition and democratization, and cultural studies.

Don Hubert is Deputy Director of the Peacebuilding and Human Security division of the Canadian Department of Foreign Affairs and a Research Fellow at the Centre for Foreign Policy Studies at Dalhousie University. He has a PhD in Social and Political Science from the University of Cambridge, and has held post-doctoral positions at the Centre for Foreign Policy Studies at Dalhousie University and the Humanitarianism and War Project at Brown University. He is author of *The Landmine Ban: a case study in humanitarian advocacy* (2000); and editor, with Thomas Weiss, of *The Responsibility to Protect: research, bibliography, background* (supplementary volume to the report of the international commission on intervention and state sovereignty) (2001); and, with Rob McRae, of *Human Security and the New Diplomacy: protecting people, promoting peace* (2001).

Ann Matear has a PhD in Politics from the University of Liverpool. She is currently a Principal Lecturer and has taught Latin American Studies at the University of Portsmouth since 1995. Her areas of research interest are Chilean politics with the primary focus on issues of equity, social justice and democratization. She has published a number of articles and a co-authored book on gender equity in public policy, and the struggle for justice and human rights in the Chilean transition to democracy.

William Pace is Convenor of the NGO Coalition for the International Criminal Court (CICC), Executive Director of the World Federalist Movement, Institute for Global Policy, and Secretary-General of The Hague Appeal for Peace.

Jennifer Schense is Legal Adviser to the NGO Coalition for the International Criminal Court (CICC).

Bridget Sleap has an MA in Understanding and Securing Human Rights from the Institute of Commonwealth Studies, University of London. She has worked, and written papers on, a number of HIV-related human rights issues including access to treatment, HIV vaccine trials in developing countries, the rights of widows, and HIV- and AIDS-related stigma and discrimination. She has worked in Mozambique and Egypt and is presently working on increasing female-initiated HIV prevention options.

Ian Smillie is an Ottawa-based development consultant and writer. He is an associate of the Humanitarianism and War Project at Tufts University in Boston, and during 2000 he served on a UN Security Council Panel investigating the links between illicit weapons and the diamond trade in Sierra Leone. His latest books are *Patronage or Partnership: local capacity* *building in humanitarian crises* (2001) and, with John Hailey, *Managing for Change: leadership, strategy and management in Asian NGOs* (2001). Ian Smillie serves as Research Coordinator on Partnership Africa Canada's Diamonds and Human Security Project and is an NGO participant in the Kimberley Process which is developing a global certification system for rough diamonds.

Carolyn Stephens is a Senior Lecturer in Environmental Health and Policy and Co-Director of the Centre for Global Change and Health at the London School of Hygiene and Tropical Medicine. She also holds positions with the Universidad Nacional de Tucuman (UNT), in North-West Argentina, as a Profesora Titular en Salud Politica y Medio Ambiente, and as a visiting Professor in the Universidad Federal de Parana in Brazil. Her research focus is on environmental inequalities, environmental justice and health in developing countries, particularly in participatory projects with disadvantaged communities and children internationally. Most recently she has moved to work on participatory ways of using epidemiology in supporting people to analyze their own health and environmental issues. Carolyn Stephens has published widely and advises international agencies, governments, NGOs and community groups.

Introduction

Paul Gready

The international politics of the 1990s was illuminated by groundbreaking events involving civil society and human rights. Numerous group- and issue-based campaigns established a politics of expanded horizons, embracing the agendas of others, elsewhere and tomorrow. Among those blazing this trail were the Zapatistas, protesters against the Multilateral Agreement on Investment (MAI) and the World Trade Organization (WTO) in Seattle, and single issue campaigns such as the International Campaign to Ban Landmines (ICBL) and Jubilee 2000, focusing on the cancellation of un-payable Third World debt. The result was that subjects including trade, development, conflict and globalization became highly politicized, subject to debate as matters of public concern and activism.

The orthodox view, however, is that this 1990s epiphany has been followed by a new millennium backlash.[1] Although the backlash preceded the September 11, 2001 attacks by al-Qaeda on New York and Washington, particularly in their aftermath the "war on terrorism" and concerns about security have challenged human rights advances and the legitimacy of and political spaces created by civil society activism. What this violent transition reveals is that the power of civil society and human rights remains fragile, swiftly challenged by threatened political elites if an opportunity arises. It does not indicate the end of an era. This collection challenges the orthodox view of decline by charting the course of campaigns that span the millennium divide, several building momentum, and, indeed, culminating in its first decade.

The dynamic is less one of beginnings and endings than of a relentless need to move on – to the next city or often a more remote and inaccessible place where a major international institution is due to meet; to sites and venues that seem most responsive to alternative agendas, creating sites and venues that are more responsive; from one single issue to the next or linking single issues to broader structural concerns – and the related need for human rights and civil society to continually reinvent themselves. Richard Falk, in the first chapter of the collection, refers to "the law of unintended effects." This is a pattern of activism and ideas that ebbs and flows, changing meaning and impact over time and from place to place, in turn exploiting and constrained by political circumstances and events. The role for human rights and civil society is currently greater than ever. They are a primary source of voices proclaiming the possibility of diversity in politics, alternative potential futures and internationalism/multinationalism. But they will have to continue to adapt to an evolving and at present hostile environment. This collection explores the ongoing dynamism and the challenges of this unfinished story.

Civil society and human rights

The link between civil society and human rights is central to campaigns for social change. Civil society here builds on but goes beyond a more neutral set of organizations/institutions, "spaces" and/or realms of social relations between the individual/family and the state or the market and the state, and the values of civility. It is a site of political action and style of political engagement and activism. It is characterized by shared political interests/ values but also sometimes fractious debate, by self-empowerment, agenda-setting, demands for accountability, and issue and identity politics. The motivation, therefore, is neither profit nor conventional political power but an attempt to link morality to power and politics in new ways. A complementary relationship between civil society and human rights is forged.

> The advantage of the human rights discourse is its globalist character and its emphasis on the individual . . . the advantage of the language of civil society is precisely its *political* content, its implications for participation and citizenship. It adds to the human rights discourse the notion of individual responsibility for respect of human rights through public action.
>
> (Kaldor 1999: 211)

For a human rights discourse that is often criticized as being unbalanced and partial for its emphasis on the individual, rights and law, civil society reasserts the importance of voluntary association and self-organization, relationships, responsibilities and a broad range of strategies for change. For civil society, human rights and the law offer campaigns moral capital and legitimacy, normative targets and potential means of enforcement, and, crucially, have helped to expand its range across national borders. At their intersection is the idea that ordinary people do not only claim rights for themselves, they also create and enforce them for others. The two key-words in combination signal a new kind of politics.

Both civil society and human rights are usually understood to have their modern origins in eighteenth-century European Enlightenment thought. They depend on the choices made by emancipated individuals and provide checks on state arbitrariness and power. Both terms carry tensions, that can be enabling or crippling, between universalism and cultural relativism, ideals and reality, and processes of debate and set, utopian outcomes. Their respective meanings have been informed and changed by historical events, diverse political ideologies, and an expanded geographical and cultural range. As a result, current meanings of the two concepts are diffuse and highly contested. As one example, both have been used to support *and* critique global capitalism and neo-liberal economic agendas. Not surprisingly, there are occasions when advocates from different camps clash, often due to opposed ideological readings of the respective keywords and global politics. Falk, in the chapter following this introduction, refers to the recent worldwide civil society campaign and actors opposing the war with Iraq and regime change, despite clear evidence of gross human rights violations by the Iraqi regime, and conversely, also refers to the use of human rights, if largely retrospectively and in the absence of weapons of mass destruction, by those supporting the US-led military invasion as a justification for intervention.

But the lack of agreed definitions, an openness and ambiguity, can be an asset. The fact that different ideologies and actors "use the same language provides a common platform through which ideas, projects and policy proposals can be worked out. The debate about its meaning is part of what it is about" (Kaldor 2003: 2). Kaldor is referring here to civil society; I have made a very similar argument elsewhere about human rights (Gready 2003). These keywords of contemporary politics represent some of the most interesting sites where political battles, sometimes camouflaged, sometimes overt, are being fought over the future of globalization and global politics.[2] Such dynamics also emerge at a national level. The Treatment Action Campaign (TAC), campaigning for a right to HIV/AIDS treatment, is the first successful social movement of the post-apartheid era in South Africa. As a bridge between anti-apartheid and post-apartheid civil societies it has critiqued the ANC government, opening the way for other criticisms and broadening policy debates (Sleap, this volume).

Transnational civil society

Echoing Howell and Pearce (2002) and Kaldor (1999, 2003), this collection views transnational civil society as a "political project" and argues that civil society has been transformed in the context of its re-emergence in the 1980s and 1990s. This transformative context includes political changes, notably the role of both national and transnational civil societies in the 1989 revolutions overthrowing communist regimes in the former Eastern Europe. It also includes the altered political alignments, agendas and opportunities of a post-Cold War world. Changing approaches to development, democracy and governance, emphasizing dialogue and partnership, privileged the role of civil society. The altered context also drew on a proliferation of non-governmental organizations (NGOs) and civil society actors, international travel, and information and communication technologies

(Hajnal 2002; Warkentin 2001). There has been a significant growth, for example, in the numbers of and density of linkages between domestic and international NGOs (Sikkink and Smith 2002). During the 1990s, registered international NGOs increased in number by a third, from 10,292 to 13,206, and their memberships grew from 155,000 to 263,000 (cited in Kaldor 2003: 89). Another source states that NGOs and their global networks increased in number from 23,600 in 1991 to 44,000 in 1999 (UNDP 2000: 8). A series of United Nations global conferences – including the Vienna Conference on Human Rights (1993) – contributed to networking among NGOs and civil society allies and to inserting such actors into international decision-making processes.

The transformation of civil society, its expansion beyond territorial borders, simultaneously reflects, drives and challenges processes of globalization. At the heart of many of the 1990s campaigns is the question of what kind of globalization is desirable. And transnational civil society itself contains some of the uncivil dimensions of globalization, such as violent nationalisms and fundamentalisms and, arguably, the deeply ambivalent effects of market capitalism (Keane 2001). The blood diamonds campaign has unmasked the underbelly of globalization and transnational civil society, highlighting the role of uncivil international networks in war, resource smuggling and corruption (Smillie, this volume). The potential for new forms of oppositional politics *and* new forms of insecurity and risk coexist side by side.

If civil society has gone global, its transformation has in part been facilitated by a parallel transformation of the already more internationally framed idea of human rights. Human rights has extended its horizons, to economic-social rights as well as civil-political rights, to non-state actors, and to the promotion of global democracy and global justice alongside its traditional focus on states (Falk, this volume). The two concepts, both of which often seem most real encircled by the boundaries of the state, have during the 1990s moved with more purpose than before to assert a global relevance and address the challenges of globalization. While the speed of these mutually enforcing processes of change has recently accelerated, the relationship between transnational civil society and norm creation has been long and fruitful.

Transnational advocacy and activism are often traced back to the nineteenth-century transnational campaigns for the abolition of slavery, women's suffrage and similarly international forms of labor organizing. Each generation of campaigns has provided templates and inspiration for their successors. Jubilee 2000 linked debt to the slave trade; both being systems of international oppression and taken for granted at one time, but both susceptible to change through mass mobilization. Civil rights organizations in the United States fed into the environmental justice movement. Some of the NGOs that participated in the landmines campaign in turn created the International Action Network on Small Arms to push for international controls on the light weapons responsible for most deaths in contemporary civil wars (Florini 2000b: 229–30; Stephens and Bullock, this volume; also see Hubert 2000: 39–71). Hubert (this volume) suggests that the landmine campaign exhibits parallels with the roles and effectiveness of civil society advocacy efforts during the 1899 Hague Peace Conference banning dum-dum bullets, and suggests more generally that it revitalizes a pre-World War II style of disarmament negotiations before the big freeze of the Cold War. This pattern is another manifestation of the capacity for renewal.

In the post-World War II era of human rights, NGOs were crucial in securing the inclusion of human rights in core documents such as the UN Charter (1945) and had significant input into the Universal Declaration of Human Rights (1948) (Korey 1998: Chapter 1). More recently, the 1970s provided a crucial springboard for subsequent transnational activities, as groundbreaking international campaigns targeted repressive regimes in Greece, Chile, South Africa and Eastern Europe, and vital international legal standards, notably the International Covenant on Civil and Political Rights (1976) and the International Covenant on Economic, Social and Cultural Rights (1976), came into force (Risse 2000: 181–4). As a further example of linkage, the transnational campaign targeting torture by the military regime in Greece set in motion a process that would lead ultimately to the UN Convention against Torture and Other Cruel, Inhuman or Degrading Treatment or Punishment (1984). The mutually enforcing relationship between NGO and transnational campaigns on the one hand, and international norms and laws on the other, therefore, has an impressive history.

Some of the key actors have been international NGOs (INGOs) that are themselves transnational in membership and the range of their concerns. Amnesty International, founded in 1961, has led a number of human rights campaigns. Clark describes Amnesty International variously as a "pioneer," a "model" and a "leader" in norm creation in the field of human rights (Clark 2001). She examines the role of Amnesty International in creating norms dealing with torture, disappearances and political killings, claiming that its ability to influence norms, its legitimacy, rests on a loyalty to principle, political impartiality and the use of information as a weapon (fact-finding, interpretation, conceptual framing, linking facts to concepts) (ibid.: 11–18). Also crucial are attempts to link shared principles to expert knowledge and public mobilization. INGOs like Amnesty International, in a style of operating taken further by the campaigns discussed in this volume, seek to work at various levels – the international arena, states/govern-ments, locally; expert knowledge and the general public – simultaneously.

Transnational civil society comes with both a history and a rather complex set of definitions. Most civil society networks and mobilizations ripple outwards from a core of a few dynamic, visionary individuals and NGO leadership. NGOs are normally defined using sometimes contra-dictory terms like autonomous, private, institutional, formal, professional/

voluntary, and non-profit/value-driven. NGOs include a range of actors from Amnesty International, Human Rights Watch and Oxfam, to Southern giants like BRAC, formerly known as Bangladesh Rural Advancement Committee, established in 1972 and now a large and multifaceted development organization, almost a parallel state in Bangladesh. Alongside large INGOs and national NGOs there are "one person and a fax machine"-type operations. The cases studies in this collection embed NGOs in broader groupings of actors – community and church groups, trade unions, women's organizations – that in turn help to constitute what is variously termed global civil society (Warkentin 2001; Anheier *et al.* 2001), transnational civil society (Florini 2000a), transnational advocacy networks (Keck and Sikkink 1998), or transnational social movements. The term transnational is preferred in this introduction as the links and networks are cross-border, not truly global.

Khagram *et al.* (2002b: 6–10) provide a useful definitional categorization, distinguishing four ascending levels of transnational collective action, involving different degrees of connection and mobilization:

- **International/transnational NGOs:** NGOs are the already-mentioned social change actors that, to define themselves as international NGOs, need to be international in their organizational structure and aims. Domestic and international NGOs are primary actors in the groups detailed below.
- **Transnational advocacy networks:** networks are the most informal grouping of non-state actors (dominant modality: information exchange).
- **Transnational coalitions:** coalitions involve a greater level of coordination on strategies/tactics to influence social change, in the form of transnational campaigns, which can be institutional and/or non-institutional, e.g. boycotts. Coordination of this kind requires more formal contacts because groups usually need to meet and report regularly (dominant modality: coordinated tactics).
- **Transnational social movements:** social movements have the capacity to generate coordinated and sustained social mobilization and collective action in more than one country to influence social change, often through protest or disruptive action. In relation to other forms of transnational collective action, they can be expected to be both more effective whilst also being the most difficult and rare (dominant modality: joint mobilization).

In the case studies considered in this collection the dominant dynamic is information exchange (transnational advocacy networks). Common characteristics include a flexible, informal and non-hierarchical organizational structure lacking centralized control; speed of mobilization and intervention; and exchanges of experience and knowledge. In this context, Pace and Schense provide an instructive insight into the role of a service-based Coalition Secretariat in the campaign for the International Criminal Court (ICC), while Buxton explores some of the weaknesses of such networks in the context of the debt cancellation campaign, for example, when trying to formulate a coherent response to partial progress in achieving objectives. Many campaigns flex their muscles at strategically important moments and events – major international meetings, precedent-setting court cases, to address complex problems – through the coordination of tactics and collective action. Interestingly, in the landmines campaign Hubert notes that sympathetic states worked together in a similar fashion. The cases considered in this collection also indicate that transnational campaigns need to be built on national civil society campaigns and social movements, often organized similarly, and rooted in local realities, contexts, activism and longer-term commitments. Campaigns are both strategically trans-national and strategic in the forms that transnationalism takes.

Normative and political contracts

The emergence of and adherence to principled rules and norms challenges a realist approach to international relations, in which global politics is dominated by states, competitive and anarchic power relations between states, and self-interest. How, then, do norms/laws based on moral principles emerge to become a part of international politics? Is it possible to create a rule-based, principle-guided global order rather than one that is too often and, increasingly it seems at the dawn of this new century, dominated by raw, uncompromising power?

Norms are shared or collective expectations, standards of appropriate behavior, accepted by and applied to a broad range of actors: "human rights norms can be understood as standards of behavior defined in terms of rights and obligations, resting on beliefs . . . of rectitude, or right and wrong" (Clark 2001: 30). Norms come in various guises. Laws, regulations, rules and international agreements are packaged in forms including bind-ing treaties, such as human rights conventions, and "softer" norms/law, such as evolving understandings of whether to privilege sovereignty or intervention in the context of gross violations of human rights and humani-tarian need and self-administered codes of conduct for Transnational Corporations (TNCs) or NGOs.

Recent history indicates that NGOs, and civil society more generally, can influence international politics and state behavior on behalf of principled norms. In fact, they are the primary champions of such a politics. Some claims in this regard are grand indeed. Risse (2000) writes: "In the absence of sustained campaigns and lobbying efforts by INGOs and particular individuals, probably not a single human right would have been written into international law" (2000: 184), and Florini (2000b) concurs: "It is clear that there would be little or nothing in the way of international human rights standards were it not for the determination of what has now become a large and entrenched transnational community of human rights activists" (2000b: 212). Contributors to this collection echo, if at varying volume, these sentiments.

A central conclusion from the case studies contained in this book is that sustainable and significant social change requires both normative and political contracts. Change often gains normative/legal recognition as a result of politically motivated civil society campaigns. Such change, once governed by norms, will only be sustained and enforced if the political mobilization is maintained. In essence, the obligation and price of failure for centers of authority, be they governments, institutions such as the International Monetary Fund (IMF), World Bank and WTO or indeed TNCs, has to be felt normatively and politically (and sometimes economically). This understanding of social change strengthens democracy and democratic accountability by insisting that it is multidimensional, national and international, political and economic, normative and political.

Normative contracts can be generated in a manner that is essentially top down or more bottom up, but principled norms, as already indicated, are invariably the outcome of civil society mobilizations. Richard Falk (2001) distinguishes between "globalization from above" (the dominance of transnational market forces and the cooption of states to their policy agenda) and "globalization from below" (criticism of and resistance towards this agenda at the local, grassroots level and on a transnational basis). Falk asks what the normative potential of "globalization from below" might be?

> The idea of normative potential is to conceptualize widely shared world order values: minimizing violence, maximizing economic well-being, realizing social and political justice, and upholding environmental quality. These values often interact inconsistently, but are normatively coherent in the sense of depicting the main dimensions of a widely shared consensus as to the promotion of benevolent forms of world order, and seem at odds in crucial respects with part of the orientation and some of the main impacts of globalization-from-above in its current historical phase.
>
> (2001: 49–50)

Civil society is the engine behind a normative agenda seeking to establish and enforce contracts from below. Ordinary people can, and should, make and monitor laws. The focus of this volume is on civil society initiatives that seek state and international recognition, so that norms aiming to establish "world order values" can be furthered from both above and below.

The political contract overlaps with its normative twin, but is also somewhat different.[3] To form a political contract, first, an issue must be politicized. Often this involves a rendering public and political of what has previously been professionalized and institutionalized as the private terrain of experts, seen narrowly, for example in economic, technical or scientific terms. Debates about development, trade and the environment provide very good examples of such processes. Politicizing problems also politicizes potential solutions. Brought into the light of public debate and media attention, issues come to be seen as a scandal. Concerns acquire a threshold of seriousness whereby they simply must happen, or, conversely, cannot be allowed to happen. To become such a transnational political cause an issue must generate cross-cultural/border recognition and outrage, moral clarity in terms of right and wrong (even over-simplification), and a related ease of identification (of victim and villain, cause and remedy). The fact that debtor countries are paying interest on loans that have effectively been repaid many times over, that net financial flows move from the South to the North, and that some countries spend more on servicing debt than on education or health care, surprises and, frankly, disgusts many people. A contract is forged as the result of a civil society movement rallying, often transnationally, sometimes in broader alliances, around such issues. Crucially, claims are made not on the basis of promises or charity, but of rights and justice. So, as this collection illustrates, campaigns for debt relief, for the eradication of anti-personnel mines, to end impunity for gross abuses of human rights and establish a positive link between human rights and democracy, for environmental justice, for access to treatment for HIV/AIDS and for an end to the trade in blood diamonds, have all been reframed in these terms.

Mutual acknowledgement of contracts between civil society, states, inter-governmental organizations (IGOs) and TNCs is a powerful political weapon. Contracts involve a commitment from, and obligation on, the relevant authority, and prevention/enforcement through forms of political accountability. Political failure is equated with illegitimacy and leads to removal from power or some other form of political price. Political contracts explain why some rights are considered sufficiently important to be guaranteed by political processes and through democratic accountability.

Contracts can have an economic dimension. Increasingly, international economic agreements have to be sold politically by governments to domestic constituencies. Even in more narrowly economic terms, corporate codes of conduct have been drawn up due to civil society and consumer pressure and will only be implemented if such pressure is maintained. They are weak norms that require primarily economic, rather than political, forms of enforcement. The price of norm violation needs to be negative media coverage, damaged public relations and consumer boycotts of particular products or brands. As documented in this volume, it is civil society that is trying to hold the pharmaceutical industry to a contract that ensures a right to treatment for HIV/AIDS. There are now real costs for those companies which link the right to life too closely to the ability to pay, prioritizing patents and profit over people (Sleap). The diamond industry has likewise been forced to address the issue of blood diamonds (Smillie).

The contractual process maps a particular mechanism for social change. Ideally, such contracts are both political and normative/legal in form, and national and international in range. Social change depends on human rights being located within ongoing civil society mobilizations and political/ legal processes, and on a patchwork of mutually reinforcing forms of political and normative/legal accountability. This is a theory of rights as historically determined and politically negotiated, and as secured through both law and politics.

Evidence for this mechanism of social change can be found within this collection. Jubilee 2000's campaign to put civil society at the heart of solutions to the debt crisis and more generally of economic decision-making has generated this kind of social change: a "self-awareness" of its potential as part of the solution that challenged both creditors and debtors. Jubilee 2000 Zambia has called for "conditionality from below" in which a tripartite "debt management mechanism" between the creditor govern-ment, debtor government and civil society "would be charged with monitor-ing debt negotiations for new loans and canceling of debts, and with overseeing the direction of freed-up resources toward poverty eradication." Placing debt and economic policy more democratically within national and international political processes might in time provide political incentives for success and attach political costs to failure (Buxton, this volume). Hubert describes the landmines campaign as involving two tracks: prepar-ation of and consultations on the text of a treaty, and a campaign to raise awareness and build political support for a landmines ban at local, national, regional and international levels. Stephens and Bullock also outline fledg-ling contractual arrangements in the environmental justice field that are local (Good Neighbor Agreements in the United States between industry and community), and, in the case of the Aarhus Convention, also driven by a cross-border and cross-generational inclusiveness. The 2001 Aarhus Convention is a European initiative developed by civil society actors in Eastern Europe and the former Soviet Union. By drawing together con-cerns for information, participation and justice in relation to environ-mental harm this represents a landmark in environmental democracy.

This theory of rights emphasizes the importance of civil society mobiliz-ation towards norms and various kinds of political commitment, but also beyond these landmarks to secure implementation. Such a momentum is often difficult to achieve. Pace and Schense note a similar challenge facing coalitions of states. International agreement provides a powerful campaign objective around which to focus energies and rally diverse constituencies, as such agreements represent a horizon of possibility, a measurable target and tangible marker of success. Norms and political commitments are too often seen as the end rather than the beginning of the process of securing human rights. The challenge for the human rights movement, civil society campaigns and sympathetic states is to acknowledge that, relatively speaking, such agreements are the easy bit. Implementation is the harder and more urgent challenge. Norm proliferation in the absence of social change breeds disillusionment. Campaigns need to be formulated with these different goals, differently prioritized, in mind.

Achieving agreement – the challenge of "partial success" – can dissipate focus, bring to the fore disagreements about priorities and strategy, and unravel coalitions. The Jubilee 2000 campaign is an example of a brilliantly devised and executed campaign, the very terms and successes of which, notably its emphasis on achieving results by the millennium, made longer-term sustainability difficult (Buxton). As the pressure for change eases, the danger is that the issue, and its newly forged agreement, recedes from the glare of public and political attention.

A further danger of partial success is of the subversion of even potentially progressive norms to power, of legal and regulatory systems operating to protect the interests of the powerful against the claims of the less powerful. The political–legal contract works only if civil society makes it work, before, during and after norm creation and official political commitments.

The WTO's Trade-Related Intellectual Property (TRIPS) provisions are interesting in this regard (as is humanitarian/military intervention in the context of evolving norms of sovereignty and (non-)intervention, discussed in more detail by Falk). Sleap argues, in relation to HIV/AIDS, that on paper intellectual property norms seem to allow a reasonable balance between the need of less developed countries to import or produce low-cost versions of drugs, and protections for the patent holder. However, given the political and economic power of the pharmaceutical industry in comparison to most less developed countries, few such countries have taken advantage of these provisions. The HIV/AIDS campaigns outlined by Sleap have sought to push the boundaries of TRIPS-compliant national legislation towards securing the right of access to treatment. The "clarification" of TRIPS provided at the WTO's Doha Ministerial Conference in 2001 reasserted that patents can be suspended on public health grounds in emergencies. But the contest between norms and power continues.

What is needed here is civil society mobilization towards a political contract to shore up the normative contract at both national and international levels. Despite some flexibility available within TRIPS, from a human rights perspective it should be noted that the challenge is a more radical one: that the right to health and the public interest be privileged more generally over intellectual property rights, and that health concerns should be integrated into a coordinated focus on poverty and basic needs rather than isolated and exceptionalized (Cullet 2003). Outcomes rest on the relationship between different strands of international law (intellectual property and human rights), and specifically which strand is prioritized, as well as how law is interpreted and applied.

In this context of norms and power, an argument outlined by Neil Stammers (1999) is illuminating. He argues that human rights have often been socially and historically constructed, from the American and French revolutions to the present day, by a range of actors including, significantly, social movements: "utilizing rights claims to challenge . . . relations and structures of power . . . Indeed, it might be accurate to see the socio-historical development of ideas of human rights emerging as social movements identified, recognized, and sought to challenge particular forms of power" (1999: 989). But this conception of the development of human rights holds within it a profound paradox. Stammers (ibid.: 996–1000) argues that it is in their institutionalized/legal form that human rights are most likely to sustain relations and structures of power, while in their pre-institutionalized, non-legal form human rights have the greatest potential to challenge relations and structures of power. Institutionalization and norm creation are ultimately the outcome of, but also effectively neutralize, "successful" social movement struggle.[4] Again, this illustrates the need for parallel normative and political contracts, for civil society mobilization driving human rights beyond norms in the service of progressive social, institutional and structural change.

The potential here is immense. Increasingly both national and transnational in range, and based on coalitions and alliances, NGO and civil society campaigns have sought to establish normative and political contracts, and to narrow the gap between principle and practice, rhetoric and reality. The result is the beginning of a global moral and regulatory infrastructure and, as we will see below, layers of global governance.

Global governance

Global governance refers to those norms and institutions that regulate cross-border activity, facilitate cooperation between relevant public and private actors, and manage the processes and challenges of globalization, in the absence of global government. The processes/challenges range from an increasingly interconnected global economy and patterns of inequality/ poverty to conflict, humanitarian emergencies, crime, the environment, human rights, various forms of population movement, and cultural and media flows. There are some stark asymmetries here. We live in a world where capital moves freely but labor does not. Governance of these processes/challenges is multilayered (local, national, regional, inter/transnational) and engages various sites of power and political actors. It is also highly uneven. Transnational civil society now has to be understood in relation to these emerging frameworks of global governance, or in the terms of this introduction, emerging global normative and political contracts. If (transnational) civil society is the medium through which many such contracts are negotiated with centers of power, then globalization requires new and renegotiated contracts with new and altered centers of power.

A central concern in the formation of such contracts is the declining role of the state in contemporary global politics. State power, relevance and legitimacy are in flux, many argue in terminal decline. Economic globalization is often depicted as bypassing the state as a major decision-maker, privileging other sites of authority, such as the IMF, World Bank and WTO, and TNCs. The former control the world of finance, the latter dominate investment, production and trade. McGrew (1998) writes that such corporations account for 80 percent of international investment, between 25–33 percent of world output and 70 percent of world trade (189). Declining state power, alongside the withdrawal of the state from areas of public expenditure and welfare provision, create challenges for a human rights regime based on an international society of states, particularly in relation to economic and social rights. These challenges can only be met by new kinds of normative and political contracts, in essence, by a new human rights regime. This requires the reimagining of sovereignty beyond the nation-state. Economic globalization occupies a place at the forefront of the multiple erosions of sovereignty, but human rights, humanitarian and military interventions, post-conflict reconstruction/nation-building, and the political decision-making of regional and international institutions, are all in hot pursuit.

A further contributory factor in state marginalization is that the self-interest and short-termism of states, and the state-based international system, are not well equipped to deal with cross-border and cumulative problems. Nor do they adequately secure broader public goods. The free market, similarly, fails to address these challenges. Increasingly, problems, even local problems, require global, long-term, managed solutions. A final component of the crisis of the state is the collapse in interest in formal politics in many parts of the world. The catalogue of woes here is familiar: falling political party membership, low voter turnouts in elections, a perceived lack of real political alternatives. As states are seen as less relevant to the issues that affect our lives, less responsive to our needs and representative of our views, we react to this perceived deficit, in relation to democracy and governance, not only through disengagement but also by seeking new political outlets.

Having said all of this, it should be noted that even in the context of globalization the state retains significant areas of influence. These include a range of functions, some, such as the rule of law, that are crucial to securing human rights and protecting civil society. But the state also oversees numerous other mechanisms of governance, security, regulation, protection, accountability and enforcement. Furthermore, the main institutions of global governance – the UN, World Bank, IMF and WTO – are all state-based, dominated by their most powerful members, chiefly today the United States. If globalization is remaking states, states are also creating and shaping globalization through conscious policy decisions. The state, finally, is important because it remains our primary model of democratic governance. One of the criticisms made of globalization is that by shifting power to other, unaccountable, sites of power, including civil society itself, it is undermining democratic gains made at the level of the nation state. The state is alive and well. Rumours of its demise are exaggerated and premature. States will remain at the heart of national and international contractual arrangements but understandings of sovereignty, democracy and governance need to change and expand to meet contemporary challenges.

The task, then, is not to replace one form of governance with another, but to get the best balance between, in particular, state and global forms of governance. Not all global governance is good governance, far from it. Alongside contractual arrangements built from below are "top-down," neo-liberal formulations. The World Bank, with its expanding role in global governance, is a good example of potential dangers. This agenda, pushed in part by civil society campaigns, has resulted in an expansion beyond more narrowly "economic" conditions for loans, such as privatiz-ation and cutting back on public spending, to other concerns such as "good governance," still targeted towards economic ends. This policy agenda marks a significant increase in the scope of World Bank activities, beyond its traditional areas of competence, and, more importantly, a ratcheting-up of its power and influence. This kind of accountability to undemocratic international institutions, which enables the North, and particularly the United States, to dictate increasingly far-reaching policy interventions to developing countries, is now under attack from civil society groups. A power-driven ideological head-lock is precisely what global governance should not be.

It is not surprising, therefore, that some civil society campaigns seek to increase the power and role of the state (such as campaigns critiquing economic globalization and structural adjustment policies which call for greater national control, democratic accountability and local participation in relation to economic policies), while others champion greater inter-national supervision (human rights, environmental protection). The challenge is to forge a more coherent and coordinated approach to sovereignty and global governance.

Can campaigners advocate greater economic self-determination for states *and* broader World Bank conditionalities? Can the world stand by and watch genocide take place again, as it did in Rwanda during 1994, selectively acceding to state sovereignty in some conflicts (where countries are too inconsequential to count or too important to challenge) while riding roughshod over it in others? What controls, from within civil society and elsewhere, can there be on US-led unilateralism in the field of "humanitarian," or more accurately military, intervention? Civil society campaigns that effectively seek regime change, at least in part on human rights grounds but targeting governments themselves, also face difficult questions about state sovereignty, consistency, the real meaning of democracy, and the morality, legitimacy and effectiveness of international efforts to influence domestic politics (Kumar 2000). Sovereignty-related concerns have similarly been raised by campaigns challenging impunity and seeking universal jurisdiction for the most serious human rights abuses. Pinochet's arrest in London in October 1998 is only the most high-profile example. Such international campaigns can be seen to challenge, and even undermine, fragile post-conflict democracies and judiciaries and/or as strengthening the hand of internal actors seeking justice and a justice-based democracy (Matear, this volume). Even given internal support and mobilization, what is the appropriate role for external actors in these campaigns? What is the place of sovereignty, and which is sovereign in this complex new governance regime: the individual, the people or the state? Clearly, collaborative, vertical governance arrangements that respect the complementary capacities of local, state and global governance are vital.

The coordination and consistency challenge is both vertical and horizontal, across a range of issues, institutions and strands of international law. The fate of HIV/AIDS medication at the intersection of intellectual property and human rights law illustrates this clearly. It also seems extraordinary that the WTO can oversee trade regulation without reference to human rights standards or outcomes, or that trade and aid policies are not better synchronized to meet the Millennium Development Goals (such as halving the proportion of people living in absolute poverty by 2015). But much global governance, like many civil society campaigns, is essentially issue-based. As both suffer from a lack of joined-up thinking, the overall outcome can be incoherent. This is a significant challenge for transnational civil society: "To the extent that the world relies on transnational civil society for its global governance, it will get a series of *ad hoc* muddlings through" (Florini 2000b: 230). Edwards describes such governance as "messy and unpredictable" (2001: 4). In part the challenge is that civil society campaigns generating contractual arrangements form around some issues and not others. These issues are not necessarily those most urgently in need of global governance arrangements. While there is an inevitable unevenness of coverage and influence, there is also potential for greater campaign coordination and more consistent linkages between specific issues and challenging broader economic and political structures. But because transnational civil society and human rights both reflect *and* seek to change vertical and horizontal governance shortcomings they provide a language and set of strategies that speak to the problem as well as potential solutions. In collaboration they provide a means of reconciliation.

The tensions within globalization and governance mean that people are seeking new ways to become political actors and enter both the domestic and global political arenas. This process, alongside the complexity and range of contemporary problems, involves not only coordination in governance, but also the already-mentioned rethinking of sovereignty, democracy and governance to include new mechanisms of supervision and accountability. This will require new voices, interests, experiences, possibilities, venues, means of political participation, and new mechanisms to achieve transparency, accountability and coherent policy solutions to complex global problems.

A powerful example is provided by the landmines campaign (Hubert, this volume). Disillusioned with established UN venues, such as the Certain Conventional Weapons Review Conference and the Conference on Disarmament, which operated by consensus, at a grindingly slow pace and with limited access for NGOs, negotiations took place outside normal multilateral channels and traditional disarmament forums. Key actors in the campaign included a diverse range of NGOs organized into the International Campaign to Ban Landmines (ICBL), the International Committee of the Red Cross (ICRC), various UN agencies (the Department of Humanitarian Affairs, UNHCR, UNICEF) and a cross-regional coalition or "core group" of small and medium-sized states. In this context, the Ottawa Process, a free-standing negotiating forum, made its own rules on participation and decision-making. For example, based on "self-selection," states participated if they supported a ban on mines; NGOs participated fully in negotiations; and, when it came to the crunch, decision-making was by two-thirds majority. This "fast track" diplomatic initiative has been heralded as a ground-breaking mechanism of global governance and international law making. The 1997 Ottawa Treaty – in full, the Convention on the Prohibition of the Use, Stockpiling, Production and Transfer of Anti-Personnel Mines and on their Destruction – is similarly multidimensional in its implementation mechanisms.

A similar alliance campaigning for an International Criminal Court (ICC) operated on this occasion within the UN system. The main partners in the alliance were the NGO Coalition for the International Criminal Court (CICC) and a diverse Like-Minded Group of states (LMG). Crucial to what Pace and Schense describe as "new diplomacy" is a concern with partnership, procedure, participation and complementary strengths. The outcome is a building of trust within and "opening-up" of governance mechanisms, and a genuine commitment and emboldening of negotiators that generates stronger international law. The campaign also seeks to support similar developments at a national level. The landmines and ICC campaigns challenged conventional understandings of sovereignty, democracy, governance and multilateralism, and developed models for vertical and horizontal coordination in governance. They represent benchmark normative and political contracts for a new human rights regime.

New thinking on governance needs to be applied to multilateral institutions themselves, many of which are undemocratic and ineffective. The IMF and World Bank, for example, need to be more accountable, as in the current situation both economic and political accountability is lacking. The International Financial Institutions Advisory Committee (the Meltzer Commission) (2000), convened by the US Congress to assess the institutions of the global economy, was highly critical of both the IMF and World Bank.

It recorded, for example, that using the World Bank's own evaluations, the failure rate of World Bank projects was 73 percent in Africa and 65–70 percent in the poorest countries. And yet borrowing of all kinds for debtor countries has become conditional on IMF/World Bank-sanctioned reform and approval, and therefore these "gateway creditors" are repaid irrespective of incompetence or failure. Politically, in terms of their own decision-making, relative economic might is translated into weighted voting by government representatives, with the result that money talks while those countries most affected in policy terms have the least say in their formulation. Normative and political contracts that ensure greater effectiveness, participation and accountability – if these institutions were businesses they would be bankrupt, if they were answerable to an electorate they would be in the political wilderness – are clearly required here too. In the absence of a global state and given prevailing global power dynamics, such contracts are most likely to be forged from below.

New thinking on governance is also vitally important for complex issues like labor and environmental standards. Civil society actors supporting such an agenda find themselves in opposition to TNCs and to many Southern states who see such standards as a kind of tax on development and point out that the industrial revolutions and colonialisms of the North notably lacked such high principles. Labor unions in countries like the United States may push for rules on a minimum wage or environmental protection in trade negotiations at least in part out of self-interest as such measures increase competitor costs. This is typical of the diversity of actors and motives, the unpredictability and fragility of alliances, and the complex moralities that require more open and accountable forms of governance.

Florini and Simmons (2000) argue that transnational civil society networks are the emerging third force in global politics, an increasingly important participant in the management and resolution of global problems and, therefore, in global governance. Phrases in the titles of recent books speak to a broad and bold agenda: reshaping world politics (Warkentin 2001), restructuring world politics (Khagram *et al.* 2002a). The case studies in this collection can be understood as examples of emerging governance mechanisms or contracts. As forms of governance are challenged and change, and new normative and political contracts are formed, civil society networks have honed their strategies accordingly.

Civil society strategies

The reasons behind NGO/civil society successes are complex and varied. Campaigns and norms can play a role in redefining state self-interest, for example, by redrawing the boundaries of acceptable behavior in such a way that states concerned about their image and standing in the international community understand that moral conduct can serve important political interests. A primary weapon here is "soft power." This form of political capital rests on the persuasive power of information, ideas and communication, often linked to moral authority and exercised in informal spaces and strategies, in shaping discourses and norms. It can change the way people think, understand the world and define their interests (Sikkink 2002: 303–6; Florini and Simmons 2000: 10–11). NGOs have been creative in their use of the media and often produce the most authoritative information on emerging issues. Hubert states that on the landmines issue, in addition to compelling NGO research, military leaders, in contrast, lacked evidence to back up their claims for the military utility of land-mines. Many tactics and strategies have been used by civil society actors and networks, of which just three will be addressed in detail here: broad coalitions, the boomerang or spiral model of human rights change, and issue framing. This selection is by no means exhaustive but it is revealing.

Broad coalitions

Most of the campaigns described in this collection are "mixed actor coalitions" (Shaw 2000), NGO-led but involving a broad range of other parties within and outside civil society. Some of the participants in the broader alliances are predictable enough, churches and trade unions, for example. Even at this predictable level of participation, however, the nature and implications of participation can be interesting. Buxton notes that church participation in Jubilee 2000 challenged North–South power dynamics. While debt activism energized a declining flock in the United Kingdom it chiefly strengthened the voice and influence of the numerically strong and growing Southern churches.

Others participants are less predictable: business, governments, IGOs, and parts of and personnel within these actors. Smillie's mapping of the participants in the Kimberley Process, the negotiations process that culmin-ated in an agreement to end the trade in blood diamonds, is illustrative. A broad and informal coalition of NGOs formed strategic alliances with the diamond industry and personal relationships with its personnel; with the United Nations, whose series of expert panel reports confirmed the link between war, weapons and diamonds, and whose unanimous General Assembly Resolution of December 2000 endorsing the Kimberley Process gave it new legitimacy; with governments and politicians, and particularly with the South African government which chaired the process throughout; and with a community of academics and research institutes (the World Bank, the International Peace Academy) that increased the audience reached by the issue and campaign.

Perhaps the most challenging alliances are with governments. These reflect what Falk in the first chapter of this collection describes as the change within human rights from "anti-statism" to "collaborative activism." This is part of the broader dynamic described earlier through which the meanings and uses of human rights have become diffuse and contested.

NGOs increasingly work with sympathetic states, or with sympathetic individuals within states. Divide – in the case of the landmines campaign dividing conventional superpower blocs and alliances (NATO, the European Union, the Non-Aligned Movement), members of the UN Security Council, foreign ministries from defense ministries (Hubert) – and if not rule, at least magnify influence and set the agenda. Clarke describes NGO-state alliances, under different types of political regimes, as a political facet of globalization (1998: 24).

Partnerships can be with certain Northern states against Southern states in the attempt to introduce labor and environmental standards into trade negotiations, or with Southern states as a way of uniting against pharmaceutical companies and allied Northern governments on the issue of access to HIV/AIDS treatment. This strategy has enabled NGOs and civil society, in alliance with core groups of sympathetic states and despite US opposition, to establish already mentioned innovative governance mechanisms such as the Ottawa Treaty, banning anti-personnel land-mines, and the ICC. Key individuals can hold various positions, cutting across the participating actors. Partnerships are flexible and often with what Edwards calls "middle-power governments" (2001: 12). Can these initiatives work in the face of US government opposition? Can opponents be brought on board at a later date? What will the implications be, for example, of ICC judgements that without the economic, political and military support of major states, notably the United States, are unenforce-able? These questions acquire increased importance in the context of the marked unilateralism of the current Bush regime in the United States. It has been suggested that such alliances represent a significant realignment in global politics, a new form of multilateralism or diplomacy over which no state has a veto.

In truth, alliances with sites of governance are not new – NGOs and civil society, for example, have for some time formed part of state delegations to international meetings and worked closely with sympathetic states when drafting new legal norms – but the proliferation in the number of alliances, and successes, does indicate an important change in activist agendas. Also, NGO-state coalitions are newer in certain areas (human security) than others (human rights). Similarly, changes in governments have always mattered enormously, sometimes reducing the prospect for human rights advancement whilst on other occasions leading to policy changes and new openings for activism. Political change boosted the landmines and ICC campaigns when Lloyd Axworthy became Canada's Foreign Minister, and when the Labour Party came to power in Britain. The impacts of regime change can, however, be paradoxical. In a pattern characteristic of political transitions, Matear describes how in Chile a civil society that had been vibrant under an oppressive military regime was soon seen as a divisive threat to the fragile post-Pinochet democracy, due to its demands for justice and a deeper democracy.

Then there is the role of NGOs as service deliverers and sub-contractors. Rather than being a check on the state (and IGOs), civil society, North and South, has, so the critique goes, been appropriated and funded by a hegemonic neo-liberalism to become a substitute for these actors in welfare, service provision, development and humanitarian relief. The state, preferred as small and non-interventionary, dismissed as corrupt and inefficient, is bypassed and undermined, for example, in the context of development and aid agendas. NGOs now deliver more aid than the whole UN system (*The Economist* 1999: 24). They are similarly ever-present in conflict zones and post-conflict reconstruction. Civil society, incorporated into policy frameworks of privatization and market reform, can smooth the running of economic globalization and undermine the developing state. It is too close to Northern states financially, rendering it anti-state ideologically. This can become global governance by cooption, with NGOs and civil society as instruments of Northern state foreign policy.

This is a reality, but a complex reality. Simplistic, generalized contrasts between service provision and advocacy, "tamed" NGOs and activist social movements (Kaldor 2003), are neither accurate nor particularly helpful. The relationships NGOs have with governments and IGOs are often layered and nuanced. NGOs and civil society can, for example, be supported in providing internal pressure for reform of corrupt and inefficient governments. In all three countries examined by Sleap in this volume (Brazil, South Africa, Kenya), NGOs are major service providers of HIV/AIDS care and prevention, whilst also campaigning for equal access to treatment and confronting their governments when necessary. The rubric suggested here is at least in part one of partnership and complementary capacities. The author argues that in Brazil the broad-based government–NGO partnership has been central to the successful response to the epidemic. A similar logic of complementary capacities can be applied to transnational campaigns. States facilitated NGO access to UN meetings and NGOs provided key research inputs in the ICC campaign (Pace and Schense). Hubert notes, with reference to landmines, that there was both a shift over time from advocacy and lobbying to partnership with the commencement of the Ottawa Process in 1996, and that even post-1996 a division remained at the level of national campaigns between those working with supporting governments and those lobbying governments opposing the ban. Much more work needs to be done on how NGOs, civil society networks and governments/IGOs seek to negotiate complex relationships with each other.

Fluid, layered and reconfigured NGO/civil society relationships with states, IGOs and the market, and broad-based coalitions more generally, have significant implications for understandings and definitions of NGOs/civil society, as well as for both national and global politics and governance. Some assume links, others see them as more recent and strategic; some cast them in a positive light whilst for others they smack of a retreat from the articulation of radical alternatives to dominant agendas to more modest goals of partnership, collaboration and reform. But given the current divisions between and within states and societies on issues such as terrorism, security and military intervention, this form of politics could be a vital source of resistance to US-led political agendas and unilateralism. Differently constituted "coalitions of the willing" are both undermining and seeking to preserve/reinvent multilateralism and justice/norm-based global governance. One way in which these broad-based networks operate has recently been given a conceptual framework.

Boomerangs and spirals

Keck and Sikkink identify what they describe as "the boomerang pattern" that characterizes the work of transnational advocacy networks (1998: 12–13). This model is interesting because it speaks to an international society remade in the era of globalization. The networks are comprised of various actors, broad coalitions, linking local, national and global politics. This too can be seen as a component of political globalization. Where national NGOs have difficulty accessing or influencing their own (repressive/unresponsive) governments, they "bypass their state and directly search out international allies to try to bring pressure on their states from outside. This is most obviously the case in human rights campaigns" (ibid.: 12). Although not without their tensions and ambiguities, these linkages provide Third World actors with access, leverage, information, security and money while for Northern groups "they make credible the assertion that they are struggling with, and not only for, their southern partners" (ibid.: 13). On issues where state hostility is contrasted with global resonance, international contacts can serve to "amplify the demands of domestic groups, pry open space for new issues, and then echo back these demands into the domestic arena" (ibid.: 13). A process of mutually enforcing internal and external legitimacy is set in motion.

Risse *et al.* (1999: Chapters 1 and 8) have subsequently expanded upon the boomerang concept in a comparative study of the role of transnational advocacy networks in the internalization and implementation of "core" international civil and political human rights norms in domestic practice. "Socialization," it is argued, takes place through material pressures, tactical or strategic adaptation and bargaining, moral argumentation and discourse (consciousness-raising, dialogue, persuasion, "shaming"), and insititutionalization. These processes are operationalized through a five-phase "spiral model" of human rights change, consisting of several "boomerang throws" which ultimately pincer abusive states from above and below. Although potentially involving a broad range of actors, including states and IGOs, "the spiral keeps spiraling only if transnational civil society makes it happen" (Risse 2000: 191). The five phases are: (1) repression, network activation and transnational mobilization; (2) denial, challenging both human rights norms themselves and specific charges of abuse; (3) tactical concessions and growing internal mobilization; (4) the "prescriptive phase," linked to regime and/or policy change (acceptance of the validity of human rights norms but possibly inconsistent practice); and (5) rule-consistent behavior.

The authors claim that there has been a significant, if imperfect and variously paced, diffusion of rights norms across borders and diverse states, political regimes, socio-economic systems and cultures, and that this model helps to explain patterns of diffusion but also difference. They argue for the existence of a "compression" of the socialization process over time as an international "norms cascade" indicates the growing influence and acceptance of human rights; for "self-entrapment" in processes of moral argumentation and accountability; and for the "power of norms" or "principles" challenging the "norms of power" (Risse 2000; Risse *et al.* 1999: Chapters 1 and 8).

How do these processes play out in the cases examined in this collection? Buxton, in his chapter on Jubilee 2000, identifies a range of different kinds of often North–South boomerangs. Campaigning was built on complementary exchanges of information and inspirational news. In Uganda, the Jubilee 2000 movement helped to open up a space for civil society to play a role in economic decision-making while in Kenya the arrest of Jubilee 2000 activists at a demonstration sparked an international network response. Transnational civil society amplified the voice and demands of Southern states with creditors in relation to debt cancellation, contributing to a growing assertiveness and confidence among Southern governments in the international arena, as illustrated in recent WTO meetings.

It is also clear that, in many cases, to achieve social change, embedding legal norms in state jurisdictions is key to implementation. While the ICC removes the power to punish from the sole domain of the state, it requires national implementing legislation because the Court's system of complementarity relies on national judicial systems to make initial efforts at investigation and prosecution (Pace and Schense, this volume). The HIV/AIDS campaigns examined by Sleap are bottom-up efforts to secure domestic legislation to enforce the right to access to treatment by law. These are set within the context of a supportive transnational access to treatment campaign led by organizations such as Médecins Sans Frontières and Oxfam, and a complex, and not always coherent, international normative regime of intellectual property law and human rights law (Cullet 2003). Finally, contrary to conventional wisdom, the justice boomerang for post-Pinochet Chile originated from the mid-1990s with prosecutions within the Chilean judicial system that had been strengthened by reforms fostering greater independence and accountability. These initiatives were in turn invigorated by international human rights law, prosecutorial processes (notably the arrest of Pinochet in London in 1998), and support networks (Matear). The struggle to implement human rights, like the architecture of governance, needs to be multi-level (local, state, global) and multi-actor in range.

Challenges remain for the boomerang/spiral model. The range of network actors needs to be matched by a similar range of campaign targets. Smillie's suggestion in relation to blood diamonds that the diamond industry moved from denial to engagement, mainly under NGO pressure, suggests that some patterns of business response might duplicate those of states. In addition, the model inadequately registers the fact that transnational civil society campaigns are invariably built on national campaigns, and that best practice, from campaign strategies to normative and policy developments, often moves from such national contexts outwards to influence international norms, governments, TNCs, IGOs and international NGOs. The dynamic is, and needs to be, an ongoing, two-way exchange.

In a related point, it is important to note that these network dynamics do not merely transmit human rights norms, they also create them. Networks are seen by Keck and Sikkink (1998) not as mere conduits for Western values, but as political sites or spaces of negotiation, where debates and disputes over the framing of issues take place. Network actors are mutually transformed through processes of interaction and exchange. The comment below returns to the diffuse and contested nature of contemporary human rights. The structures of networks and the discourse of human rights provide a mutually enforcing flexibility.

> Western human rights norms have indeed been the defining framework for many networks, but how these norms are articulated is transformed in the process of network activity . . . human rights provide[s] a language for negotiation . . . [W]ithout doubt, human rights is a very disciplining discourse. But it is also a permissive discourse. The success of the campaign in making the point that women's rights are human rights reveals the possibilities within the discourse of human rights. Because international human rights policies came simultaneously from universalist, individualist, and voluntarist ideas *and* from a profound critique of how Western institutions had organized their contacts with the developing world, they allowed broader scope for contradictory understandings than might be expected. These critiques led in a very undetermined fashion to the emergence of human rights policy; theorists in the late twentieth century should not assume that the trajectory was predetermined by homogenizing global cultural forces.
> (Keck and Sikkink 1998: 211–12)

Illustrative is the story of how, through a series of major UN conferences – particularly three during the UN Decade for Women (1975–85), and the UN World Conferences on Human Rights in Vienna (1993) and on Women in Beijing (1995) – violence against women became the "master frame" of the women's movement, overcoming significant divisions and moving beyond a focus on discrimination. It did so by encompassing common experiences and structural problems but also difference, in terms of specific manifestations (from domestic violence to female genital mutilation), notably across cultures. This example also represents a link to a human rights frame, within the broader campaign for "women's rights as human rights," that achieved significant normative advances in the 1990s (Bunch *et al.* 2001; Joachim 1999; Keck and Sikkink 1998: 165–98). Networks, then, are sites where the human rights debate between universalism and cultural relativism/diversity is being engaged and producing enabling, evolving reconciliations.[5] A benefit of acknowledging difference within unity is that it enables a diversity of local campaign strategies and tactics to be employed.

These important processes of communication, norm construction, solidarity and reconciliation are linked to a key component of civil society strategy: issue framing.

Framing

Framing forms part of broader strategies of information management and the exercise of "soft power." A frame for any particular issue, forged in both discourse and action, is an interpretation or explanation, an attempt to create shared understandings as the basis for campaigning, and to communicate an issue in a way that engages the general public and sets the terms of the debate (Keck and Sikkink 1998: 2–3, 17; Khagram *et al.*, 2002b: 11–17). Frames forge shared identities, expectations and action from often diverse constituencies. When effective, they enable civil society coalitions to "create" an issue and insert it onto the international agenda. Frames, like campaigns, form templates for the future.

Frames are characterized by choices, implicit and explicit. A given frame implies a choice of target audience, venue, relevant strategies and partners. Reframing an issue entails a different set of strategic choices. Sometimes simply renaming can reframe an issue, as when traditional and technical terms like female circumcision, clitoridectomy, or infibulation were replaced by feminists with female genital mutilation, which much more overtly highlights violence and violation. Issue linkage is a related strategy. Placing an issue within a human rights frame, for example, can form links between issues and strategies not previously considered together. Choices can be strategic but controversial. In relation to HIV/AIDS, Sleap argues that the goal of equal access to health care in the public sphere has overshadowed a more complex, but arguably more empowering alternative: challenging control over sexual relationships in the private sphere. Although a lack of power in the private sphere entails greater vulnerability and risk, the private sphere poses challenges for a human rights framework that is more developed in relation to regulating public life. Framing the issue as the right to equal access to treatment is a right behind which many different sectors of civil society can comfortably unite. But it does not question existing social norms, sexual/power relations or patriarchy. Other HIV/AIDS frames emphasize poverty and the absence of health infrastructure.

Frames are also contested. What is at stake in such contests is how an issue should be understood, and what, if anything, needs to be done. As with the forming of political contracts, one of the main disputes over framing is whether the relevant issue should be framed in narrow economic, technical or scientific terms, and therefore remain the province of experts, or in more political and accessible terms that engage a broader public. Where civil society networks win such contests issues are reframed in sometimes quite dramatic ways. Both the landmine and blood diamond campaigns have reframed our sense of contemporary conflict, stressing linkages between human rights abuses/war, civilian casualties and environmental degradation/resources, and prioritizing humanitarian and human security concerns over trade and military agendas (Hubert; Smillie).

The growth of civil society is linked to but not identical to processes of democratization. For Kaldor (1999, 2003), the reformulated civil society agenda, rooted in the democracy movements of Eastern Europe and now part of transnational activism, is concerned with the radicalization, deepening and global extension of democracy. In Chile, the contest was whether democracy should be framed in narrow, institutional and technical terms that left the status quo largely unscathed, or as rooted in justice as well as a broader agenda of structural change. In this clash between elite/military and alternative agendas, Matear argues that human rights organizations' pursuit of justice for human rights abuses and equality before the law has reframed and deepened democracy. Post-Pinochet arrest legacies include the marginalization of the military politically and their subjection to greater democratic control, whilst the political right has also been freed from the military's shadow. This reframing has wider relevance for societies undergoing processes of democratization.

The environmental justice movement is framed as a critique of resource appropriation and displaced injustice. The former, a characteristic of "consume and waste" societies, has driven the historical pattern of excess consumption in Northern, industrialized countries; while displaced injustice involves the exporting of environmental hazards and risk geographically, onto the poorest and powerless, both nationally and internationally, and temporally, on to future generations. Two sides of the same unjust distributive coin. In a related set of linkages, environmental justice connects the social and environmental aspects of sustainable development. Environmental hazard/resource inequalities are linked to other inequalities (in access to information, decision-making processes and in policy impacts; in income, employment opportunities, health, education) creating cumulative injustices across issues, space and time/generations. Any potential solution requires the framing of justice and human rights as procedural and substantive, international and intergenerational (Stephens and Bullock).

Having outlined a generally positive picture of the interface between (transnational) civil society and human rights, and their impacts on global politics and governance, this introduction ends with a more cautionary analysis of future challenges.

Future challenges

The opening up of international politics raises questions about who the players should be, and their respective roles and powers. As NGO and network numbers, effectiveness and influence have increased so have challenges to their authority and legitimacy. Challenges have emerged on issues such as:

- internal democracy (what are the mechanisms for decision-making, strategy choices and addressing differences of opinion?)
- transparency (is there published information on personnel, purpose and activities, funding and expenditure?)
- accountability (are actors accountable to members/supporters, donors, victims/survivors/local actors, accurate information?)
- representivity (are participants all members of middle-class elites? is there a solid grassroots constituency? who speaks on behalf of whom? what consultation procedures exist and with whom?)

These concerns are crucial to legitimacy. Is this gained through representation, other above-mentioned democratic credentials or effectiveness/usefulness? Does it confer the right to voice or vote in global fora (Edwards 2001: 6–8)? These challenges and questions inform vital debates about the role and responsibilities of NGOs and civil society. These actors are not themselves democratically legitimate in the conventional sense but can deepen democratic processes – providing ideas, expertise and alternative viewpoints, empowering individuals and states that might otherwise be voiceless, demanding greater transparency and accountability, generating publicity, public awareness and greater levels of political participation. Codes of conduct for NGOs and similar agreements among diverse actors around particular issues/institutions could form part of the response to the above concerns. Four challenges merit further discussion as they emerge forcefully from the case studies that follow: whether to work on single issues or structural causes; the dynamic of cooption by states and IGOs; the danger of reflecting what is ostensibly the subject of critique; and the need to find ways of positively combining norms and power.

A single-issue focus can resonate with and mobilize broad publics, creating effective raw material for civil society campaigns. But such campaigns may end up addressing symptoms rather that causes and depoliticizing highly political issues. The HIV/AIDS campaign focus on access to treatment side-steps causative issues such as sexual and power relations, privileging aspects of public over private politics (Sleap). Campaigns may be conceived as ways of tackling structural concerns through single issues. Environmental justice links into sustainable development; debt to debates about national and global economic policies and policy-making; resource exploitation fuels conflict and poverty (Stephens and Bullock; Buxton; Smillie). Patterns of campaign spill-over, mentioned earlier, can also provide a ripple effect, linking issues to structures. Debt campaigners moved on to champion fairer global trade and the Tobin Tax (a global tax on currency speculation). Linkages, between issues and between issues and structures, and a consideration of difficult trade-offs, need to be more self-consciously mapped and addressed in civil society campaigns and within human rights, as part of a more coherent governance agenda. Otherwise one danger, as illustrated by Buxton's discussion of debt relief, is that the power structures responsible for the problem end up presiding over its supposed solution.

The ambiguities of working with governments and IGOs are considerable and well documented. Cooption takes place in many forms and for different reasons (to deflect criticism and neutralize opponents, to increase efficiency and capacity, to draw on expertise and new ideas). It can take place through funding, and the previously mentioned channeling of welfare, service provision, development aid and relief through civil society actors. The outcome is upwards accountability to funders instead of or alongside other forms of accountability. A recent survey of transnational human rights organizations found that 52 percent of the NGOs studied received grants from governments or IGOs (Smith *et al.* 1998: 410). Human rights NGOs receive funding for capacity-building and training work fostering the rule of law, for example, that could be considered the responsibility of states.

Many core ideas have been appropriated over time, including human rights, civil society and good governance. Furthermore, NGOs have been incorporated into national and international decision-making processes, for example, at the UN through being granted "consultative status" with the Economic and Social Council (ECOSOC) and attendance at UN global conferences, and through dialogue and alliances with the World Bank. While contacts often span service delivery/partnership and advocacy/critique, such cooperation can be critiqued as global governance by co-option that legitimizes all the actors involved while reinforcing the status quo. Buxton states that divisions within Jubilee 2000, caused by tension about whether to work with or against governments and institutions such as the World Bank and IMF, accept change through a process of gradual reform or push for a more radical agenda ("consensual" or "contestual" visions of civil society), eventually caused splits within the movement. More conventional sites of power can also engage in the tactic of divide and rule.

These are difficult strategy choices and complex relationships. Most forms of cooption are contested, and despite unequal power dynamics can operate in both directions. But important questions remain. At the international level, mixed actor campaigns that seek to bypass the UN and other international institutions in pursuit of progressive agendas can create exciting new political processes, circumventing UN Security Council and super-power obstructionism. But is there not also a danger that they undermine, rather than work with and seek to reform, existing global institutions of governance, in the same way that development and aid agendas can bypass and potentially undermine the state? More generally on the issue of partnership, and at both domestic and international levels, is it possible to be simultaneously within and without, both collaborating with and contesting dominant agendas? What impact on policy is possible through collaboration, and what sacrifices are necessary and acceptable in advocacy potential to achieve these gains? Is the price of idealism irrelevance, in the sense of isolation from policy debates and influence? Is it possible for civil society movements to democratically manage differences between reformists and radicals? Do NGOs end up preoccupied with servicing and training for participation in such collaborations? As mentioned above, more research is needed on the negotiations taking place within these new forms of politics and governance.

There is an unsettling danger, implicit in discussions of legitimacy and cooption, and raised by Buxton in relation to Jubilee 2000, that NGOs and civil society networks reflect the imbalances of power and participation that they purport to critique. Through issues ranging from a lack of democracy to North–South divisions, they can reproduce and accentuate existing patterns of injustice and inequality, creating new ways for the North to dominate global policy debates. Again, nowhere are the challenges starker than in relation to funding. Whether within civil society networks or from governments, foundations and IGOs, such funding invariably flows from North to South, potentially creating new structures of dependence. Within networks and NGO partnerships, local partners may be used as a source of information but often have no input into policy and campaign strategy; a lack of consultation can undermine local initiatives and even endanger people and organizations. To challenge existing patterns of power and inequalities, to open up debates, NGOs and civil society networks need to acknowledge that they both reflect and challenge global power structures and, as part of the agenda of ongoing reinvention, continually work to accentuate the latter.

The relationship between norms and power is central to the campaigns outlined in this collection and to the argument of this introduction. One of the major challenges for such campaigns, and for human rights in general, is how to move more consistently beyond the promise and rhetoric of norms to substantive social change. As mentioned above, campaigns that work well "towards norms" are often singularly ineffective in the "beyond norms" phase. This is the challenge of partial success. In the boomerang/ spiral scenario, there is a danger of external pressure and attention easing off too soon, as gross or high-profile violations of human rights decrease, as policy changes, which may be largely tactical, are announced, and even simply as regimes learn to say the right thing. Similar patterns can be identified in the campaigns considered in this collection. The debt cancellation campaign secured certain commitments by its millennium target date, but these have been very imperfectly delivered and the campaign itself has suffered from internal divisions and a decline in public profile (Buxton). NGOs involved in the Kimberley Process, having secured an agreement built around a global certification scheme for all rough diamonds, face the prospect of having to monitor the agreement themselves as it lacks adequate monitoring mechanisms (Smillie). However, precedents exist in the monitoring of human rights NGOs and in the Landmine Monitor project set up by the International Campaign to Ban Landmines (ICBL). The latter, complementing other mechanisms such as state-based reporting, monitors states' compliance with the Ottawa Treaty notably through a weighty annual report. The subversion of norms to power, however, is a constant threat. This returns to the need for normative *and* political contracts, and for civil society mobilization towards and beyond normative agreement.

The balance between different kinds of contracts and the form of contracts themselves will need to be flexible. Florini (2000b: 235–6) argues that networks are increasingly bypassing governments and targeting or forming partnerships with the private sector. She claims that this is happening in connection with human rights and, in particular, in the environmental field. In the latter case a disillusionment with the ineffectiveness of state-based norms is being superseded by direct approaches to consumers and producers.

NGOs and civil society networks are having to readjust to a globalized and increasingly unequal world, in which their influence is growing but also continually questioned and sidelined. They have a central role to play in processes that are reconfiguring power, sovereignty, democracy and governance; in ensuring that different voices are heard and alternative futures contemplated. But their role needs to be a reflective one, shored up by rigorous self-criticism and the acknowledgement of weaknesses, failures and appropriate limits to power. They will have to continue to reinvent themselves within an environment of both great potential and considerable hostility, reaching out beyond like-minded people to broader publics and providing an affirmative vision of issues such as the governance of globalization and the links between security and human rights. All of the chapters in the collection speak to these challenges. The first chapter, by Richard Falk, addresses both the history and the post-September 11, 2001 interface between civil society and human rights through "the law," good, bad and paradoxical, "of unintended effects." In the remainder of the volume authors from both academic and practitioner backgrounds examine a series of case studies that in various ways and to varying degrees span the millennium divide.

Notes

1 Much literature on this subject, certainly pre-September 11, 2001, was celebratory, even triumphalist. For more critical views, see Chandhoke 2002; Edwards and Gaventa 2001; Laxer and Halperin 2003.

2 See, for example, the distinction made by Howell and Pearce (2002) between "mainstream" visions of civil society and an "alternative" set of views in the context of development, where the latter is "reinventing" civil society as a space where power relations and dominant values can be challenged as well as reproduced, and in which, registering a critique of the neo-liberal market orthodoxy, an inclusive debate can occur about development options, alternatives and futures. See Buxton's chapter in this volume for an application of their related concepts of "consensual" and "contestual" civil society.

3 This discussion of political contracts is adapted from Alex de Waal's (1997) work on famine prevention that is rooted in state-based structures and processes; also see Slim 2002.

4 For an interesting discussion of institutionalization in relation to global civil society and HIV/AIDS, see Seckinelgin 2002.

5 Kaldor (1999, 2003: Chapter 3) provides an earlier example of this transnational dynamic, as the Western European peace movement and East European opposition debated the prioritization of nuclear disarmament/peace and democracy/human rights, across the ideological divide in Cold War Europe: "Gradually, however, the readiness of peace activists to share risks, the intense discussions, and the new ideas and language led to a coming together around new concepts, in which the inseparability of peace and democracy, disarmament and human rights, came to be mutually recognised" (1999: 200).

Bibliography

Anheier, H., Glasius, M. and Kaldor, M. (eds) (2001) *Global Civil Society 2001*, Oxford: Oxford University Press.

Bunch, C., with Antrobus, P., Frost, S. and Reilly, N. (2001) "International networking for women's human rights," in M. Edwards and J. Gaventa (eds) *Global Citizen Action*, London: Earthscan: 217–29.

Chandhoke, N. (2002) "The limits of global civil society," in M. Glasius, M. Kaldor and H. Anheier (eds) *Global Civil Society 2002*, Oxford: Oxford University Press: 35–53.

Clark, A. M. (2001) *Diplomacy of Conscience: Amnesty International and changing human rights norms*, Princeton, NJ: Princeton University Press.

Clarke, G. (1998) *The Politics of NGOs in South-East Asia: participation and protest in the Philippines*, London: Routledge.

Cullet, P. (2003) "Patents and medicines: the relationship between TRIPS and the human right to health," *International Affairs* 79 (1): 139–60.

De Waal, A. (1997) *Famine Crimes: politics and the disaster relief industry in Africa*, Oxford: James Currey (in association with African Rights and The International African Institute).

The Economist (1999) "The non-governmental order," 11 December: 22, 24.

Edwards, M. (2001) "Introduction," in M. Edwards and J. Gaventa (eds) *Global Citizen Action*, London: Earthscan: 1–14.

Edwards, M. and Gaventa, J. (eds) (2001) *Global Citizen Action*, London: Earthscan.

Falk, R. (2001) "Resisting 'globalization-from-above' through 'globalization-from-below'," in B. Gills (ed.) *Globalization and the Politics of Resistance*, Basingstoke: Palgrave: 46–56.

Florini, A. M. (ed.) (2000a) *The Third Force: the rise of transnational civil society*, Tokyo: Japan Center for International Exchange, and Washington, DC: Carnegie Endowment for International Peace.

—— (2000b) "Lessons learned," in A. M. Florini (ed.) *The Third Force: the rise of transnational civil society*, Tokyo: Japan Center for International Exchange, and Washington, DC: Carnegie Endowment for International Peace: 211–40.

Florini, A. M. and Simmons, P. J. (2000) "What the world needs now?" in A. M. Florini (ed.) *The Third Force: the rise of transnational civil society*, Tokyo: Japan Center for International Exchange, and Washington, DC: Carnegie Endowment for International Peace: 1–15.

Gready, P. (2003) "The politics of human rights," *Third World Quarterly* 24 (4): 745–57.

Hajnal, P. I. (ed.) (2002) *Civil Society in the Information Age*, Aldershot: Ashgate.

Howell, J. and Pearce, J. (2002) *Civil Society and Development: a critical exploration*, Boulder, CO: Lynne Rienner.

Hubert, D. (2000) *The Landmine Ban: a case study in humanitarian advocacy*, Thomas J. Watson Jr. Institute for International Studies, Brown University, Providence, RI, Occasional Paper 42.

International Financial Institution Advisory Commission (Meltzer Commission) (2000) "The Meltzer Commission final report," http://www.house.gov/jec/imf/meltzer.htm (accessed 6 November 2003).

Joachim, J. (1999) "Shaping the human rights agenda: the case of violence against women," in M. Meyer and E. Prügl (eds) *Gender Politics in Global Governance*, Lanham, MD: Rowman and Littlefield: 142–60.

Kaldor, M. (2003) *Global Civil Society: an answer to war*, Cambridge: Polity Press.

—— (1999) "Transnational civil society," in T. Dunne and N. Wheeler (eds) *Human Rights in Global Politics*, Cambridge: Cambridge University Press: 195–213.

Keane, J. (2001) "Global civil society?" in H. Anheier, M. Glasius and M. Kaldor (eds) *Global Civil Society 2001*, Oxford: Oxford University Press: 23–47.

Keck, M. and Sikkink, K. (1998) *Activists Beyond Borders: advocacy networks in international politics*, Ithaca, NY: Cornell University Press.

Khagram, S., Riker, J. and Sikkink, K. (eds) (2002a) *Restructuring World Politics: transnational social movements, networks, and norms*, Minneapolis: University of Minnesota Press.

Khagram, S., Riker, J. and Sikkink, K. (2002b) "From Santiago to Seattle: transnational advocacy groups restructuring world politics," in S. Khagram, J. Riker and K Sikkink (eds) *Restructuring World Politics: transnational social movements, networks, and norms*, Minneapolis: University of Minnesota Press: 3–23.

Korey, W. (1998) *NGOs and the Universal Declaration of Human Rights: "A Curious Grapevine,"* New York: St. Martin's Press.

Kumar, C. (2000) "Transnational networks and campaigns for democracy," in A. M. Florini (ed.) *The Third Force: the rise of transnational civil society*, Tokyo:

Japan Center for International Exchange, and Washington, DC: Carnegie Endowment for International Peace: 115–42.

Laxer, G. and Halperin, S. (eds) (2003) *Global Civil Society and its Limits*, Basingstoke: Palgrave Macmillan.

McGrew, A. (1998) "Human rights in a global age: coming to terms with globalization," in T. Evans (ed.) *Human Rights Fifty Years On: a reappraisal*, Manchester: Manchester University Press: 188–210.

Risse, T. (2000) "The power of norms versus the norms of power: transnational civil society and human rights," in A. M. Florini (ed.) *The Third Force: the rise of transnational civil society*, Tokyo: Japan Center for International Exchange, and Washington, DC: Carnegie Endowment for International Peace: 177–209.

Risse, T., Ropp, S. and Sikkink, K. (eds) (1999) *The Power of Human Rights: international norms and domestic change*, Cambridge: Cambridge University Press.

Seckinelgin, H. (2002) "Time to stop and think: HIV/AIDS, global civil society, and people's politics," in M. Glasius, M. Kaldor and H. Anheier (eds) *Global Civil Society 2002*, Oxford: Oxford University Press: 109–36.

Shaw, T. (2000) "Overview – global/local: states, companies and civil society at the end of the twentieth century," in K. Stiles (ed.) *Global Institutions and Local Empowerment: competing theoretical perspectives*, Basingstoke: Macmillan: 1–8.

Sikkink, K. (2002) "Restructuring world politics: the limits and asymmetries of soft power," in S. Khagram, J. Riker and K. Sikkink (eds) *Restructuring World Politics: transnational social movements, networks, and norms*, Minneapolis: University of Minnesota Press: 301–17.

Sikkink, K. and Smith, J. (2002) "Infrastructures for change: transnational organizations, 1953–93," in S. Khagram, J. Riker and K. Sikkink (eds) *Restructuring World Politics: transnational social movements, networks, and norms*, Minneapolis: University of Minnesota Press: 24–44.

Slim, H. (2002) "Not philanthropy but rights: the proper politicisation of humanitarian philosophy," *International Journal of Human Rights* 6 (2): 1–22.

Smith, J., Pagnucco, R. with Lopez, G. A. (1998) "Globalizing human rights: the work of transnational human rights NGOs in the 1990s," *Human Rights Quarterly* 20 (2): 379–412.

Stammers, N. (1999) "Social movements and the social construction of human rights," *Human Rights Quarterly* 21 (4): 980–1008.

UNDP (2000) *Human Development Report 2000: human rights and human development*, New York/Oxford: Oxford University Press.

Warkentin, C. (2001) *Reshaping World Politics: NGOs, the internet, and global civil society*, Lanham, MD: Rowman and Littlefield.

1 Human rights and global civil society

On the law of unintended effects

Richard Falk

The rise of human rights

From the time *international* human rights became a topic of interest in the years following World War II, civil society was integral to the process, although *global* civil society was not even an imaginary in this early period. As time passed, and grassroots struggles to promote human rights deepened and widened, an impetus toward transnational collaboration evolved, and from this dynamic, in conjunction with some related civic initiatives associated with environmental activism, feminism, global economic justice, and, more recently, anti-globalization and anti-war militancy, there has emerged a historically significant social construction that can be duly named "global civil society" (Colas 2002; Edwards forthcoming; Lipschutz 1992; Kaldor 2003; Keane 1998). This chapter seeks to narrate the interplay of human rights and global civil society by depicting certain peaks and valleys that help shape our current understanding about how best to advance the international protection of human rights in the early twenty-first century.

There is an assumption that guides this inquiry to the effect that major geopolitical turning-points, such as the end of World War II, the Cold War and its abrupt ending, a decade of transition in the 1990s and the aftermath of the September 11 mega-terrorist attacks on the United States, bear strongly and distinctively on the pursuit of human rights. Attention will be given to how these shifts in the overall global setting seem to alter the outlook and priorities of state actors, international institutions and civil society actors. Global civil society provides multiple arenas within which creative perspectives on the future of world order are being fashioned, and offers a principal source of resistance to present trends toward global dominance associated with American behavior since 1989, but especially in the course of the presidency of George W. Bush (Broad 2002). The challenge confronting global civil society, at present, is to revive the forward momentum of the 1990s in the altered political setting of a global war against terrorism and an American political leadership that throws its weight around unilaterally, while opportunistically conflating "human rights" with the spread of universally valid "American values" by coercive means, as necessary.[1]

But even aside from this issue of American dominance, the attitude of civil society actors toward human rights was complex from the beginning, and included some concerns. In the Cold War setting, leftist outlooks were suspicious of some prominent Western human rights groups that seemed to use their influence to mount anti-Soviet propaganda. At the same time, in the 1980s, civil society was the main force behind the European movement to promote détente-from-below, essentially a formidable movement for peace and human rights that innovatively linked activists in Western Europe with those in Eastern Europe (Kaldor *et al.* 1989). More problematic were the grassroots concerns throughout the South that human rights NGOs in the North did not regard economic and social rights with nearly the legal *gravitas* associated with civil and political rights, nor did they devote their resources or energies to such issues.[2]

A further set of concerns have been associated with recourse to "humanitarian intervention" in the years since the end of the Cold War. There was a certain skepticism among countries of the South that humanitarian pretensions were a pretext for a post-colonial reassertion of Western control. This concern mounted in 1999 when a NATO coalition, directed from Washington, bypassed the UN Security Council to avoid a veto by China and Russia, to conduct the Kosovo War, which was undertaken to save the Albanian Kosovars from the prospect of imminent ethnic cleansing at the hands of the Serbs, and in response to human rights atrocities attributed to the Serb rulers of Kosovo (Independent International Commission on Kosovo 2000). Civil society opposition to "humanitarian intervention" undertaken without a UN mandate reached a climax during the pre-war debate on Iraq policy, and was not assuaged by further evidence of oppressive practices of the Baghdad regime uncovered after the war. Especially in the aftermath of the Iraq War, the US government vigorously claimed that it had liberated the Iraqi people from an abusive government, even insisting that this rescue served as a sufficient justification for the war, an argument given added weight by Washington in view of its awkward failure to produce any proof that Iraq, in fact, possessed weapons of mass destruction. Recalling the Iraq threat associated with this weaponry provided the principal *pre-war* rationale for the war, argued with special vigor by the American Secretary of State, Colin Powell, in the course of the Security Council debate. Those who had opposed such a war all along as dangerous and illegal have become even more dubious about entrusting leading states, and particularly the United States, with the authority to wage wars for humanitarian goals (Chomsky 1999). There remains ambiguity because the UN and governing elites and citizenry of certain countries facing catastrophe call upon the United States to lead peacekeeping efforts, as in Liberia during the summer of 2003.

At this point, civil society, while not formally united on these issues, is overwhelmingly and militantly opposed to relying on human rights justifications for recourse to a war that lacks a Security Council mandate and seems inconsistent with international law on the use of force.[3]

These issues are complex, multi-dimensional and contested. The United States during the 1990s was often faulted for doing too little on behalf of vulnerable peoples, being especially criticized for its abrupt withdrawal from Somalia after encountering warlord resistance to its presence, its opposition to UN efforts to prevent, or at least mitigate, genocide in Rwanda during 1994, and its refusal to fund or authorize an adequate UN mission and capability in Bosnia to cope with ongoing Serb ethnic cleansing. The responsibilities of the UN system and the United States as global leader have not been clearly defined or agreed upon, and tend to shift from context to context (International Commission on Intervention and State Sovereignty 2001; Wheeler 2000). Since the Bush presidency, the issue has been further confused by the initial expressions indicating US reservations about the humanitarian diplomacy of the Clinton years, and the post-September 11 enthusiasm in Washington for the spread of American values to the furthest reaches of the planet, including the provisional acceptance of huge state-building projects in the shattered societies of Afghanistan and Iraq. There are widespread doubts as to whether the United States is prepared to pay the costs of such reconstructive efforts in Afghanistan, and even in Iraq there are growing concerns about the American willingness and capacity to restore Iraq to conditions of political normalcy. But the problems of sub-Saharan Africa still seem to place a premium on the willingness of the North and the UN, including the United States, to undertake humanitarian interventions to prevent dire suffering on a massive scale.

One of the persisting legacies of the 1990s was the expansion of the human rights agenda to encompass several high-profile topics *additional* to the development of an international law framework based on human rights norms and their implementation (Steiner and Alston 2000; also Falk 2000). Among these concerns were the inclusion of "international humanitarian law of war" (Geneva Conventions and Protocols and the customary law of war), individual criminal accountability for official wrongdoing (the Pinochet litigation), redress of historic grievances and, more controversially, humanitarian intervention (Barkan 2000; Minow 1998; Thompson 2002). This more comprehensive understanding of international human rights significantly reflects the success of civil society actors in promoting a multi-dimensional global justice movement, acting both as an innovative locus of agency in international life and in creative collaboration with socially minded governments (Keck and Sikkink 1998; also Risse *et al.* 1999). But this success seemed, in part, a reflection of the geopolitical pause that was occasioned by the end of the Cold War, producing a ferocious backlash among American neoconservatives that long before the al-Qaeda attacks succeeded in reestablishing the primacy of "power politics" and a related preoccupation with global security issues as a result of George W. Bush's contested, yet operative, electoral victory in the 2000 elections (Project for a New American Century 2000). Whether this shift in the global policy climate is a temporary aberration or represents a more enduring return to the more habitual structures of power and authority relating to the control of human behavior is impossible to anticipate at this point. But the resolution of this uncertainty is central to the assessment of whether human rights will again flourish in the years ahead, and how civil society will pursue human rights in this altered atmosphere. As of late 2003, defensive concerns about the abridgement of domestic liberties and fears of a global fascist future are dominating the efforts of human rights activists, especially in the United States (Falk 2003a; Leone and Anrig 2003).

The demise of Westphalia: the escape of the human rights genie

Ideas matter, but not necessarily or automatically, and certainly not often in the manner expected by the original proponent. The launch of "self-determination" by Woodrow Wilson in the setting of the peace settlement after World War I surely helped subvert the world colonial order by changing the calculus of legitimacy as between the status quo and its opponents (Danspreckgruber with Watts 1997). And yet Wilson had no such intention, seeking mainly to influence the shape of political communities emerging out of the collapsed Ottoman Empire, arguably with the rather cynical objective of discouraging the expansion of European colonialism in the Middle East at the expense of emerging American global interests. That the ethos of self-determination would go on to have such a tempestuous journey was due to many factors, mostly unforeseen, including the rising nationalism of the non-Western world, the weakening of the colonial order brought about by the Great Depression of the 1930s and World War II, and evolving political support for a consensual and humane relationship between governmental authority and the territorial society.

Human rights has had a comparable journey, and indeed has partially, although ambiguously, incorporated the self-determination idea.[4] When World War II ended there were somewhat opposed political imperatives: the overriding structural imperative was to establish order on the basis of sovereign states treated as black boxes not to be opened, whereas a parallel strong ethical imperative was to project a future world order in which oppressive regimes would not be free to hide behind the walls of sovereignty while abusing their citizenry in the extreme manner associated with the Nazi experience. To pursue this latter goal seemed to require some sort of commitment with respect to the *internal* relations between state and society, an undertaking at variance with Westphalian pretensions of unconditional sovereignty (Booth 1995; also Falk 2002a). It was in this contested and ill-defined space between piety and interventionism that international human rights was formally launched as a doctrinal reality through the adoption in 1948 of the Universal Declaration of Human Rights in the UN General Assembly. This document encapsulated the prevailing moral wisdom of the 1940s about the humane treatment of individuals, especially with respect to state/society relations. The UDHR combines a series of minimal specific standards of respect for human dignity with rather grand aspirations for a world order that is dedicated to meeting the material needs of every person on the planet (see especially Articles 25 and 28 of the UDHR). But the idea of compliance, and enforcement, are nowhere to be found in the document.

And what was to be found in the world was not reassuring about the prospects for voluntary compliance and self-enforcement. Many of the states that joined in support of the Declaration were organized on bases that flagrantly contradicted the fundamental premises of rights for individual citizens. The liberal democracies of the West that were more or less in compliance were themselves not ready to waive their sovereign rights, and winked at the hypocrisy of including the Soviet bloc states and the various authoritarian states scattered around the non-Western world in 1948. Intriguingly, the UDHR would never have been accepted even as "a declaration" if it has pretended to be a framework of enforceable rights. What made it politically acceptable was precisely its unenforceability, which was consistent with the Westphalian ideology of world order.

It is against this background that civil society emerged, some of its most energetic representatives taking seriously the obligation of governments to uphold the standards embedded in the UDHR, and to give those standards greater specificity, political support and a higher status as legal claims. What followed is the now familiar proliferation of human rights instruments addressing in greater detail certain issue areas that were treated vaguely in the declaration, such as racial discrimination, the rights of women and children, and the treatment of refugees (Weston *et al.* 1997: 368–670). At the same time, the framework of the UDHR was split into the two covenants, acknowledging a difference between "civil and political rights" and "economic, social and cultural rights." Both covenants were concluded in 1966, and have now been widely ratified by states throughout the world. The influence of civil society actors in this process is difficult to assess with precision, but the pressure for elaboration and implementation was mounted by important transnational human rights organizations, often focusing on a single issue of wrongdoing. For many years, Amnesty International concentrated almost all of its energies on seeking the release from confinement of "prisoners of conscience" and on inducing governments to end their reliance on torture. Without this pressure emanating from civil society, it is quite likely that human rights would have never overcome their marginality, being largely dismissed as either a display of moral sentimentality or the output of opposed Cold War propaganda machines.[5]

This dynamic of strengthening the global regime of human rights reached its climax at the 1993 UN Conference on Human Rights and Development held in Vienna, and also the related conferences on population and women in 1994 and 1995, as well as the Social Summit held in Copenhagen in 1995. On each occasion there were several elements present: a high-profile civil society presence capable of gaining media attention and of providing information and guidance to weaker and poorer governmental participants; an atmosphere where the relevance of human rights was taken for granted as part of the inter-governmental undertaking; and a tension and interaction between the formal governmental proceedings and the civil society policy agenda. These UN conferences became vibrant occasions for the practice of an incipient global democracy during the 1990s, and were accordingly terminated by leading states threatened both by the subversion of Westphalian authority structures and the corresponding emergence of global civil society.[6]

The enhanced stature of international human rights contributed to two historically significant moves that seemed to cast aside Westphalian deference to the authority of oppressive states. The first of these was a kind of Faustian Bargain struck with the Soviet Union in the mid-1970s, the Helsinki Accords, which exchanged the stabilization of the borders of East Europe, a high priority for Moscow, for a commitment to monitor through annual hearings and reports adherence to human rights standards. This commitment by East European governments both compromised their legitimacy and appeared to strengthen the resolve of internal opposition movements which, when the Gorbachev leadership emerged a decade later, were able to challenge successfully oppressive governments without firing a shot.[7]

The second momentous development related to the rise of the anti-apartheid movement, which was based on the growing consensus that the South African racial policies were violative of human rights and constituted crimes against humanity, warranting concerted international action by way of censure and sanctions. Humanitarian intervention was not entertained as a serious option, but boycotts and sanctions had the effect of isolating apartheid South Africa, apparently leading their white elite to initiate a process that produced an entirely unexpected peaceful transition to a multi-racial constitutional order dominated by black South Africans. It was the militancy of civil society anti-apartheid activity that exerted decisive pressure on the conservative governments of the United States and United Kingdom in the 1980s, which in turn turned moral outrage into a viable political project that produced dramatic success in the early 1990s. Also relevant was the inspirational leadership of Nelson Mandela and the African National Congress generally, which was disposed to overlook decades of persecution and oppression in the course of cooperating with the white apartheid elite in moving bloodlessly toward a constitutional multi-racial society.

These two transformations of oppressive circumstances demonstrated the potency of human rights as a focus of transnational political action by civil society, at least when historical circumstances were supportive of the changes being sought. At the same time, the experience of this period also disclosed limits on transnational human rights activism. The Chinese pro-democracy movement was effectively crushed, stabilizing autocratic rule, and several other Asian movements aiming at constitutional democracy either petered out or were brutally suppressed. The Westphalian box can still be tightly closed in a variety of circumstances, and even a generally mobilized global civil society cannot pry it open. The frustrations associated with efforts to allow the people of Tibet to enjoy the fruits of self-determination is indicative of these limits. The Dalai Lama has inspired civic activists around the world to dedicate their energies to a free Tibet for decades, and yet China has not significantly weakened its colonial hold, and has managed to gain entry into the World Trade Organization, and to participate fully in the structures of international society without stigma or constraint. The theme of this chapter is the evolving role of civil society in relation to human rights, given the altered geopolitical climate that exerts such an influence on global politics.

Perhaps, the area of greatest controversy has been and continues to be associated with "humanitarian intervention." Part of the erosion of Westphalia was the willingness of the United Nations to erode the inhibition on its own initiatives contained in the Charter admonition in Article 2(7) to "refrain from intervening in matters essentially within the domestic jurisdiction of states." The last three secretary-generals of the United Nations have each weighed in with observations that, given the increased attention to human rights abuses, it is no longer acceptable for the organized world community to remain on the sidelines when such severe abuses as ethnic cleansing and genocide are occurring.[8] But whether such interventionary diplomacy can be disentangled sufficiently from geopolitical priorities is what makes this development so problematic from a civil society perspective. Is humanitarian intervention either a cover for disguised goals such as access to energy or upholding the viability of alliances? Is humanitarian intervention so selectively practised that some countries are neglected because they don't count, as in Africa, or their behavior overlooked because of their geopolitical status or alignment, as with Israel or Russia?

And in light of the Iraq War it is necessary to consider a further question. To what extent can recourse to war justified on a theory of defensive necessity be rationalized after the fact as vindicated on grounds of humanitarian intervention? The issue is important because the law, morality and politics of global society is more receptive to arguments related, however loosely, to self-defense, whereas the tendency is to be more resistant to humanitarian justifications for recourse to war, especially lacking a mandate from the UN. To the extent that such retrospective arguments are accepted within United Nations circles it further weakens constraints on recourse to force in the context of international disputes.

At the same time, where abuses are severe, and geopolitical factors favor intervention, is it not better to protect vulnerable people wherever possible, recognizing the imperfections of world order? True, the rule of law presupposes that equals are treated equally, but the geopolitical structure of world order is based on hierarchy and inequality. Under these circumstances, where factual conditions validate contentions of humanitarian catastrophe, then intervention as a last resort seems beneficial, although the hidden cost may be to loosen the restraints on waging war (Chomsky 2001; Vidal 2002).

The new globalism: from anti-statism to collaborative activism

Global civil society self-constructed as a political reality arose out of an oppositional mentality. Such attitudes were shaped in the crucible of activism associated with human rights during the Cold War, and in relation to the anti-colonial and anti-apartheid movements. The state was perceived as the adversary, especially the authoritarian state, which by definition pursued policies drastically at variance with the moral, political and legal expectations associated with adherence to human rights standards. The liberal democratic state tended to do better domestically, especially with regard to civil and political rights, and the countries of Northern Europe, with their highly evolved social democratic orientations and levels of development, also did well with economic and social rights. But even European states struggled to achieve acceptable levels of compliance with respect to cultural rights, as reflected especially in the treatment of ethnic and religious minorities, notably those of non-European race and religion.

But when foreign policy was taken into account, the picture was less positive. The relations between the North and the Third World were dominated by the anti-colonial and Cold War struggles. In the anti-colonial settings, to differing degrees, the colonial powers resorted to a variety of policies violative of human rights, particularly when faced with a rising tide of revolutionary nationalism and associated movements of armed resistance. In the wider contest of East and West, dominated by the policies of the two superpowers, each side seemed motivated almost exclusively by considerations of geopolitical advantage and alignment arising from the political outcome of a particular struggle, rather than its merits as seen from the vantage point of the right of self-determination. Until the Carter presidency American strategic goals were specified in terms antithetical to the pursuit of human rights, especially in the period between 1950 and 1975.[9] US foreign policy adhered to the notorious admonition of George Kennan, delivered while he was Director of the Policy Planning Staff at the State Department, to the effect that the main challenge facing the United States was how to stabilize relations in a global setting in which its

6 percent of the world's population was consuming up to 50 percent of the world's resources, and matters such as the promotion of democracy and human rights had to be put aside as sentimental and essentially obstructive.[10] During virtually the entire Cold War it was viewed as preferable for the United States to support reactionary political leadership with strong anti-Marxist and anti-Communist credentials than to risk backing more populist elements dedicated to social justice, including the reform of land tenure arrangements and support for the rights of workers and peasants. This governmental position of Washington was also backed by business interests, which sought to ensure that Third World countries were governed by elites friendly to foreign capital, which meant refraining from the nationalization of industries and keeping organized labor under strict constraints.

In the aftermath of the Vietnam War, the Carter presidency appeared to reverse the American approach to human rights. It was President Carter's contention that American values should be more influential in the shaping of American foreign policy, which meant giving weight to human rights considerations. This new approach was tested, and challenged, by the Iranian Revolution, in which the forces aligned against a crucial American ally in the Cold War, the Shah of Iran, seemed to gain confidence as a result of the alleged priority being accorded human rights. The Carter administration backed away from its all-out advocacy of human rights, backing the Shah until the last minute despite the atrocious human rights record of the Tehran regime, and even sending a high US military official to Iran at the height of civic turmoil to explore whether the Iranian military could be rallied to fight against the Iranian Revolution, despite the evidence of its huge popular backing. And indeed, during the last two years of the Carter presidency, almost nothing was heard about human rights, and the emphasis of US foreign policy meekly returned to strategic concerns about Soviet expansionism.

At the same time, a symbolic and bureaucratic momentum was initiated by the Carter administration that had longer-term reverberations, including unintended effects. It was in this period that the Helsinki Accords unexpectedly gave human rights political relevance in relation to Europe, a relevance greatly heightened by the degree to which European civil society activists on both sides of the Iron Curtain picked up the torch of human rights in the 1980s. Beyond this the upgrading of human rights within the US government persisted, with the post of Assistant Secretary of State for Human Rights being created, as well as the Congressional effort to tie foreign economic assistance to human rights. In this process, again unexpectedly, human rights became an issue for political conservatives who sought to portray the oppressive circumstances in countries organized around socialist principles or aligned with the Soviet Union and China. To this day, American sanctions directed at Cuba find their sole justification in the human rights record of the Castro government, although the politics surrounding their longevity is a tribute to the persistence and effectiveness of the anti-Castro lobby, particularly in the Congress where anti-Communist antipathies linger.

The central point remains, despite some qualifications and nuances, that the state was seen by civil society as responsible for the most serious and systemic abuses of fundamental human rights. This responsibility pertained both to state/society relations and to the bearing of geopolitics and capitalist pressures on the foreign policy of leading states. For these reasons the human rights struggle directed its attention toward correcting the abuses of states, and challenging the foreign policy approach of the liberal democracies. But this pattern began to change in the 1980s. For one thing, the United States, and even capitalist interests, became disenchanted with dictatorial and military rule as a source of political stability and economic advantage. America actually welcomed the collapse of military rule, which Washington had covertly promoted earlier, in the main countries of Latin America and even watched passively as their Filipino ally, Fernando Marcos, was driven from power by the People Power movement of 1986. It was in the late 1980s that strategic thinking shifted to the view that American economistic interests were best realized for world capitalism in settings where constitutionalism, the rule of law and consensual government flourished. The Cold War ended with a formal endorsement of "market-oriented constitutionalism" as the foundation of legitimate government, implicitly endorsing liberal conceptions of human rights, while at the same time challenging socialist forms of political organization. It was this challenge that was given various triumphalist interpretations by Western ideologues, most prominently in Fukuyama's "end of history" portrayal of world order (Fukuyama 1992; also Mandelbaum 2002).

The UN conferences on global policy issues touching on human rights helped forge a less confrontational attitude between states and civil society representatives. It was evident that the goals of civil society could be furthered in such settings by working with sympathetic governments, and the evolution of civil society/state collaboration was initiated. This process took on more far-reaching dimensions in the late 1990s when a coalition of civil society groups mounted significant global pressure in support of the inter-governmental drive to achieve a treaty banning anti-personnel land mines, and later, to establish an International Criminal Court. What is significant in both instances is that a treaty was negotiated and brought into force, despite the strong opposition of the United States and several other significant states. The potency of this collaboration disclosed a way to advance the wider agenda of human rights even in the face of formidable geopolitical obstacles. How far such advances can proceed in the face of the determined and relentless opposition associated with the Bush presidency is difficult to say at this point, and depends on the durability of the current US leadership and worldview.

While the results and prospects for further collaboration suggest an important way forward in promoting the wider agenda of human rights (including issues relating to international humanitarian law and account-ability of leaders for crimes of state), the behavioral impacts of such initiatives have so far had a mixed record. The effective use of UN conference agendas to promote these and other world order goals by civil society up through 1995 induced a geopolitical backlash that has dis-couraged the organization of high-profile conferences under UN auspices that address global policy issues.[11] The Land Mines Treaty, although widely ratified, has still not formally inhibited the behavior of China and the United States, the leading producers of land mines, although it may have informally led these governments to a search for alternative "cost effective" ways to fulfill military missions. The ICC, although successfully established in 2002, and gaining more and more ratifications, has yet to act, and has not attracted the participation of several leading states. The United States government continues to oppose the ICC, and has exerted various pressures to assure that its citizens will not be subject to prosecu-tion, including the Congressional passage of the Servicemen's Protection Act that goes so far as to envision recourse to force to prevent the ICC from proceeding against an American citizen.[12]

What is at stake is a political encounter between shifting collaborative relationships between civil society actors and congenial governments on one side and the geopolitical leadership of the United States, and its supporters, on the other. Since the encounter relates to the locus of global lawmaking authority as much as to the substantive issues at stake, the United States tends to be joined to varying extents on different issues by states otherwise deemed as adversarial, especially, China. The United States invokes its sovereignty while itself evolving into a global state that increasingly disregards the sovereign rights of other states (Falk 2003b). The international protection of human rights, especially given the expanded agenda of the 1990s, gives rise to an appearance of Westphalian defensive-ness, which is misleading, because it is coupled with a post-Westphalian assertiveness that seems associated with ambitions to establish a global empire associated with the coercive dissemination of American values as the only legitimate foundation for state/society relations.[13]

Globalization, anti-globalization and the global justice movement

The 1990s were dominated by economistic preoccupations that seemed to fill the geopolitical vacuum left at the end of the Cold War, accentuated by the breakup of the Soviet Union into its constituent parts (Falk 1999; Gray 1997; Korten 1995). It was a period of ideological hegemony for the precepts of neo-liberalism, a market-driven world economy in which the role of states was to facilitate trade, investment and growth, with a minimal regard for either poverty or the unequal distribution of material benefits. The institutional infrastructure of the world economy, especially its triad of economic institutions (International Monetary Fund, World Bank, World Trade Organization), acted as "the enforcer," imposing a fiscal discipline on poor countries, and encouraging privatization and open currency markets. In this atmosphere there arose grassroots resistance to this neo-liberal world order, not only to its economic consequences, but also its association with the values of consumerism and its linkage with a globally networked media that celebrated American values and life style. This resistance became the unifying theme for the disparate forces of global civil society.

The seriousness of this resistance became evident, first of all, in the course of "the Battle of Seattle," street demonstrations in Seattle that had a paralyzing effect on ministerial meetings of the WTO at the end of 1999. This militancy was perceived in the mainstream as an "anti-globalization movement," but it was regarded by its main spokespersons as an expression of support for economic, social and cultural rights, as the beginnings of a global justice movement that sought to put the well-being of individual persons and the peoples of the world in place of the neo-liberal commitment to the well-being of capital. It was also, and increasingly, a protest against the formation of global economic policy behind closed doors by small, unaccountable elites representing the world of finance and trade, as in such settings as the World Economic Forum, the decision-making processes of the international economic institutions and the annual meetings of the Group of Seven (G7, now G8 with the addition of Russia) (Bello 2002).

The outlook and orientation of this movement of resistance has evolved in recent years, seeking to express a more affirmative worldview, thereby overcoming the criticism that globalization, as such, was an expression of technological innovation, particularly with respect to information technology and economic interdependence, which was potentially beneficial for the countries of the South, spreading the benefits of modernity and giving countries a chance to raise dramatically the standards of living within their societies. The problematic side of globalization was not its integrative reach, but its tendency to accentuate inequities, consolidate American dominance and associate itself with a market-driven ideological orthodoxy. Instead of being an anti-globalization movement, it was important to project a vision of a different type of globalization that incorporated values of democracy (participation, accountability, transparency, rule of law) and balanced concerns about capital efficiency with commitments to overcome poverty, health hazards and the pervasive effects of income and wealth disparities.[14] The creation of the World Social Forum as a civil society replicate of the World Economic Forum, and its locus of activity in the South, is indicative of this new emphasis, with its energizing slogan "there are alternatives" capturing the essence of a twenty-first century mood to *fight for* global justice, as well as *against* global injustice.

Given the expanded agenda of human rights, as including the framework of global authority structures, this effort to promote global democracy and global justice by transnational social activism could be understood as the new direction of the world human rights movement. If the period between 1945 and 1990 was the time in which the normative architecture of human rights was established in law and converted into a political project (largely thanks to civil society pressures), then the period since 1990 has been devoted to the reorientation of global institutions and ideology so as better to enable the realization of human rights. Part of this adjustment involves the recognition that the struggle for civil and political rights cannot be cordoned off from the pursuit of economic, social and cultural rights, and most fundamentally, that the achievement of a human rights culture depends as much on *global reform* as it does on governmental practices *within national societies* (Donnelly 2003: especially 173–81). At the same time, national developments in relation to the global economy should not be ignored, as the implementation of human rights continues to depend crucially on national procedures, especially in the United States, given its stature as the only political actor that claims and exercises a global reach. The Alien Tort Claims Act has a very important role as a legislative weapon for the judicial enforcement of human rights claims against corporations operating abroad in a manner that is complicit with the commission of crimes against humanity or severe abuses of workers.

The legislation, which is an old law, allows plaintiffs to recover civil damages for violations of international law wherever in the world the operative facts occurred. In pending cases before American courts involving American corporate involvement in governmental abuses in Burma (Myanmar) and Indonesia, the US Justice Department has sought to intervene on behalf of the corporate defendants, claiming that such cases interfere with the conduct of US foreign policy, which according to the Constitution should be entrusted *exclusively* to the Executive Branch of government.[15]

Part of the ongoing struggle to implement human rights needs to be waged domestically, maintaining and extending the capabilities of national judicial institutions to give victims of overseas abuses an important source of symbolic and monetary relief. The symbolic importance of such litigation should not be underestimated. The media attention given to lawsuits of this kind, almost independent of their outcome, tarnishes the reputation of the corporate defendants who evidently thought that their nefarious actions in remote foreign countries were beyond the domain of legal, moral and political scrutiny. And it seems that the current American government, despite the Bush administration claims of liberating oppressed peoples by war as a contribution to human rights, is determined to give higher priority to the pursuit of foreign business interests than it is to the use of its overall legal authority to reconcile corporate operations with minimal human rights standards (Brysk 2002).

The uncertain relevance of September 11, 2001

The al-Qaeda attacks of September 11, 2001 on the World Trade Center and Pentagon appear to have had a huge impact on the global policy agenda, but whether that impact is a temporary phenomenon, or of more enduring significance, is impossible to tell at this point (Glasius and Kaldor 2002). The importance of these attacks relates directly to the role of the United States in the world and to the revival of peace and security issues as dominating the political imagination of leaders and citizens. Prior to September 11 the prominence of human rights was unprecedented, and although the Bush administration has already disclosed a skeptical attitude to what has been referred to above as "the wider agenda" of humanitarian diplomacy (humanitarian intervention, international criminal account-ability, human security), the ongoing momentum associated with what I have elsewhere called "the first global normative revolution" seemed likely to produce forward progress (Falk 2002b; also Barkan 2000). After the attacks, the future is far more clouded. The United States' response to September 11 by way of wars against Afghanistan, and then Iraq, has elevated peace and security issues, backgrounded the dialogue about the future of globalization, and cast a long dark shadow over the global justice movement.

The response of global civil society is still in gestation. On the one side was the mobilization of unprecedented popular opposition around the world to the war against Iraq, climaxing in the form of demonstrations in more than 50 countries, involving street protests by more than 5 million demonstrators on February 15, 2003. Despite the political failure to stop the war, there was created the sense that there is a receptive worldwide constituency ready to mount challenges against the American embrace of militarism and the pursuit of global empire. What is yet to be tested is whether this anti-war constituency overlaps in values and personnel with the global democracy and justice constituency that was forming in the 1990s. The outlook and action plans of future gatherings of the World Social Forum will be indicative, as will the continuing protests against the WTO and other global economic policies. Will the energy remain? Will media interest persist? Can the participants, priorities and visions be given a new coherence that combines the earlier agenda of social, economic and political justice with the recent agenda of peace and security? It may be that a reconsideration of "human security" might provide a comprehensive framework that takes account of the dangers posed by mega-terrorism and the geopolitical response, as well as sustaining concern for protecting an array of victims of abuse and injustice, including those locked in the annals of history and those potentially among future generations.

There is another puzzling aspect to this new global context. It un-expectedly puts anti-war civil society activists opposed to a reliance on war-making as the basis of a response to mega-terrorism up against ultraconservative advocates of "humanitarian intervention." This tension was revealed in various ways during the debate preceding and following the Iraq War of 2003. Prior to the war civil society activists were being urged to join with advocates of regime change because of an Iraqi threat mainly associated with the possession of weapons of mass destruction (WMD) on the grounds that a side-effect of war would be to remove from power a brutal abuser of human rights. This line of reasoning was generally rejected by spokespersons for civil society mainly because of a disbelief in the justification for war under these circumstances, widespread civic and governmental opposition based on international law, a general sense of prudence, and strong suspicions that the pretexts for war were designed to secure oil and military bases for the victors rather than human rights for the Iraqi people. Beyond this, the inter-governmental debate in the UN Security Council and the media focused almost exclusively on the WMD controversy, whether Iraq possessed such weaponry and the degree of threat posed thereby.

But now that the Iraq War has occurred, that the country has been occupied by US/UK military forces, and that evidence has been disclosed of mass atrocities by the Baghdad regime that were even more serious than had earlier been alleged, it is suggested by President Bush and supporters that the war should be retroactively vindicated on human rights grounds.[16] The same justification was proposed earlier after the Afghanistan War, pointing to the removal of an oppressive Taliban regime as a victory for the Afghan people, although the war had been undertaken to remove to the extent possible the al-Qaeda capabilities that were centered in the country and to capture or kill the leadership, especially Osama Bin Laden. In both instances, the human rights effects rose to the surface in the aftermath of the wars partly to compensate for the unconvincing contributions to global security made via battlefield victories. In the Iraq case the threat dimension has almost disappeared from official explanations of the war given the absence of WMD, while in relation to Afghanistan there was definitely a threat, although its extent and how best to address it continue to be disputed, especially in view of the failure to establish political stability in the country. As of mid-2003, it seems evident that cooperative international criminal law enforcement has yielded far more useful results in the struggle against the al-Qaeda threat than has reliance on international warfare, and at a far lower cost and with much less damaging side-effects.

But the double irony should not be lost. The Bush administration, earlier so blatantly opposed to undertaking humanitarian missions of even modest proportions, has, under the protective cloak of anti-terrorism, accepted significant casualties and incurred huge costs of occupation and reconstruction so as supposedly to promote humanitarian goals in distant countries. At the same time, those who were most closely associated with humanitarian activism, especially in civil society, refused to affirm an outcome that was produced by recourse to aggressive war based on a misleading rationale.[17] In the background is the further irony that the American people who reacted so negatively in 1993 when 18 Americans engaged in peacekeeping were killed in Somalia, have so far accepted with overwhelming approval the outcome in Iraq even though Americans are continuing to die in their role as occupiers on almost a daily basis. Of course, the political illiteracy of the American public needs to be considered. Recall that almost a majority of Americans held Saddam Hussein partly responsible for the September 11 attacks and that after the war a significant minority believed that WMD had been found by the American forces and that such weapons had *actually* been used by Iraqi forces during the war!

A further concern is the degree to which anti-terrorist security imperatives give governments a pretext for denying human rights to their own citizens. Such a process has been particularly disturbing in the United States, blending reasonable precautions at airports and soft target areas with a widespread claim of sweeping powers of surveillance and detention. Arab male immigrants, in particular, have been subjected to harassment in many forms, including arbitrary deportation. The USA Patriots Act, passed in a climate of fear and anger with hardly any debate, has circumscribed freedoms well beyond reasonable security measures. And now the Justice Department is calling for more extensive authority, seeking additional legislation (Falk 2003a; Leone and Anrig 2003).

The challenge facing civil society actors is to reassert the relevance of human rights in arenas of global policy, and to insist that security concerns, however real, do not provide any excuse for overlooking the plight of more than half of the world's population mired in poverty, disease, backwardness and victimized by various forms of oppressive rule and practices.

A concluding note

The ebb and flow of the human rights narrative makes any anticipation of the future exceedingly problematic. If anything, the pattern of the last 50 years or so suggests that apparent trends are deceptive, subject to rapid and unexpected reversal. Among the illustrative milestones, the adoption of the Universal Declaration and the negotiation of the Helsinki Accords were both perceived at the time as modest steps from the perspective of the international protection of human rights, yet both produced historically significant results that helped put human rights on the global policy agenda. But such shifts in expectations are not always positive. The 1990s were extremely hopeful from the human rights perspectives of widening and deepening, with the emergent sense that human rights had become the moral discourse for foreign policy as well as the test of political legitimacy used by global civil society. And then came September 11 and its aftermath, producing a drastic shift in priorities for both states and civil society activists, pushing human rights into the background, especially the wider agenda.

But even September 11 had some rather positive human rights effects, concealed within the anti-terrorist campaign and its militarist tactics. Two of the regimes in the world with the worst human rights records were removed from power as an accident of wars waged for essentially geo-political reasons, especially the Iraq War. Even though the Iraq outcome is to be welcomed from a human rights perspective, this positive result does not begin to offset the larger negative effects of recourse to a non-defensive war unauthorized by the United Nations. The broader point is that in the post-September 11 world "humanitarian intervention" is likely to proceed *indirectly* if dependent on American participation and *directly* if under UN auspices, but even then mainly without significant US participation, as is the case with respect to Liberia and the Republic of the Congo, where UN peacekeepers who have been sent in June 2003 to protect the population of these countries from genocidal ethnic warfare are essentially French forces.

The challenge now facing civil society actors is to revive the effort to promote a vision of humane globalization, including a viable and equit-able structure of global governance, in the altered setting brought about by the American response to September 11, and provide a coherent alter-native to either warfare between a terrorist network and a global state or the establishment of an American global empire (Bacevich 2002). The tactical implications of such a vision includes flexibility as to partners, keeping open collaborative possibilities with likeminded states, as well as efforts to influence the policies and procedures of international institutions.[18] In some circumstances, it may also be possible to advance human rights by way of cooperative arrangements negotiated with market forces willing to trade adherence to human rights standards for an improved public image. One important institutional innovation that could be adopted as a project for civil society would be the establishment of a global people's assembly either within the United Nations system or in some free-standing mode (Falk and Strauss 2000, 2001; Mendlovitz and Walker 2003).

It is important for civil society to reassert human rights priorities in the present world climate, including the protection of peoples menaced by ethnic cleansing and impoverishment, the acceptance of an expanding role for the International Criminal Court, the adherence of belligerents to the Geneva Conventions and international humanitarian law generally, and the resumption of effort to address unresolved historic grievance, including the search for redress by indigenous peoples. The vitality and political relevance of global civil society will be tested by whether it can give renewed energy to the worldwide movement of peoples to advance human rights in the face of terrorist and imperialist diversions.

Notes

1 See the covering letter signed by President George W. Bush to the authoritative statement of American foreign policy in this period, *The National Security Strategy of the United States of America*, Washington, DC, September 2002.

2 An important exception to this generalization is the Center for Economic and Social Rights that has been established in the late 1990s, and has since been doing invaluable work on these issues. Also see Felice 1996, 2003.

3 The Bush administration has tried to expand the right of self-defense under international law since the September 11 attacks, claiming a right of anticipatory self-defense, which has been usually describe as "the doctrine of pre-emptive war." It is given a prominent place in the new statement of United States security policy (see note 1). For legal discussion of this doctrine, and its application to Iraq, see Falk 2003.

4 The right of the self-determination of *peoples* is impressively set forth in the common Article 1 of both the International Covenant on Civil and Political Rights and the International Covenant of Economic, Social, and Cultural Rights, both negotiated under United Nations auspices and readied for ratification in 1966. For further discussion see Falk 2002: especially 36–7.

5 Incidentally, such an observation pertains even more forcefully to the Nuremberg Tradition of holding responsible leaders accountable for political crimes of state. Without civil society activism, especially in the setting of the Vietnam War and in relation to nuclear weaponry, this tradition of accountability would probably have disappeared. For a narrative of these efforts as presented by one of the leading lawyer scholars concerned with these issues, see Boyle 1987.

6 For a suggestive account of the closely interrelated phenomenon of "parallel summits" organized under the auspices of global civil society see Pianta 2001, 2003.

7 Romania was an illustrative exception, the regime responding violently to the rise of popular resistance, indicating the deeper roots of authoritarianism in a country that had earlier been admired in the West because of its degree of political independence as compared to other countries in "the Soviet bloc."

8 The culmination of this debate is reflected in the influential report of an independent commission of eminent persons entitled *Responsibility to Protect* (International Commission on Intervention and State Sovereignty 2001). For some skeptical views that are much less sanguine about the role of humanitarian intervention see Jokic 2003.

9 For a systematic critique of the American championship of human rights see Chomsky and Herman 1979; for a more tempered argument along the same lines see Falk 1981. For an argument in support of the American human rights policy during the Cold War, see Kirkpatrick 1982.

10 This assessment was put forward in a notorious "Top Secret" memo written by George F. Kennan while he was Director of the Policy Planning Staff in the US State Department. PPS 23, February 1948.

11 This has led civic activism into other channels, especially those associated with the administration of the global economy. The UN conference on Racism and Development held in Durban, South Africa, in 2001 deepened this encounter within a UN framework. See the Pianta (2001, 2003) discussions of the rise of parallel summits.

12 In this vein also are the bludgeoning attempts by US diplomacy to secure exemptions from the jurisdiction of the ICC for American peacekeeping forces, as well as bilateral agreements with a series of foreign governments to refuse cooperation with the ICC in relation to nationals accused of international crimes.

13 See the opening paragraphs of the cover letter associated with the American strategy document cited in note 1. For a more comprehensive presentation of this drive for global empire, including its historical and ideological antecedents, see Bacevich 2002.

14 For a recent collection of writings on "democracy" that combines concerns for values, as well as forms, and assumes the need for a global scope, see Archibugi 2003; also see the earlier volume, Archibugi and Held 1995.

15 See Michael O'Donnell, "Capitalism v. Conscience," *LA Times*, June 9, 2003: B11; Ka Hsaw Wa, "Court is Villagers' Only Hope," *LA Times*, June 9, 2003: 11.

16 Arguably, UN Security Council Resolution 483, adopted unanimously on May 22, 2003, without explicitly acknowledging such issues, accepts without question the outcome of the Iraq War, including US/UK occupation and political control, as the basis for reconstructive efforts. For a more skeptical rendering of this outcome, without the slightest mention of humanitarian benefits, see the transcript of the Al-Jazeera interview with Abdallah al-Nafisi, June 4, 2003. The attack on the UN Headquarters of August 19, 2003 has produced much discussion around these issues, including the suggestion that the UN was to a degree tainted by its support of the American approach to post-Hussein Iraq, as epitomized by its unanimous "welcome" given to the US-generated Governing Council of Iraq and its establishment of a United Nations Assistance Mission in Iraq. See Paul Reynolds, "Why the UN is a target," BBC News Online world affairs correspondent, August 19, 2003.

17 For criticisms of such postures see Robert Kagen, "A plot to deceive?" *Washington Post*, June 8, 2003: B7; also, William Shawcross, "Because he was right," *Wall Street Journal Europe*, June 5, 2003.

18 See for example, Larry Rohter, "Latin lands don't share Powell's priorities," *New York Times*, June 10, 2003: A14.

Bibliography

Archibugi, D. (ed.) (2003) *Debating Cosmopolitics*, London: Verso.

Archibugi, D. and Held, D. (eds) (1995) *Cosmopolitan Democracy: an agenda for a new world order*, Cambridge, UK: Polity.

Bacevich, A. J. (2002) *American Empire: the realities and consequences of U.S. diplomacy*, Cambridge, MA: Harvard University Press.

Barkan, E. (2000) *The Guilt of Nations: restitution and negotiating historical injustices*, New York: W. W. Norton.

Bello, W. (2002) "Toward a deglobalized world," in R. Broad (ed.) *Global Backlash: citizen initiatives for a just world economy*, Lanham, MD: Rowman and Littlefield: 292–5.

Booth, K. (1995) "Human wrongs and international relations," *International Affairs* 71: 103–26.

Boyle, F. A. (1987) *Defending Civil Resistance under International Law*, Dobbys Ferry, NY: Transnational.

Broad, R. (ed.) (2002) *Global Backlash: citizen initiatives for a just world economy*, Lanham, MD: Rowman and Littlefield.

Brysk, A. (ed.) (2002) *Globalization and Human Rights*, Berkeley, CA: University of California Press.

Chomsky, N. (2001) *9–11*, New York: Seven Stories Press.

—— (1999) *The New Military Humanism: lessons from Kosovo*, Monroe, ME: Common Courage Press.

Chomsky, N. and Herman, E. S. (1979) *The Political Economy of Human Rights*, Boston, MA: South End Press, 2 vols.

Colas, A. (2002) *International Civil Society*, Cambridge, UK: Polity.

Danspreckgruber, W. with Watts, A. (eds) (1997) *Self-Determination and Self-Administration: a sourcebook*, Boulder, CO: Lynne Rienner Publishers.

Donnelly, J. (2003) *Universal Human Rights*, 2nd edn, Ithaca, NY: Cornell University Press.

Edwards, M. (forthcoming) *Civil Society*, Cambridge, UK: Polity.

Falk, R. (2003) "What future for the UN Charter system of war prevention?," *American Journal of International Law* 97: 590–7.

—— (2003a) "American civil liberties and human rights under siege," 2nd Annual Frank K. Kelly Lecture on Humanity's Future, Santa Barbara, CA: Nuclear Age Peace Foundation.

—— (2003b) *The Great Terror War*, Northampton, MA: Olive Branch Press.

—— (2002) "The challenges of humane governance," in G. J. Andreopoulos (ed.) *International Human Rights: concepts and strategies*, New York: Peter Lang: 21–50.

—— (2002a) "Revisiting Westphalia, discovering post-Westphalia," *Journal of Ethics* 6: 311–52.

—— (2002b) "The first normative revolution? The uncertain political future of globalization," in M. Mozaffari (ed.) *Globalization and Civilizations*, London: Routledge: 51–76.

—— (2000) *Human Rights Horizons: the pursuit of justice in a globalizing world*, New York: Routledge.

—— (1999) *Predatory Globalization: a critique*, Cambridge, UK: Polity.

—— (1981) *Human Rights and State Sovereignty*, New York: Holmes and Meier.

Falk, R. and Strauss, A. (2000) "On the creation of a global people's assembly: legitimacy and the power of popular sovereignty," *Stanford Journal of International Law* 36 (2): 119–219.

—— (2001) "Toward global parliament," *Foreign Affairs* 80 (1): 212–20.

Felice, W. F. (2003) *The Global New Deal: economic and social rights in world politics*, Lanham, MD: Rowman and Littlefield.

—— (1996) *Taking Suffering Seriously: the importance of collective human rights*, Albany, NY: State University of New York Press.

Fukuyama, F. (1992) *The End of History and the Last Man*, New York: Free Press.

Glasius, M. and Kaldor, M. (2002) "The state of global civil society: before and after September 11," in M. Glasius, M. Kaldor and H. Anheier (eds) *Global Civil Society 2002*, Oxford: Oxford University Press: 3–33.

Gray, J. (1997) *False Dawn: the delusions of global capitalism*, New York: New Press.

Independent International Commission on Kosovo (2000) *The Kosovo Report: conflict, international response, lessons learned*, Oxford: Oxford University Press.

International Commission on Intervention and State Sovereignty (2001) *The Responsibility to Protect*, Ottawa, Canada: International Development Research Center.

Jokic, A. (ed.) (2003) *Humanitarian Intervention: moral and philosophical issues*, Peterborough, Ontario: Broadview Press.

Kaldor, M. (2003) *Global Civil Society: an answer to war*, Cambridge, UK: Polity.

Kaldor, M., Falk, R. and Holden, G. (eds) (1989) *The New Détente: rethinking east-west relations*, London: Verso.

Keane, J. (1998) *Civil Society: old images, new visions*, Cambridge, UK: Polity.

Keck, M. E. and Sikkink, K. (1998) *Activists Beyond Borders: advocacy networks in international politics*, Ithaca, NY: Cornell University Press.

Kirkpatrick, J. J. (1982) *Dictatorships and Double Standards: rationalism and reason in politics*, New York: Simon and Schuster.

Korten, D. (1995) *When Corporations Rule the World*, San Francisco, CA: Kumarian Press.

Leone, R. C. and Anrig, Jr., G. (2003) *The War on Our Freedoms: civil liberties in an age of terrorism*, New York: Public Affairs.

Lipschutz, R. D. (1992) "Reconstructing world politics: the emergence of global civil society," *Millennium: Journal of International Studies* 21 (3): 389–420.

Mandelbaum, M. (2002) *The Ideas That Conquered the World: peace, democracy, and free markets in the twenty-first century*, New York: Public Affairs.

Mendlovitz, S. H. and Walker, B. (eds) (2003) *A Reader on Second Assembly and Parliamentary Proposals*, Wayne, NJ: Center for UN Reform Education.

Minow, M. (1998) *Between Vengeance and Forgiveness: facing history after genocide and mass violence*, Boston, MA: Beacon Press.

Pianta, M. (2003) "Democracy vs. globalization: the growth of parallel summits and global movements," in D. Archibugi (ed.) *Debating Cosmopolitics*, London: Verso: 232–56.

—— (2001) "Parallel summits of global civil society," in H. Anheir, M. Glasius and M. Kaldor (eds) *Global Civil Society 2001*, Oxford: Oxford University Press: 169–94.

Project for a New American Century, The (September 2000) "Rebuilding America's defenses: strategy, forces and resources for a new century," Washington, DC.

Risse, T., Roppe, S. C. and Sikkink, K. (eds) (1999) *The Power of Human Rights: international norms and domestic change*, Cambridge, UK: Cambridge University Press.

Steiner, H. J. and Alston, P. (eds) (2000) *International Human Rights in Context: law, politics, morals*, 2nd edn, Oxford: Oxford University Press.

Thompson, J. (2002) *Taking Responsibility for the Past: reparation and historical justice*, Cambridge, UK: Polity.

Vidal, G. (2002) *Perpetual War for Perpetual Peace: how we got to be so hated*, New York: Thunder's Mouth Press.

Weston, B. H., Falk, R. and Charlesworth, H. (eds) (1997) *Supplement of Basic Documents to International Law and World Order*, 3rd edn, St. Paul, MN: West.

Wheeler, N. (2000) *Saving Strangers: humanitarian intervention in international society*, Oxford: Oxford University Press.

2 Debt cancellation and civil society

A case study of Jubilee 2000

Nick Buxton

Introduction

In the space of four years, a retired Professor Martin Dent's visionary idea to mark the millennium with a "Jubilee" cancellation of third world debt developed into a movement that transformed the international political debate on debt and development. Jubilee 2000's goal to cancel the unpayable debt of the poorest countries is yet to be achieved, but the campaign made more progress than many imagined possible. Most significantly it brought together an international civil society movement that had an impact on the highest levels of political power, and has had ongoing effects in the area of development. Jubilee 2000's growth came at a time of unprecedented activism and interest in global issues and was heralded by commentators from the *Economist* to President Castro of Cuba as evidence of the emergence of civil society.

Yet three years after the campaign's set deadline of 2000 for radical debt relief, the international anti-debt movement has lost much of its momentum and the promises made by creditor governments and institutions appear increasingly hollow. This chapter will explore the reasons for both Jubilee 2000's success but also its fundamental weaknesses and contradictions. It will look at the interplay between civil society and the Jubilee 2000 campaign worldwide, in the context of growing activism on a broad range of global issues. It will cover Jubilee 2000 growth as a civil society movement from its launch in 1996 to its peak in 1999 and 2000 as an international movement of almost 70 national Jubilee campaigns. It will highlight the campaign's self-awareness of its own role in combating the debt crisis, and the political impact it made. Finally it will examine the political and economic context that led to the emergence of the Jubilee 2000 movement and highlight some of the implications and lessons of the new growth in civil society activism, based on Jubilee 2000's experience.[1]

Defining "civil society"

Civil society has become an everyday but rarely analyzed phrase, particularly in the world of development, so it is important to define the term.

Civil society has traditionally been understood as one of the three sectors of the nation state, complementary to the government sector and business sector – an "arena in which people come together to advance the interests they hold in common, not for profit or political power, but because they care enough about something to take collective action" (Edwards 2000: 7). It is best to understand these different sectors as overlapping spheres rather than distinct entities: an international study showing that 33 percent of civil society funding comes from government highlights the dangers of a narrow interpretation (Salamon and Anheir 1999: 11–13). There are also limitations in understanding civil society from only a sectoral perspective as civil society has increasingly been viewed as a "process," one of resistance to government and business or at least a way of holding these sectors to account.[2] In this process of resistance, very different views of what civil society is and what its roles should be have emerged, both from government and business sectors and from within civil society itself.

Jubilee 2000 – a global civil society movement

Jubilee 2000 certainly reflected the growth of an increasingly assertive civil society sphere that posed significant challenges to government and business. The campaign from its inception sought to bring together many existing civil society groups, independent of government and business,[3] in unity behind its common goal. Jubilee 2000's founders believed that canceling debt would only happen with massive public support, and that reaching the public by directly involving other civil society organizations was the most effective way to multiply support. The focus and timetabled goal of the campaign proved immensely successful in rapidly forging unity across a broad range of groups. The timing, which related to the millennium; and the idea of celebrating the year 2000 in a unique way also turned out to resonate with an extraordinary number of people.

Civil society groups had been active on debt since the 1980s protesting against the IMF and World Bank's Structural Adjustment Policies (SAPs), which included the removal of food subsidies and introduction of charges for health and education. Jubilee 2000 built on both their experience and existing networks. However, Jubilee 2000 stood out from previous civil society movements in several ways: the breadth of its alliances, the rapid growth and size of its mobilization, its nature as a "global civil society" campaign and the strong self-awareness it had of its own role.

First, Jubilee 2000's idea of a "debt-free start to the new Millennium" acted as a unique catalyst for bringing organizations together to form coalitions in almost 70 countries. In Uganda, the campaign was launched in 1998 by an organization that undertook research work on debt, the Uganda Debt Network. However, to promote the campaign nationally they set up a coalition, which included churches, trade unions, community associations and individuals. In Germany, the campaign mirrored the country's federal structure and was backed by over 2,000 regional organizations.

In particular, Jubilee 2000 was successful in mobilizing church members. Churchgoers were the bedrock of the activist base, many inspired by the biblical principle of Jubilee. Michael Taylor, President of the UK Coalition and a long-term church activist on social issues said: "The Jubilee 2000 campaign saw churches at their best . . . more than once I have sung forlornly *O Church of God awake*, on this occasion it did!" The paradox is that the UK churches, which were so crucial to the distinctive growth and energy of Jubilee 2000 had seen their membership fall from 33 percent to 12 percent of the population in the last century (Brierley 2000/ 2001).[4] However, decline in UK church attendance contrasted with growing church populations in many other parts of the world including many indebted nations. This may have encouraged UK churches to listen more attentively to their expanding sister churches, who had been making the call for radical debt cancellation since the late 1980s. This was evident in the 1998 Lambeth Conference of the world Anglican churches when African bishops, such as Archbishop Ndungane of South Africa, led radical calls for debt cancellation which were eventually endorsed by the whole conference.

Once Jubilee 2000 had engaged the churches, the movement managed to build broader alliances of all faiths and none, and from across the political spectrum. The campaign also succeeded in reaching out beyond traditional community-based civil society groups by winning the support of the music and global entertainment industry.

Second, Jubilee 2000 managed to mobilize people on a development issue with a scale and speed that had not been achieved before. Within four years, Jubilee 2000 grew from an UK-based organization with one member of staff and 80 contacts on its database to an international movement made up of 69 national campaigns and a record-breaking 24 million signatures on its petition.[5] In May 1998, Jubilee 2000 shocked the media and many political observers when 70,000 people turned up to form a 10-kilometre human chain around the Birmingham summit venue of the G8 leaders. In Brazil, in September 2000, 5.5 million people voted in an unofficial referendum against debt repayments organized by Jubilee 2000 Brazil, despite heavy opposition from the government who dismissed the poll as a "stupid" initiative which would undermine the economic stability gained through years of spending cuts and free market reform.

Third, Jubilee 2000 was distinctive because of its nature as a "global civil society" campaign. International relationships between civil society groups in the North and South were at the heart of the campaign. Northern campaigns used their Southern partners' experiences of the impact of debt in public awareness-raising and in government lobbying, whilst Southern campaigns shared debt information gathered in the financial capitals of the North with people in their own country. The knowledge that only global pressure would lead to an eventual solution also meant that campaigns in the North and South gained inspiration from each other. In 1997, Jubilee 2000 supporters in the United Kingdom were motivated by news that 30,000 women had marched in South India to push for debt cancellation for Africa. Similarly, news reports in Zambia of the 70,000-strong debt demonstration in the United Kingdom convinced Zambian campaigners that there was a large Northern constituency supporting their struggle, and gave them a huge boost in morale.

These international relationships made up a complex web of networks and organizations, sometimes acting relatively independently and consisting of members with diverse alliances and commitments. For example aid agencies like the Catholic Agency for Overseas Development (CAFOD) were members of the UK Coalition but had strong independent relationships with Catholic development networks and Southern campaigns that they funded, with whom the Jubilee 2000 UK secretariat had limited contact. Unlike other international campaigns, an international secretariat was never established, so Jubilee 2000 remained at international level largely an informal non-hierarchical movement. This had its shortcomings, which will be explored later, but did facilitate involvement by a wide variety of actors and limited the formation of over-bureaucratic structures that impede some international organizations.

Most importantly, Jubilee 2000 was distinctive from previous movements in the strong self-awareness of its own role. The Jubilee 2000 campaign did not just call for debt cancellation but asserted that the "civil society" make-up of the campaign provided a solution to the debt crisis. This self-awareness was the key to why so many different groups were prepared to act on an issue that was not directly in their remit.

Jubilee 2000's belief in its unique role was a response to the criticism that most campaigners became all too familiar with: that debt relief would be wasted and misspent by corrupt Southern leaders. Jubilee 2000's analysis turned the spotlight on the creditors as well as the debtors, and identified the lack of civil society involvement or knowledge about lending as the central cause of the debt crisis. Western banks and governments had made corrupt loans for ill-thought-out projects or their own political interests, in connivance with mercenary Southern leaders.[6] IMF policies imposed as a result of the debt crisis have long been acknowledged to have increased poverty and indebtedness, and have had very little positive economic effect (Cornea *et al.* 1987).[7] The IMF has gone on to control the debt relief process – arguing for tight economic conditions to prevent mismanagement of funds. Not surprisingly, debt campaigners argued that the IMF should be the last agency to control the debt relief process. As Hanlon, in the report *Kicking the Habit*, argues: "This is like putting cigarette makers and drug pushers in charge of the health service" (in Hanlon and Pettifor 2000: 16). Faced with the question of who could effectively monitor debt relief and future lending, campaigners put "civil society" at the heart of the development debate and the proposed solution to the crisis.

Jubilee 2000 campaigns argued that conditions should be set within the country to control resources released by debt relief and to ensure future loans are used for development. The Rome Declaration, signed by 39 Jubilee 2000 campaigns in November 1998, stated:

> Creditor governments, international financial institutions and commercial banks, which are chiefly responsible for the debt crisis, should not set the conditions for debt cancellation. Civil society in the South must play a significant and influential role in a transparent and participatory process which will define and then monitor the use of resources released by debt for the benefit of the impoverished.

A meeting of Southern-based campaigns in Lusaka in May 1999 went further:

> Debt is a manifestation of the neo-liberal world order, the power of international banks to push loans on Southern borrowers without the democratic inputs of parliaments and civil societies. We believe that without a dramatic increase in our own power, we will not succeed.

Jubilee 2000 Zambia made concrete proposals for civil society's role by calling for "conditionality from below." It proposed an official tripartite "debt management mechanism" between the creditor government, debtor government and civil society "that would be charged with monitoring debt negotiations for new loans and canceling of debts, and with overseeing the direction of freed-up resources toward poverty eradication."[8]

Whilst the Jubilee 2000 movement was united in a belief in its own role in solving the debt crisis, there were much larger divisions on how to achieve this. At the heart of opposing views on tactics was the fact that Jubilee 2000 encompassed what Howell and Pearce call "consensual" and "contestual" views of civil society. A consensual view sees civil society "as a self-regulating arena of the private economic individual" which counters "the unequal tendencies of global capitalism while retaining the market principle of economic organization." A "contestual" view sees civil society as "a realm of emancipation, of alternative imaginations of economic and social relations and of ideological contest, one that seeks to show the embedded power relationships and inequalities that make development an often conflictual rather than consensual process" (Howell and Pearce 2001: 9).

Both views were represented within many national campaigns and across the wider movement. Most, although not all, campaigns were prepared to work inside the spheres of national governments and international financial institutions to make steps towards the goal of debt cancellation. Yet these same campaigns would also question the legitimacy of governments and undemocratic financial institutions, saying that their past responsibility for the debt crisis and their undemocratic, unaccountable nature made them entirely unsuitable for presiding over debt relief and poverty reduction. These contradictory but simultaneously held viewpoints were a constant tension within Jubilee 2000. In fact they were later to cause a split within the movement, as some Southern campaigners went on to form Jubilee South, arguing that it was a waste of time trying to engage the institutions whose values they fundamentally opposed and whose structures for decision-making had no legitimacy.

Political impact of global civil society

Despite the tensions within the movement, the combination of broad, popular alliances in both the North and South under the umbrella of Jubilee 2000 had a sizeable political impact. Anthony Gaeta of the World Bank said in 1999:

> It [Jubilee 2000] has managed to put a relatively arcane issue – that of international finance and development – on the negotiating table throughout the world. The pledges Clinton and Brown have made would not have happened without Jubilee 2000. It's one of the most effective global lobbying campaigns I have ever seen.[9]

In this section, the political impact that Jubilee 2000 made is examined through looking at the political pressure it applied on the Northern creditors to respond, the influence it had on Southern debtor governments, and finally the ways in which it transformed the debate on debt and neo-liberal economic policies.

The campaign pushed debt and the concept of civil society participation in development firmly up the political agenda by putting unprecedented political pressure on Northern creditors. The UK government alone received over 9,000 letters, 300,000 postcards and 300,000 emails from UK supporters on debt in the year 2000. In the run-up to Germany chairing the G8 Summit in Cologne in 1999, the German Finance Ministry received 58,000 postcards from international campaigners citing the case of Germany receiving generous debt relief after World War II as a reason why Germany should lead on the issue. Juergen Kaiser, Co-ordinator of Erlassjahr 2000 (German Jubilee 2000 campaign), commenting on the impact said: "There was a strict order not to reveal that figure, nor to respond to any letter, and to give the impression that they absolutely did not care, although everybody became more and more nervous every day. These guys [from the finance ministry] are quite different today."[10]

The remarkable participation by churches on a political issue, combined with pressure from a broad array of organizations, made a noticeable impression on Northern governments. In the United States, President Clinton acknowledged the political power that came from the breadth of Jubilee 2000's coalition:

You know, we have a lot of Democrats who represent inner city districts with people who have roots in these countries – allied for the first time in their entire career with conservative, Republican, evangelical Christians who believe they have a moral responsibility to do this, because it's ordained . . . it's given us a coalition that I would give anything to see formed around other issues . . . if we can actually pull it off, it can change the nature of the whole political debate in America.[11]

This level of political pressure helped change the terms of the debate on debt and development. In the 1980s, debt cancellation was largely dismissed by the political and financial elite as likely to cause "moral hazard" (a seemingly perverse use of the word moral to indicate the perceived threat to the financial system from debt default). There was no suggestion of consulting popular civil society groups over economic policy. The poorest countries were instructed to tighten their belts, adopt a set list of economic policies and then the economic situation would improve. Jubilee 2000, together with others, transformed the arguments for debt cancellation and the need for civil society involvement in economic decision-making, and raised serious questions about neo-liberal policies (usually called the "Washington Consensus") imposed as a result of the debt crisis. It also helped ensure that the goal of reducing poverty was made central to determining the success of development policy.

The argument now is not about whether debt cancellation is necessary, but how much is needed and how it should be processed. Debt cancellation has been shown to be successful where it has happened. In ten African countries, all of which had started to receive some debt service relief by the end of 2000, education spending rose from only $929m in 1998, or less than the amount spent on debt service, to $1,306m in 2002, more than twice the amount spent on debt service (Jubilee Research 2002). Even more significantly, the language has changed completely – so that arguments for "pro-poor growth," "poverty reduction," "empowerment of civil society," "consultation" and "sustainable development" have moved from appearing in civil society declarations to inclusion in government and World Bank documents. There is growing criticism and questioning of the orthodox economic prescriptions applied by the IMF and World Bank in the last 20 years to highly indebted poor countries. Joseph Stiglitz, former Chief Economist of the World Bank, has been unambiguous in condemning the development policies imposed as a result of the debt crisis. Talking about IMF-imposed structural adjustment policies, for example, he says:

When a single car has an accident on the road one is inclined to blame the driver or his car; when there are dozens of accidents at the same spot, however . . . it is likely that something is wrong with the design of the road.

(Hanlon and Pettifor 2000: 109)

The political pressure of an international movement helped open up new opportunities for Southern civil society organizations to play the active role in economic decision-making that they were demanding. In Uganda, the Jubilee 2000 campaign initiated an anti-corruption network and became active in a Poverty Action Fund, set up to manage the proceeds of debt relief. This fund was responsible for increasing primary school enrolment in the country from 54 percent to 90 percent. The campaign also succeeded in lobbying for all loans to receive parliamentary approval – in this way they blocked a loan for a controversial electricity project in March 1999. Ann Kamya, Campaign Co-ordinator for Jubilee 2000 Uganda said:

> This campaign has uniquely engaged civil society through a variety of activities. They are now demanding increased activity in their respective districts. Civil society is becoming a force to reckon with and is rightfully demanding effective debt relief as well as appropriate utilization of government revenues, debt relief funds and other resources.
>
> (Barrett 2000: 14)

In Bolivia, campaigners who were concerned about the direction of their government's consultation on how debt relief should be invested, organized their own consultation. This was an impressive process with regional workshops in nine districts, involving 4,000 individuals and 800 organizations. Sometimes this challenge to government had to be supported at international level. When 58 activists from Jubilee 2000 Kenya were arrested during a demonstration in Nairobi in March 2000, Jubilee 2000 campaigners from around the world sent letters and faxes of protests leading to the dismissal of charges. Brother André Hotchkiss, one of those arrested said: "Without the avalanche of e-mail, fax, and letters that poured into Kenya, this thing may have pushed on for a longer time."[12]

Interestingly, whilst international civil society often challenged Southern governments, the knowledge of such a large civil society constituency in support of debt relief seemed to play a role in strengthening Southern governments' demands on the issue. Since Peru was frozen out of the financial world after putting a cap on debt repayments in 1985, debtor governments had been highly cautious about challenging creditors to cancel debt. However, during the late 1990s Southern governments increasingly spoke out for more radical debt cancellation, and had their voices amplified by Jubilee 2000 campaigns. The Nigerian Government cited Jubilee 2000 heavily in booklets calling for debt cancellation. President Obasanjo of Nigeria, Prime Minister Mkapa of Tanzania along with the Angolan government specifically cited the role Jubilee 2000 played in advancing progress on the issue. In November 2000, the Zambian Finance Minister Katele Kalumba copied letters to the IMF about inadequate debt relief to Jubilee 2000, and made increasingly strident calls for total debt cancellation. Noticeably, Zambia, as well as the other leading Southern government advocates of such policies, have strong national Jubilee 2000 campaigns. Jubilee 2000 fitted into and in part-shaped an increasing pattern of assertiveness and confidence amongst Southern governments. This has been demonstrated since the end of Jubilee 2000, most noticeably at the World Trade Organization (WTO) summit in Qatar in November 2001 where it was widely acknowledged that Southern governments were a much stronger and more effective political and lobbying force than at previous trade negotiations.

Of course the emerging consensus and impact on debt, development and civil society participation was clearly a result of more factors than just the political impact created by Jubilee 2000. Many of the "new" arguments about debt and development had been articulated before Jubilee 2000, for example, in UNICEF's report *Adjustment with a Human Face* in 1987 (Cornea *et al.* 1987) and in the UN World Summit for Social Development in Copenhagen in 1995. Moreover, the increasingly globalized economic system and the election of center-left governments in the 1990s in Europe and the United States all played a part in changing ideas on development.

The changing debate also reflected growing support for the vital role of civil society in development, superseding previous development paradigms of national planning and the unfettered neo-liberal approach of the 1980s. In response to the continued failure to solve world poverty, this new consensus has been backed by institutions such as the World Bank (and to a lesser extent the IMF) alongside influential thinkers such as Amartya Sen. In part this new consensus and the emergence of civil society as an influential political force came out of the political vacuum caused by the end of the Cold War and the bipolar approach to politics. Without Cold War imperatives, rich creditor nations started to put the blame for the failure of Structural Adjustment Policies (SAPs) on bad governments. This has led to increasing focus on the need for "good governance." Civil society organizations in debtor countries were seen as agents that could provide the necessary internal pressure for reform considered necessary for development.

This "consensual" view of civil society was key to institutions such as the World Bank and IMF creating "institutional space" for civil society participation. Initially this took the form of joint World Bank/NGO forums; more recently it has meant requiring civil society participation, which has often been led by organizations within the Jubilee 2000 movement, in drawing up debtor countries' Poverty Reduction Strategy Papers (PRSPs).[13] These developments have in turn generated a range of controversies concerning the role of the state and state capacity in development, the good faith of the international financial institutions' engagement with civil society, and tensions between advocates of "consensual" and "contestual" views of civil society.

The limits to Jubilee 2000's political achievements

The political impact of Jubilee 2000 only went so far. Even at the level of language, debates continue with some conservative commentators such as Martin Wolf of the London *Financial Times* calling talk of empowerment "foolish and naïve" (Wolf 2000). In reality, there has been very little evidence of creditors and international financial institutions enacting the rhetoric they espouse. Fundamentally there has been no shift in terms of democratization of institutions such as the IMF and World Bank. Power in terms of decision-making is still firmly in the hands of rich creditor nations.

The contradictions are becoming increasingly clear between language emphasizing poverty reduction and civil society participation and the reality which still sees institutions in Washington imposing development policies that lead to increases in poverty. For example, the Senegalese government in 2002 was required to end its involvement in and privatize the collection of its peanut crop in order to earn debt relief. At the same time, the government has also been required to show what steps it is taking to reduce poverty. The consequences of peanut privatization, however, were that private companies did not have the infrastructure to pick up the crop and farmers were forced to accept low prices at a fraction of the previous set rate. This together, with recent poor rains threatened up to 6 million people in Senegal with further impoverishment and widespread hunger (MacCuish 2002).

In Zambia, civil society organizations including the Jubilee Zambia campaign called in 2003 for a de-linking of privatization of state firms from the debt relief process, saying "that any honest evaluation of the past ten years of privatisation will acknowledge that overall it has done great damage to Zambian people's livelihood." They were supported by the Zambian parliament that voted to stop privatization of the Zambia National Commercial Bank (ZNCB) in December 2002. However, the IMF threatened to withdraw a promised $1billion in debt relief if the government did not privatize Zambia's national bank (ZNCB) and consequently forced the government to agree to privatization. Crispin Mphuka from the Jubilee Zambia campaign says from experience: "there is actually no major change in the shift by the two financial institutions. The move of renaming ESAF [Economic Structural Adjustment Facility] as PRGF [Poverty Reduction Growth Facility] is only an attempt to add poverty reduction into SAPs without changing the actual policy conditions" (Hardstaff 2003: 7, 15, 22).

The contradictions between the rhetoric and ongoing reality of creditor control of the debt relief process has led to a fall in debt relief on offer to the poorest countries. By April 2002, the World Bank was already admitting that the Highly Indebted Poor Country Initiative (HIPC) was not going to provide the "sustainable exit from the debt burden" that it had formerly promised. By May 2003, only eight of the poorest countries had received substantial debt relief – less than one third of the $110 billion promised in 1999 and not much more than 10 percent of the $300 billion (at a minimum) identified as unpayable by the Jubilee 2000 campaign (Greenhill *et al.* 2003: 18). Four countries who have entered the debt relief process (Mali, Niger, Sierra Leone and Zambia) are predicted to have higher annual debt service payments in 2003–5 than they paid in 1998– 2000.[14] It is still far from clear whether, as Ann Pettifor, former Director of Jubilee 2000 has argued, these contradictions are indicative of a paradigm shift that will eventually lead to a new consensus on development in the future (Pettifor 1999).

Empowerment: the arrival of the "global citizen"

Yet despite the ongoing failure of creditor governments to deliver on their promises, the most lasting and exciting impact of Jubilee 2000, has been its impact in empowering ordinary people on economic affairs – in other words convincing thousands of people in North and South that they could have an impact on issues such as the allocation of public resources and the world of international finance. The message and slogan "Drop the Debt" were very simple, but once convinced of the morality of debt cancellation, many activists became highly educated on the development issues surrounding debt. Russell Price who worked with church groups in the UK coalition explained that "high quality and in-depth information by Jubilee 2000 proved vital for giving activists the confidence to articulate support for debt cancellation at church policy meetings."[15] Many people who became involved in Jubilee 2000 have continued campaigning on debt as well as started to take on and make progress on new issues including demands for fairer trade relations and proposals for an introduction of a Tobin Tax on financial speculations.

In the South, a similar process took place. Zie Gariyo, from the Uganda Jubilee 2000 campaign, recounts a time when he was contacted by a local government official complaining that a local villager was talking about how Uganda was paying more on debt than the local school. The official was keen to dissuade the villager as it involved government business and should not be a subject for popular discussion.[16]

The growing level of confidence by ordinary activists has put a spotlight on the impact of economic policies which were previously left for discussion by policy experts and government and financial officials. Practical demands for changing the unjust financial system and in the long term building greater control over public resources have been popularized. This was not only evident in the Jubilee 2000 movement, but is also evident in the popular demonstrations that have erupted around various international meetings, such as the 250,000 who demonstrated at the G8 summit in Genoa in July 2001 or the lobbying of 500 UK Members of Parliament

(MPs) by supporters of the Trade Justice Movement in June 2003. It has led to the emergence, as Hazel Henderson of the New Economics Foundation noted, of a "new identity; the global citizen; even before the arrival of global governance structures" (Barrett 2000: 5).

Globalization of resistance

The arrival of the "global citizen" can be attributed in part to Jubilee 2000's tactics and vision to build an international movement, but it also took place in the context of significant global political-economic changes known as "globalization." Globalization has become synonymous with the rapid increase in capital flows and trade across borders, growth of multi-national companies, and the dramatic expansion in communications particularly through the internet. Some of these developments have themselves been shaped by debt – in particular liberalization of trade and capital, which has been one of the key conditions imposed on indebted countries. However, the changes that have resulted from globalization have in turn shaped the growth of civil society movements, especially the Jubilee 2000 movement.

Support for civil society movements has, firstly, grown in response to the shift of economic and political power from governments to companies and from the growth in decision-making at an international level. Companies and global institutions like the IMF are increasingly seen as having power without accountability, whereas state governments are to varying degrees accountable but have decreasing power.[17] This process has driven people in the South to support civil society organizations to defend their rights, and in the North has led to more people expressing their activism through international civil society organizations rather than through traditional party-political channels.[18]

The rapid growth of processes that have allowed the interchange of goods, culture and communications also helped to build civil society movements, especially on an international level. People have become more aware of our international interconnectedness – a basket of shopping at an American supermarket now can take in the entire globe with mangetout from Kenya and wine from Chile. Organizations such as the churches and trade unions also started to place more emphasis on their international make-up and used conferences to formulate shared positions on issues such as international debt. This feeling of internationalism was a central feature of Jubilee 2000. From regional to national level, campaigners actively linked up with activists in other countries. Groups in Germany regularly invited Bolivian campaigners to meet with them; American campaigners visited Nicaragua to inspire their own campaigning. These links were often made without the involvement of national secretariats and have gradually led to a web of civil society groups linked at all levels across the globe.

This international interconnectedness has been dramatically assisted by the growth in speed and efficiency of global communications, especially the impact of the internet. Jubilee 2000's growth from a powerful idea to an international movement coincided with the take-off of the internet.[19] The internet proved to be ideal technology for building an international civil society movement for three reasons. First, the internet provided an ideal structure of networks upon networks to spread and multiply the campaign's message. Second, it allowed rapid, efficient and cheap communication – email was used to circulate the initial ideas of the campaign, and then for daily communication and information-sharing between 300 key campaign coordinators worldwide. Third, it was a flexible global communication medium that campaigners controlled – for example through the website, Jubilee 2000 was able to provide high-quality information which reached a weekly international audience of between 8,000 and 12,000 international visitors. Dynamic local supporters in Seattle used information from Jubilee 2000 UK's website to build a powerful local coalition which brought together a 30,000 strong human chain for debt cancellation on 29 November 1999, the first day of the WTO summit. Equally, shortly after the announcement of the Cologne Debt Initiative at the G8 Summit in June 1999, Jubilee 2000 was able to use the website to provide detailed analysis and warn supporters not to believe the spin given by government press spokespersons.

The internet was a highly significant and effective tool in the growth of Jubilee 2000's civil society movement. However, it still cannot match the global reach of television, which as a result of globalization is being controlled by fewer and fewer companies. In general, this monopolization of media is making it harder and harder to promote political or global issues, which is why the internet has become so popular amongst civil society groups for raising awareness. On the four British terrestrial TV channels alone, the total output of factual programs on developing countries dropped by almost 50 percent between 1989 and 2000 (Stone 2000). However, the monopolization of media is also an opportunity: if you are able to win press coverage you have more chance of receiving global coverage. To reach an international mass audience, Jubilee 2000 was forced to work hard at courting the mass media's favorite partner: the entertainment industry, and international celebrities in particular. Individuals such as rock group U2's Bono, pop star Sakamoto in Japan and opera singer Pavarotti in Italy mobilized support from individuals worldwide not reached by traditional civil society networks. When the *Brits* music awards decided in 1999 to back the campaign after Muhammad Ali and Bono both said they would attend, their promotion of Jubilee 2000 onstage reached a global TV audience of more than 100 million in 130 countries and received massive coverage in the popular press (Buxton 2002).

Criticisms and challenges

Jubilee 2000 has undoubtedly been part of a process that has led to civil society emerging as a significant player on the world stage. This is to be celebrated, as Jubilee 2000's experience has demonstrated. However, this section examines the difficulties and challenges Jubilee 2000 faced in terms of internal divisions, issues of accountability, bringing together campaigns with unequal resources and the challenge it faced in working with states. At the root of many of these difficulties lies the fact that the successful rise of global civil society reflects in part the democratic deficit in the national and international political economy. There is a danger in this void: as van Rooy points out: "cornucopian expectations for social change [are] heaped on the idea [of civil society as a] . . . solution to the enduring problems of development and democratic change" (van Rooy 2000: 1). Jubilee 2000's own experiences again have revealed that the rise of a global civil society movement does not come without problems and does raise considerable issues that future civil society movements will need to resolve.

Whilst the Jubilee 2000 movement had some success in challenging the sectional self-interests of elites involved in international lending, it was certainly not immune from these problems itself. Many national campaigns were coalitions and whilst remaining united around their central goal still suffered considerable internal conflicts, personality clashes and sectional interests. Coalitions were often comprised of organizations which competed against each other and the national secretariats for profile and funding. This led to tensions or compromised decisions that did not serve the best interest of the campaign. Whilst there remained the conviction that working together would have a greater impact, it was not always easy. The dissolution of the UK Jubilee 2000 coalition into two separate organizations at the end of the year 2000 reflected in part the fact that without the binding nature of the millennium deadline some members no longer wished to unite in one coalition to take work forward.

Jubilee 2000 also revealed some of the tensions inherent in a civil society coalition that bridged North and South. For while the united aim of the coalition was to seek debt cancellation as a vital step in addressing the inequality between North and South, the coalition could not help reflecting the divide itself. The imbalance of resources along with a historical context of colonialism and imperialism shaped the campaign's message but also affected the relationships between North and South. Northern campaigns were almost invariably better funded and resourced, and therefore had a distinct advantage in terms of access to information, ability to implement strategy, and mobilizing and lobbying key politicians. Southern campaigns were usually small, with poor access to information, and with considerable constraints in terms of mobilizing, communicating and lobbying decision-makers. Nearly all Southern campaigns were ultimately dependent on

Northern campaigns and organizations for funding. Campaigns based in the North were aware of this division in resources and context and many sought to provide opportunities for Southern voices to be heard; however, the relationship between Northern and Southern campaigns was never an equal one. At international meetings, such as the World Bank and IMF meetings in Washington and Prague, Northern campaigns far outnumbered Southern campaigns. Those Southern voices represented had to secure funding from Northern organizations – many of whom inevitably chose voices that most closely aligned with their own regardless of whether the "Southern voice" represented a broad constituency in the indebted country. The lack of a formal international structure also meant that the international strategy of the campaign was often pushed by well-resourced campaigns in the North, especially Jubilee 2000 UK. This situation led at times to tension, with Southern campaigns claiming that the North was seeking to speak on their behalf and the North querying what constituency the Southern voice claimed to represent.

Some Southern campaigns claimed the fact that they suffered the effects of the debt crisis meant that they had a unique role to play in decision-making on international strategy. The reality and international balance of political power meant that the key arena for challenging the global economic injustice of the debt crisis was in the North. As a result a "Jubilee South" movement emerged which questioned the "politically expedient" tactics of Northern campaigns which it felt undermined the radical and longer-term demands of Southern campaigns.

The formation of Jubilee South by some, but not all, Southern campaigns did not just reveal North–South divisions but also the constant tension between a "contestual" and "consensual" view of civil society. This came to a head at the Cologne G8 Summit, where some Northern campaigns felt they had to welcome the "Cologne Debt Initiative" as an "important first step" alongside recognizing its shortcomings in order to keep their constituency mobilized and to help continued engagement with creditor governments. Jubilee South however was scathing:

> Do not ask us, as we are often asked by debt coalitions and Jubilee Campaigns in the North, to accept the lesser of many evils, to settle for a piece of the loaf and not the whole, to be realistic about the HIPCs as the 'only game in town'. If that is the only game in town, then the problem is not the game but the town.

> (Jubilee South 1999)

Cologne proved to be a watershed in Jubilee 2000's history. Whilst Jubilee 2000 internationally continued to grow and make a sizeable political impact in the following two years, divisions remained that undoubtedly prevented the consolidation of the international movement. This limited its effectiveness up to the initial millennium year deadline and has limited the continuity and ongoing impact of "Jubilee debt" campaigns since 2000.

Similarly, while the Jubilee 2000 movement challenged the undemocratic nature of lending and borrowing governments, the movement itself had its own weaknesses in terms of internal democracy. The rapid formation of networks around the debt issue meant that there were no criteria for becoming a national campaign, and no democratically accountable international campaign secretariat. This limited the movement's effectiveness as it was difficult to agree a coordinated international campaign strategy, which meant that some of the better-resourced campaigns took strategic campaign decisions which had international relevance without proper consultation. The lack of criteria for becoming a national campaign also raised questions of legitimacy – at international meetings or in lobbies of international institutions, a one-person "think-tank" or a national coalition of 100 organizations would have equal weighting as a "national" campaign. Whilst most of the national campaigns had the backing of, and therefore could be said to be accountable to, a broad section of civil society movements, a few failed to even fully engage civil society organizations in their country. Others may have had national groups involved, but were not engaging participation from local community level. Moreover one or two campaigns suffered from accusations of corruption – and it is likely that the growing popularity of the Jubilee 2000 campaign and the explosion of civil society groups attracted some people to participate who saw an opportunity for funding rather than because they shared Jubilee 2000's vision. Peter Henriot, part of a highly effective Jubilee 2000 campaign in Zambia, noted the formation of "civil society groups formed primarily to benefit the organizers and their narrow interests. In Zambia, besides NGOs, we also have NGIs – Non-Governmental Individuals, and GONGOs – Government Organised NGOs!" (Henriot 2001).

This issue of how democratic and accountable the coalitions were to their national population applies in the North as well as the South. In Finland, the Jubilee 2000 campaign was almost exclusively funded by the Finnish government, which undoubtedly influenced the direction of the campaign. In the United Kingdom, while the Jubilee 2000 secretariat received no government funding directly, many of its strongest national members were aid agencies who were mainly accountable to their funders, which included the UK government Department for International Development. Whilst their campaigning, policy work and partnership with Southern organizations was invaluable to the overall success of the campaign, aid agencies do not have a democratic constitution. Given growing criticism of civil society organizations and their power, it will clearly be vital that internal accountability of civil society organizations and coalitions is continually improved to both their supporters, and particularly to those they seek to represent. As Michael Edwards in *NGO Rights and Responsibilities* points out: "More democracy in global governance is the key to a peaceful and prosperous international order . . . but in order to claim their seat at the global negotiating table, they [NGOs] must put their own house in order" (Edwards 2000: 28).

Jubilee 2000's experience also highlighted the broader question of the relationship between civil society, democracy and the state. In indebted countries where democracy has often been undermined by debt and poverty, it is clearly more difficult for civil society to operate independently and there is much greater likelihood of repression. Although democratic forces are growing in indebted continents such as Africa, it has led to a legacy in some countries of a weak and vulnerable civil society. In the year 2000 alone, anti-debt demonstrators were attacked by police in, amongst other countries, Malawi, Angola, Bolivia and Nigeria. The UK NGO, World Development Movement, has documented 100 fatalities from demonstrations against World Bank and IMF policies between 1999 and 2002 (Hardstaff 2003: 21).

In other developing countries, civil society organizations in the Jubilee 2000 campaign were able to make an impact on national government and were involved in helping to draw up their country's national Poverty Reduction Strategy Papers (PRSPs). However, part of the reason for the principle of unprecedented involvement of civil society organizations in development was the weakening of the state particularly as a result of policies promoted by the World Bank and IMF – which radically cut back government and the public sector. Civil society, as has been mentioned, was encouraged by institutions such as the World Bank and IMF as an attempt to reinforce pressure on governments to reform, to create good governance and to mediate the harmful costs of neo-liberalism. There was some evidence that Jubilee 2000 helped strengthen Southern government voices and bolstered their calls for debt cancellation. However, as civil society organizations also tended to be critical, quite rightly, of many Southern governments, there was a danger that Jubilee 2000 may have inadvertently supported a process of undermining the role of the state particularly in the areas of delivery of essential services.[20] Given the increasing evidence of the need for effective national government to build development, this process must be questioned. As Howell and Pearce summarize in their study of civil society and development:

> In emphasizing the role of civil society as a democratic force against oppressive states, donor discourse has added to the dominant anti-statist theme in civil society debates . . . [and] ensured that a serious debate on the problems and prospects of the developmental state has not happened, and the neo-liberal critique of the State remains the uncontested paradigm.
>
> (Howell and Pearce 2001: 12)

Criticisms of civil society's increased profile has also come from more predictable quarters. In the United Kingdom, Clare Short, former Secretary of State for International Development, regularly held a series of regional policy forums open to local community organizations which have consulted on debt, but at the same time has accused anti-globalization protestors who espouse similar views of being "undemocratic." In May 2001, Larry Summers, former US Secretary of State to the Treasury, questioned the World Bank's increased emphasis on consulting civil society: "I am deeply troubled by the distance that the Bank has gone in democratic countries towards engagement with groups other than governments in designing projects." He claimed that a "large number of things those organizations say are not true and if they were acted on would be inimical to the goal of reducing poverty around the world."[21]

This type of critique is likely to be backed by many democratic governments, as a backlash against the increased strength of civil society organizations – particularly in a post-September 11 era where the space for dissent has shrunk. It is also likely to expose more clearly the very different and opposing views that make up the new consensus on civil society participation in development. A more "consensual" view of civil society's role was very clearly shown by the G8 governments in Cologne in June 1999 when they both increased the number of conditions required by indebted countries to receive relief alongside proposing greater involvement in economic decision-making by civil society groups.

This approach could divide civil society actors. In contrast to the World Bank's consensual view and, as already been mentioned, many civil society groups including groups within Jubilee 2000 hold a "contestual" view of civil society that sees itself as not just challenging governments and institutions but challenging an entire economic system. The danger of this contestual view is that it could create a scenario of two parallel universes rather like the two civil society consultations held in Bolivia in 2000: one run by the Bolivian debt campaign and the other by the Bolivian government. In one universe, civil society remains uncompromised by political power but fails to engage with national political institutions, which remain vital for development. In the other universe, the lack of engagement by dynamic social forces in national politics leads to an increasingly weak national parliamentary democracy speaking for an ever-declining electorate and large financial interests. It will be essential for development and poverty reduction that civil society organizations find a way to combine challenging the state with renewing democracy and building up effective and accountable democratic institutions.

Responding to partial success

These North–South and consensual–contestual tensions are sure to emerge in future global civil society movements, such as the broad "alternative globalization movement" that has gained media profile since the Seattle WTO summit in 1999. In particular these tensions are likely to surface at occasions like the Cologne G8 summit. Cologne represented the first partial victory Jubilee 2000 had achieved. Up to then, the movement had been united in its call for debt cancellation and its opposition to the policies of creditor governments and institutions on the basis of the immorality of the debt crisis. The paltry but first steps taken by the G8 governments under enormous popular pressure at the summit opened up the divisions on how to respond. At such moments, in any campaign, these tensions will emerge and will never be easily resolved. However, tensions do not necessarily need to turn into divisions. In the case of Cologne, the existence of an accountable democratic structure, alongside careful communication within the movement, could have balanced responses from all sides of the debate. A consensus could have been reached: on the one hand marking the impact the movement had made and demonstrating this to their supporters; and on the other holding on to the moral argument that clearly showed that the Cologne debt agreement failed in every respect to live up to an ideal of justice. The divisions could also have been diminished if there had been a greater attempt by both sides to appreciate, learn and respect each other's different political and economic contexts, and even to realize that different approaches within the same movement could be complementary rather than contradictory.

As the campaign formally came to an end at the end of the year 2000, it was noticeable that the movement seemed to be united again in the view that it was still very far from its goal of a "debt-free start for a billion people." Trying to understand the lack of progress despite unprecedented pressure and even promises from the richest nations highlights perhaps the most important lesson from Jubilee 2000's experience, which is never to lose sight of tackling the power relations that affect change. The creditor nations and international financial institutions that bear so much responsibility for the debt crisis are still the institutions that ultimately decide on debt relief, set the conditions and monitor how proceeds from debt relief are spent. It is not in their interest to cancel debt and as a result, despite many promises, very little debt has been cancelled.

Redistributing power will require democratization of the international economic order, particularly institutions like the IMF, so that poorer countries may have a greater say. It will also require strengthening of national governments' ability to regulate multinational companies to ensure their economic activities bring benefit to ordinary people. Most importantly it will involve long-term investment in building up civil society. The new Poverty Reduction Strategy Papers (PRSPs) may talk about country "ownership" and include a new process which allows countries to draw up poverty reduction strategies in consultation with civil society, but the ultimate veto still lies with the creditor-dominated IMF. As Angela Woods and Matthew Lockwood have argued: "All too often ownership relates to persuading the public that reforms are necessary and good in order to minimize political opposition to them" (Woods and Lockwood 1999: 13).

Whilst all Jubilee 2000's declarations talked about putting civil society at the heart of decisions about lending and finance in order to achieve development, the reality was that this conflicted with its short-term goals of debt cancellation by the end of the year 2000. Very few Jubilee 2000 campaigns had the capacity either to engage the whole civil society sector in their country or even then had the capacity to challenge the government and develop alternative policy proposals. Despite unprecedented recent growth of non-governmental organizations in the South, civil society remains weak. Only long-term and substantial funding for Southern civil society organizations and a strong commitment to democracy alongside partnership in development and advocacy have the potential to rectify this balance.

Since the formal end of Jubilee 2000 UK in December 2000, debt campaigning has continued in many countries, but noticeably with less of a coordinated focus and its public visibility dissipated by campaigning on a broader range of issues. Henry Northover of the Catholic Agency for Overseas Development (CAFOD), speaking after meetings with World Bank officials at their autumn 2002 meetings, said:

> It's clear that we are unlikely to get more aid or debt relief without the sort of domestic political pressure applied by the Jubilee 2000 movement. The challenge is to refocus the different themes and campaigns that have emerged around a common, clear and targeted message.[22]

This will be difficult to achieve, although the rewards could be far greater than those won through the pressure of the Jubilee 2000 movement. For civil society mobilization around international issues has, if anything, grown since 2000, despite fears that a post-September 11 world could constrain it. 250,000 people demonstrated at the World Bank and IMF meetings in Barcelona in March 2002 under the banner "Another world is possible." Millions marched against the war on Iraq in the largest-ever international mobilization on an international issue on February 15, 2003. Yet global civil society has also become a more complex and less united force. This was evident at the G8 summit in Genoa in July 2001. With the killing of one protestor by police and widespread use of repressive tactics, divisions on the way forward for the "alternative globalization movement" were highly apparent as different civil society groups attacked each other. It remains to be seen whether the "alternative globalization movement" will come to respect and manage the "contestual" and "consensual" views within it or whether it will split and let its energies dissipate.

Conclusion

In response to protests outside the IMF and World Bank, in April 2000, Michel Camdessus, former President of the IMF is reported to have said: "Who are these people? Who do they represent? If anyone is the voice of the people, it is me."[23] The emergence of civil society movements such as Jubilee 2000 and the broader anti-globalization movement at the turn of the millennium has surprised many commentators and shaken those in power. Ironically, the roots of the movement that Camdessus saw outside his multi-storied building lay inside his own institution. The IMF's response to the debt crisis in the 1980s contained in it some of the seeds of the civil society movement that would rise against it – their policies on capital account liberalization, export-led growth, deregulation, privatization and a weakened state helped fuel globalization, a widening gap between rich and poor and linked up a global movement of resistance. "Global civil society" has emerged as a politically powerful player with a confidence in its own role, and growing popular support.

The fact that essentially voluntary associations with an international awareness are standing up for or representing the excluded at an international level heralds many opportunities. The arrival of the "global citizen" who is highly informed and connected with creative popular networks around the world has the potential to hold to account and challenge the increasing concentration of economic power in the hands of a few governments and multinational companies. Whilst international institutions like the United Nations lack political power, and global bodies like the WTO and the World Bank continue to be controlled by the rich few, the role of the "global citizen" is vital to balance the democratic deficit inherent in the current highly unequal global order. This will involve combining targeted campaigns for specific policy changes with a clear challenge to the power structures that perpetuate injustice.

However, citizenship also carries with it responsibilities and a critical examination of civil society's own make-up. The IMF, controlled by a few creditor governments, is clearly not representative of the "people" as Camdessus would like to think. But civil society movements themselves are far from democratic, and have been shaped by the unequal world they are trying to change. To ensure their power and moral force, civil society organizations will need to demonstrate how they represent people. This is particularly important for the more diffuse, broader "alternative globalization movement" if it is to embody the ideals of participation that it promotes. This will involve an ongoing process, by which civil society organizations seek to make themselves more accountable, and seek to strengthen democracy and popular participation. It will involve civil society organizations continually challenging themselves with the same vigor as their unprecedented challenge to the established political institutions in the last ten years.

Acknowledgements

The author would especially like to thank Marlene Barrett, Graham Gordon, Henry Northover, Duncan Green and Juergen Kaiser for their constructive and helpful comments. He would also like to thank all the international activists in Jubilee 2000 who provided immense inspiration in his work, and hopes this analysis will be useful to future civil society organizations as they struggle for social and economic justice.

Notes

1 Jubilee 2000 UK officially dissolved on December 31, 2000, although work on debt has continued in many countries or been carried on by new organizations and coalitions such as the Jubilee Debt Campaign in the United Kingdom and the Uganda Debt Network. This chapter will mainly limit its examination in terms of timing to the period up to the UK coalition's official dissolution at the end of the year 2000, but in terms of geography it examines Jubilee 2000 as a global movement.

2 Alison van Rooy (2000) describes this latter definition of civil society as the "anti-hegemonic model" in her excellent introduction to the concept of civil society.

3 Jubilee 2000 did have two business members namely, the Co-operative Bank and Triodos Bank. However, they were businesses with a strong "ethical mandate" who signed up to the campaign without playing any role in steering its strategic direction.

4 This decline in membership of traditional civil society organizations was also true of the trade union members of Jubilee 2000. In the UK, membership of trade unions fell from 13.3 million in 1979 to 7.1 million in 1998, although there has been some growth recently. Source: TUC website www.tuc.org.uk

5 The Jubilee 2000 UK office was opened in April 1996, after several years of campaigning on the issue by Martin Dent, who launched the idea in the early 1990s and promoted it with Bill Peters. However, its beginnings could also be traced to the call for a "Year of Jubilee for Africa" by the All-African Council of Churches in 1990.

6 For example, the late President Mobutu of former Zaire was lent $8.5 billion by Western lenders including the IMF over 15 years, despite clear evidence of corruption. Yet the moment he died, the IMF came in to advise the new government on how to ensure repayment.

7 Despite this research, IMF's policies have changed very little. In the 1990s, the UN Conference on Trade and Development (UNCTAD) found that those countries that liberalized the most had the highest levels of poverty (Hardstaff 2003: 11).

8 The full proposal was detailed by Jubilee 2000 Zambia in the *Times of Zambia* on August 12, 1999.

9 Anthony Gaeta, spokesman for the World Bank, quoted in *PR Week*, April 16, 1999.

10 J. Kaiser, quoted in email correspondence with author, September 2000.

11 Quote from a speech by President Clinton at a White House prayer breakfast in September 2000.

12 Brother Hotchkiss, quoted in email correspondence with the author, April 2000.

13 President Wolfensohn of the World Bank has strongly endorsed this "consensual" view of Jubilee 2000's role. Speaking in 1999 he said: "[We need]

coalitions with civil society and communities to mobilise the kind of grass roots support we have seen behind the debt campaign – and to extend it to health, to education for all, to participation, and to poverty reduction."

14 World Bank statistics http://www.worldbank.org. The World Bank itself admitted in August 2002 that to meet the Millennium Development Goals agreed by the UN, which commit the international community to halve poverty by 2015, will require full debt cancellation for impoverished countries and additional aid. See World Bank 2002: 91.

15 R. Price in email to author, September 2000.

16 Z. Gariyo in conversation with author, June 1999.

17 The votes of the IMF are determined by the contributions made by its members – consequently in 2000, the ten richest countries controlled 45 percent of the votes of the IMF.

18 Sarah Parkin, chair of the Real World Coalition put this question in an article on the legitimacy of the G8 in the *Guardian* on July 11, 2001: "What is it that governments are getting so wrong that prompts so many people to give up voting in elections every four or five years, and to go elsewhere for the services and political campaigning that matter most to them?" In part as she points out it is the failure of the G8 leaders to tackle the issues that concern people, but it also reflects a growing sense that the power to effect economic decisions lies elsewhere. This was reflected in polls held during the UK General Election campaign in May 2001, which revealed both a strong apathy for domestic politics but also an unprecedented prioritizing of international issues. Polls undertaken and reported in the *Scotsman*, May 15, 2001.

19 The internet had a global online population of 44 million (mostly based in the United States) at the end of 1995. Four years later, the number of people online had gone up by 700 percent. See Press Release, *Computer Industry Almanac* (August 18, 1999), at http://www.c-i-a.com/199908iu.htm.

20 Some debt campaigns went further in undermining the role of the state in their call for debt-for-development swaps. This involves releasing funds from debt cancellation directly to civil society organizations, a step that goes further than PRSPs by taking the state completely out of the picture.

21 L. Summers in a speech at the US World Bank Country Director's retreat, May 2, 2001.

22 H. Northover in email to author, October 2002.

23 Quoted in "Focus on the Global South," *Focus on Trade Issue No. 46* (February 2000), at http://www.focusweb.org/focus/pd/apec/fot/fot46.htm.

Bibliography

Barrett, M. (2000) *The World Will Never Be the Same Again*, London: Jubilee 2000.

Brierley, P. (ed.) (2000/2001 edition) *Religious Trends*, No. 2, London: Harper Collins.

Buxton, N. (2002) "Dial up networking for debt cancellation and development: a case study of Jubilee 2000," in S. Hick and J. McNutt (eds) *Advocacy, Activism and the Internet: community organization and social policy*, Chicago: Lyceum Books.

Cornea, G. A., Jolly, R. and Stewart, F. (eds) (1987) *Adjustment with a Human Face, Vol. 1: Protecting the Vulnerable and Promoting Growth*, Oxford: Clarendon Press.

Edwards, M. (2000) *NGO Rights and Responsibilities: a new deal for global governance*, London: NCVO and Foreign Policy Center.

Greenhill, R., Northover, H., Pettifor, A. and Sinha, A (2003) *Did the G8 Drop the Debt? Five years after the Birmingham human chain what has been achieved and what more needs to be done?* London: CAFOD/Jubilee Debt Campaign/ Jubilee Research.

Hanlon, J. and Pettifor, A. (2000) *Kicking the Habit: finding a lasting solution to addictive lending and borrowing – and its addictive side-effects*, London: Jubilee 2000.

Hardstaff, P. (2003) *Treacherous Conditions: how IMF and World Bank policies tied to debt relief are undermining development*, London: World Development Movement.

Henriot, P. (2001) "Democracy, development, debt and disease in a globalising Africa: what is our future?," speech at SEDOS Catholic Religious Conference, Rome, 28 June.

Howell, J. and Pearce, J. (2001) *Civil Society and Development: a critical exploration*, Boulder, CO: Lynne Rienner Publishers.

Jubilee Research at New Economics Foundation (August 2002) "Relief works: African proposals for debt cancellation and why debt relief works," at http://www.jubileeresearch.org/analysis/reports/reliefworks.pdf.

Jubilee South (December 1, 1999), "Jubilee South and the call for a new strategic alliance," at http://www.jubileesouth.org.

Lipschutz, R. D. (1992) "Reconstructing world politics: the emergence of global civil society," *Millennium: Journal of International Studies* 21 (3): 389–420.

MacCuish, D. (2002) "Privatizing peanuts: no debt relief without it," *Upstream Journal*, September, Social Justice Committee, Montreal, Quebec, at http://www. s-j-c.net.

Pettifor, A. (1999) "What does the Köln agreement mean for the Jubilee 2000 campaign worldwide?", June 24 at http://www.jubilee2000uk.org/jubilee2000/ comment/koln0107.html.

Salamon, L. M. and Anheir, H. K. (1999) *The Emerging Sector Revisited: a summary*, Baltimore, MD: Center of Civil Studies, Johns Hopkins University.

Stone, J. (2000) *Losing Perspective: global affairs on British terrestrial television 1989–1999*, London: Third World Environment and Environment Broadcasting Project.

van Rooy, A. (2000) *Civil Society and the Aid Industry*, London: Earthscan.

Wolf, M. (2000) "The power to banish poverty," *Financial Times*, September 13, London.

Wolfensohn, J. (1999) 'Coalitions for Cange, Address to the Board of Governors at the IMF and World Bank Annual Meetings, September 28, Washington, DC, at http://www.worldbank.org/html/extdr/am99/jdw-sp/jdwsp-en.htm.

Woods, A. and Lockwood, M. (1999) *The Perestroika of Aid? New perspectives on conditionality*, London: Bretton Woods Project and Christian Aid.

World Bank (2002), *HIPC status of implementation report*, August 16, at http://www.worldbank.org.

3 "New" humanitarian advocacy?

Civil society and the landmines ban[1]

Don Hubert

The campaign to ban landmines has been widely celebrated as one of the most successful examples of humanitarian advocacy. At the outset of the campaign in the early 1990s, estimates suggested that more than 100 million mines had been scattered through over 60 countries and each month 2,000 civilians were either killed or severely injured. In addition to the direct human cost, the presence of landmines impeded the distribution of humanitarian aid, obstructed access to infrastructure and agricultural land, deterred the repatriation of refugees and diverted vital resources from reconstruction efforts. In the most mine-affected countries, clearance pro-grams were expected to take decades, and in spite of growing resources dedicated to the task, the number of mines sown worldwide far outpaced demining efforts.

Seemingly from nowhere, the International Campaign to Ban Landmines (ICBL) emerged. It mobilized grassroots activists, galvanized public opinion, lobbied governments and by the fall of 1997 had secured an treaty comprehensively banning the production, transfer, stockpiling and use of anti-personnel landmines. In recognition of their efforts, the Campaign and its coordinator Jody Williams were awarded the 1997 Nobel Peace Prize.

Lessons from the landmine campaign are being applied by governments and activists to a range of other humanitarian concerns. Yet confidence in the "conventional wisdom" is often misplaced. Learning lessons depends both on an accurate account of the campaign itself and a rigorous assessment of the reasons for its success. This chapter provides a detailed account of the emergence and development of the campaign from the initial attempts to restrict landmines in the 1970s, through the birth of the international NGO campaign in the early 1990s, to the signing ceremony of the Land-mines Convention in December 1997. It also provides a thorough assessment of the key factors accounting for their success and a discussion of the broader significance of the campaign.

The origins of the campaign to ban landmines

Although landmines were first used in the American Civil War, their widespread deployment began during World War I. These anti-tank mines were used predominantly to secure defensive positions. But as they were easily found, removed and redeployed by the enemy, the anti-personnel mine, a smaller device designed to maim rather than kill, was developed. Mine warfare played a greater role in World War II, where the anti-personnel mine was deployed not only to protect anti-tank munitions but also to defend military bases and installations, deny strategic positions and channel enemy forces. As the objective was to alter the pattern of enemy movements, in most cases the devices were laid within clearly identified minefields. Given the longevity of the explosive charge and the difficulties in maintaining adequate markings, however, even properly laid minefields became serious hazards to civilians, as the contemporary casualties of World War II mines in Libya and Poland attest.

Technological advances in the production and deployment of mines through the 1960s, however, radically transformed the scale of the problem. The Vietnam War witnessed the initial widespread use of remotely delivered mine systems, first from aircraft and later from ground vehicles and artillery. In contrast to the laborious process of hand emplacement, the capacity for remote delivery allowed for rapid deployment and spurred production in the tens of millions. Predominantly defensive purposes began to give way to offensive tactics. In Vietnam, the United States used mines in an attempt to stop the flow of men and material to South Vietnam from the North and also through Laos and Cambodia, but they were also used as area denial weapons, rendering villages, fields and grazing lands unsuitable for civilian use. Remote delivery precluded the possibility of marking minefields or keeping accurate records of mined areas.

As recognition of the effects on civilians of a range of emerging anti-personnel weapons increased, efforts were made to restrict their use further through the development of international humanitarian law. Two basic principles relevant to the use of anti-personnel weapons already existed: a prohibition on weapons causing "superfluous injury" and "unnecessary suffering" and a prohibition on the use of indiscriminate weapons. A diplomatic process attempting to apply these two principles emerged in the mid-1970s.

The International Committee of the Red Cross (ICRC), at the prompting of the Swedish government, convened two conferences of governmental experts, one in 1974 and another in 1976, on Weapons that May Cause Unnecessary Suffering or Have Indiscriminate Effects. The second conference reached consensus on three proposals: a ban on undetectable fragments, restrictions on remotely delivered mines and a prohibition on incendiary attacks against civilian areas. Priority was placed on universal acceptance of minimum standards rather than pursuit of stringent prohibitions unlikely to attract broad support.

The Diplomatic Conference of the 1977 Additional Protocols to the Geneva Conventions, following up on the conclusions of the ICRC meetings, recommended that a formal Conference of Governments be convened not later than 1979 to pursue "agreements on prohibitions or restrictions on the use of specific conventional weapons." The UN General Assembly acted later that year to set into motion two preparatory conferences in 1978 and 1979 leading to the UN Conference on Prohibitions or Restrictions of Certain Conventional Weapons which May Be Deemed to Be Excessively Injurious or to Have Indiscriminate Effects (Certain Conventional Weapons Conference or CCW).

The 1980 CCW Convention and its three Protocols on non-detectable fragments, landmines and booby traps, and incendiary weapons represented the first formal ban on conventional weapons since the 1899 Hague Declaration banning dum-dum bullets. The second Protocol on landmines and booby traps prohibited their indiscriminate use, and included modest restrictions on the use of remotely deliverable mines. Calls for more stringent restrictions on landmines came from the ICRC and NGO observers. The ICRC stressed that military utility alone was insufficient grounds on which to base the legality of a weapon and argued that the principle of proportionality required that utility be balanced against humanitarian costs (Aubert 1990). But these views were given little consideration by the military experts and diplomats working in relative obscurity. The Convention entered into force following ratification by the twentieth state on December 2, 1983.

The modest advances made through the 1980 Convention, however, were to be rendered totally inadequate in the face of the continued use of readily available anti-personnel mines in countries such as Cambodia, Afghanistan, Angola and Mozambique. The CCW failed to achieve broad ratification, with only 31 states committed by 1990. But the emerging landmines crisis was not merely the result of insufficient ratification or respect for existing provisions. The scope of the treaty failed to cover non-international or civil wars while technological advances including non-detectable mines and anti-handling devices were transforming the character of the landmines problem.

Although largely neglected by diplomats after 1980, a growing landmines crisis was apparent to ICRC field surgeons and NGOs working in medical assistance programs and demining operations. The origins of the NGO campaign can be traced back to three organizations working in Cambodia: the Coalition for Peace and Reconciliation, Handicap International (HI) and Mines Advisory Group (MAG). The head of the first group, a Jesuit priest, had worked in the area since 1979 and by the early 1990s was including reports on landmines in the Coalition's newsletter. HI was founded in 1979 by young doctors working in Cambodian refugee camps to help handicapped people in poverty situations, in particular some 5,000 victims of anti-personnel landmines. In its first decade of operations, HI had fitted more than 15,000 amputees with prostheses, but the number of amputees had grown to over 30,000 and was getting steadily worse not only in Cambodia but also in over half of the 26 countries in which it worked. Sensing that it was losing ground, HI began to take a proactive approach to the landmines crisis in 1992. The third group, a British demining organization called the MAG, was founded only in 1992, although its director Rae McGrath had been working on demining for several years in Afghanistan and Cambodia.

In this context of growing alarm came the first two influential accounts of the scale of the landmines crisis, testimony by the Women's Commission for Refugee Women and Children to a US Congressional Committee in 1991 and *Landmines in Cambodia: the coward's war* (Stover and McGrath 1991). Information, particularly from ICRC surgeons, also began to appear in Western medical journals (Coupland 1989; Coupland and Korver 1991; McGrath and Stover 1991). These activities in the early 1990s laid the foundation for the campaign to ban anti-personnel landmines that emerged in 1992. Advocacy for a ban came from four different sets of actors: NGOs, the ICRC, the UN and individual governments. Each is reviewed in turn.

The advocates

NGOs

The International Campaign to Ban Landmines (ICBL) emerged out of nascent campaigns among NGOs from different countries. In November 1991, the Vietnam Veterans of America Foundation (VVAF) and Medico International, a German-based medical assistance organization, agreed to launch a campaign of advocacy and bring together NGOs to call for a global ban on mines. At the launch of the French translation of *Landmines in Cambodia: the coward's war* the following spring, HI, MAG and Physicians for Human Rights (PHR) began a signature campaign to stop the "Coward's War." These two efforts were merged in October 1992 when the five organizations, together with Human Rights Watch (HRW), agreed to coordinate their campaigning and co-sponsor an NGO Conference on Landmines in London the following year. The London Conference in May 1993 brought together 50 representatives from 40 NGOs to strategize. A steering committee of the original six organizations was agreed, with VVAF taking the role of coordinator. The conference also set out three central objectives:

(a) an international ban on the use, production, stockpiling and sale, transfer or export of anti-personnel mines;
(b) the establishment of an international fund, administered by the UN, to promote and finance mine victim aid programs and landmine awareness, clearance and eradication programs worldwide; and
(c) ensuring that countries producing and disseminating anti-personnel mines contribute to the fund.

The ICBL invited other NGOs that supported these objectives to become part of the campaign and within two years the number of supporting organizations exceeded 350. A further NGO conference was held in Geneva in May 1994 with logistical support from the United Nations Children's Fund (UNICEF). If the first conference represented the launch of the NGO campaign, the second meeting, with 110 representatives from 75 organizations, represented its consolidation, with both greater cohesion and more articulate demands.

Lobbying for a total ban on landmines and for more intensive mine clearance was a central component of the NGO contribution to addressing the global landmines crisis. Equally important, however, was the production of authoritative reports on the scale and character of the crisis in countries such as Cambodia, Iraqi Kurdistan, Somalia, Mozambique and Angola, and the compilation volume, *Landmines: a deadly legacy* (The Arms Projec, HRW 1993). NGOs also advanced the cause of a global ban on landmines through more than a dozen national campaigns launched over the next two years. In addition to lobbying political leaders and meeting with government officials, national efforts also included public awareness programs and signature campaigns.

The ICRC

The ICRC played an important and under-appreciated role from the earliest stages of the campaign to ban mines. Although individual ICRC medical personnel had publicized the human costs of landmines through the late 1980s, the ICRC's first explicit response to the crisis came in the form of a 1992 publication entitled *Mines: a perverse use of technology*. It stressed the importance of upholding international humanitarian law and called for responsible use of landmines, including the development of self-destruct and self-neutralizing mechanisms, halting the use of non-detectable mines and calling for forces employing mines to be responsible for their removal.

As it did in the early 1970s, the ICRC initiated expert conferences to examine the possibilities of additional legal restrictions on the use of mines. In April 1993, the Montreux Symposium on Anti-Personnel Mines brought together representatives of governments, manufacturers, militaries, NGOs and mine clearance personnel. The objectives were to collect facts regarding the actual use and humanitarian consequences of mines, to analyze the mechanisms and methods to limit use and alleviate suffering, and to establish a strategy for future action. The final report reflected the broad range of opinion among participants, ranging from calls for an immediate and total ban to cautions that a ban would reduce military capability.

A further symposium on the military utility of anti-personnel mines followed in January 1994. The participants, mostly military combat engineers, produced five main conclusions: landmines were an indispensable part of the conventional battlefield; the current landmine crisis stemmed from irresponsible use; properly employed anti-personnel mines represent no greater risk to civilians than other conventional weapons; technology could help to minimize the risk to civilians; and a comprehensive ban would be unworkable and easily circumvented (Hays Park 1995: 54). Although the prognosis of the military experts was bleak, the ICRC the following month declared its full support for a global ban on anti-personnel mines as the only effective solution to the humanitarian disaster. Shortly thereafter it abandoned its tradition of quiet diplomacy and published *Landmines: time for action* (ICRC 1995), including a call for a total ban on use, trade and production of landmines.

UN agencies

Within the United Nations system, the early campaign to ban anti-personnel mines received support from the Secretary-General and three key agencies. Boutros Boutros-Ghali first expressed concern regarding their effects in "An agenda for peace" (1992). He followed this with an article published in *Foreign Affairs* (1994), and a foreword to the proceedings of a Council on Foreign Relations symposium on landmines in 1995, in which he argued that the UN should aim "to build widespread support for an international agreement on a total ban on the production, stockpiling, transfer, and export of mines and their components" (Boutros-Ghali 1995).

Within the UN, the Department of Humanitarian Affairs (DHA) was designated focal point for mine-related activities. As early as 1992, DHA and the Department of Peacekeeping Operations (DPKO) hosted a series of meetings with UN departments and NGOs to share information on mine clearance and legal controls on the use of mines. By 1994, DHA was calling for a complete ban as the only effective response to the crisis. Two other UN agencies also got involved. In September 1993, UNICEF declared landmines to be a priority issue and instructed its national committees to begin advocacy work. It also held a consultative meeting on mines in Geneva in early 1994, with UNICEF executive director James Grant soon advocating a complete ban. The UN High Commissioner for Refugees (UNHCR) joined UNICEF in May of that year to call for a complete ban, a position it restated at the International Meeting on Mine Clearance in Geneva in July 1995. UNICEF also produced a major report documenting the deleterious effects of mines on children and reviewing the prospects for restrictions on their use (UNICEF 1994). Thus by late 1994 the key UN humanitarian agencies had become vocal members of the international campaign.

States

State-initiated measures to attack the global landmines crisis began in the United States in October 1992 with the successful effort of Senator Patrick

Leahy and Congressman Lane Evans to impose a one-year moratorium on the sale, transfer and export of landmines. While relatively uncontroversial at the time, this was an extremely bold step as the moratorium prohibited export even to NATO allies. In August 1993, the United States drew further attention to the problem with the publication of the State Department's influential report *Hidden Killers: the global problem with uncleared mines*. The United States also first raised the subject within the UN General Assembly, where Senator Leahy introduced a resolution in November 1993 urging states to agree to and implement a moratorium on export. Within two years, 15 countries were observing such moratoria. The following year Leahy again submitted a General Assembly resolution reiterating the appeal for a moratorium on export and calling for the "eventual elimination" of landmines.

The European Union also undertook early action to address the proliferation of landmines by passing a resolution in December 1992 requesting a five-year moratorium on the export of anti-personnel mines. In further high profile steps, the Swedish Parliament called for a complete ban in June 1994 and, in November of that year, the Netherlands undertook to destroy its entire stockpile of mines. Belgium passed legislation banning the use, production, procurement, sale and transfer of anti-personnel mines in May 1995.

Multilateral focus for the anti-mine campaign, however, came with a request of the French Minister of Foreign Affairs for a review of the 1980 CCW Convention. The French initiative had its origins in a lobbying campaign by Handicap International (HI) and particularly its Director, Philippe Chabasse. In the summer of 1992, he met with French Ministry officials sympathetic to greater legal restrictions on mines. A Ministry review of existing humanitarian law concluded that the 1980 CCW Convention offered the most promising avenue for such restrictions. While opposition from the French Defense Ministry slowed progress, renewal of the Leahy moratorium in the United States provided an important spark for the French. In February 1993 at a symposium on landmines co-sponsored by HI, the French government indicated that it would formally request a review of the 1980 Convention.

The path to the landmines treaty

The CCW Review Conference

The states parties to the convention, responding to a call from the UN General Assembly, scheduled four expert groups meetings beginning in February 1994 to prepare for the review conference. Conducted on the basis of consensus, the first of these meetings focused almost entirely on the question of NGO participation. In contrast to the preparatory meetings for the 1980 Convention, those organizations with the greatest expertise on the landmines crisis were denied observer status. Nevertheless, more than 100 representatives from 70 NGOs attended the conference to monitor negotiations and lobby in the corridors.

Lacking official status, they nonetheless attempted to set the broad context by highlighting the humanitarian costs of landmines and their disproportionate effects on civilians. The ICRC had commissioned a special report designed to quantify the social and economic consequences of landmines. Written by members of the VVAF, *After the Guns Fall Silent: the enduring legacy of landmines* (1995) was released on the eve of the review conference.

The conference was scheduled to last for three weeks beginning in September 1995. Discussions of the draft Protocols had focused almost entirely on the military utility of mines and only modest control measures were seriously discussed. Detailed negotiations soon revealed a deadlock between some governments wanting credible new restrictions in the face of an emerging public backlash and others opposed to almost any strengthening of the Protocol. As a result, the decision was taken to suspend the conference and resume work through a technical session in January and a concluding session in April 1996.

The humanitarian consequences of landmines were given serious consideration only in the context of a joint US–British proposal to establish a landmines control regime banning all anti-personnel mines which did not self-destruct or self-deactivate. Prior to the opening of the review conference, the two governments had hosted a meeting in Budapest, attended by 31 countries, at which they set out a detailed program that would bind signatories to cut stocks of conventional anti-personnel mines, bar their export and replace stocks with self-destruct mines. The ensuing debate between "smart" and "dumb" mines was to be a major turning point for the campaign. The essential logic behind the CCW measures – that the mines problem was simply the result of improper use – was losing credibility in the face of the effective NGO campaign. A fall-back argument for those advocating continued use was that the crisis was the result of mines that remained active indefinitely, and the solution was self-neutralizing mines.

Opposition came from less industrialized countries which argued that while the technologically advanced North was already using these devices, countries from the South were less able to replace their stockpiles with expensive new mines. Proponents of a total ban also challenged this technological solution to the crisis, arguing that the self-neutralization mechanisms were unreliable, that even these mines are indiscriminate while active, that civilian exposure during the active period was highly likely and that a false sense of safety might encourage their use in greater numbers. The claim that self-neutralizing mines are a sufficient response to the crisis continued to be raised in subsequent years. However, an effective ICBL advocacy campaign helped undermine strong initial support for the technological approach among Western governments and ensured that the US/UK control regime was rejected.

The ICBL continued its campaign for a total ban between sessions of the review conference. These efforts were complemented by a renewed push from the ICRC. In November 1995, the ICRC launched an international campaign calling for a total, immediate and definitive ban on landmines. Not since the campaign against chemical weapons following World War I had the organization publicly lobbied for such a cause. The objective was to "to rally public opinion and muster political support so as to stigmatize the use of anti-personnel landmines and strengthen the international community's resolve to clear mines and care for victims" (ICRC 1995a). With this initiative, the ICRC not only contributed legitimacy to the larger campaign but also raised international awareness of the issue through its access to the international media and through distribution of materials by the extensive network of national Red Cross Societies.

The ICRC also commissioned a report to assess the military utility of landmines. Highlighting the humanitarian costs of landmines attracted 450 organizations to the ICBL and brought over 30 countries to call for a complete ban on landmines, but it had little direct effect on the negotiations at the review conference. Recognizing the insulated nature of the official debate, the ICRC report attempted to challenge the military logic on its own grounds. Written by former British Army combat engineer and later UN demining specialist Patrick Blagden, *Anti-personnel Landmines: friend or foe?* (1996) challenged the two central military arguments regarding landmines use: first, that the present problem can be attributed to the irresponsible use of mines by irregular armies; and second, that landmines remain essential components of land warfare. Noting that the use and effectiveness had not been the subject of systematic study, Blagden concluded from a review of the open literature that responsible mine use is the exception rather than the rule even for so-called "developed armies," and that even when used on a massive scale, the devices had little effect on outcomes. He also argued that the costs and dangers to the forces employing mines have been systematically underestimated and may in fact mean that the use of mines is counter-productive.

Challenges to the presumed military utility of landmines also emerged within the United States. An open letter to President Clinton, sponsored by the VVAF, was signed by 15 senior retired military personnel, including the US commander in the Gulf War, General Norman Schwartzkopf, and published in the *New York Times* on April 3, 1996. According to these prominent individuals, landmines were not a necessary component of the American military arsenal. Around the same time, another Leahy-sponsored bill calling for a one-year moratorium on the use of landmines by US troops, to come into effect in 1999, was passed unanimously in Congress. By the time the review conference reconvened in late April 1996, events had clearly overtaken the modest measures being negotiated. Within the consensus-bound negotiations, the lowest common denominator had prevailed. Minor advances were made with respect to broader coverage of non-international conflicts, regular Convention reviews and restrictions on non-detectable mines. But most provisions would not come into effect for at least a decade, no restrictions were made on anti-handling devices, and implicit encouragement was given to self-neutralizing and self-destructing mines. Furthermore, the Convention had actually been weakened with a reworked definition of an anti-personnel mine to include only those devices *"primarily* designed to be exploded by the presence, proximity or contact of a person." While some diplomats hailed the Conference as a success, many concluded that the new Protocol would have no noticeable effect on the landmine crisis and it was denounced by the ICBL as a humanitarian failure.

In terms of raising the profile of the issue, however, the review conference had been an enormous success. Over 40 countries were on the ICBL "good-list," having endorsed a comprehensive ban; an equal number were observing some kind of export moratoria; and still others had renounced the use of mines and were beginning to destroy their stockpiles. Pro-ban activists had also managed to draw attention to the humanitarian consequences of landmines through innovative campaigning techniques and effective use of the media. A front-page article summarizing the conference in the *International Herald Tribune* on May 3, 1996 is a clear example of successful ICBL campaigning. Three of the first six paragraphs clearly convey the ICBL's message "that the agreement would not go far enough to ban these indiscriminate weapons . . . [and that] the new agreement will be little better than a fig leaf behind which governments will continue to produce ever more sophisticated weapons" (James 1996).

Yet the direction forward for the campaign was unclear. In the absence of an alternative to the CCW Convention, the ICBL agreed to pursue the two-fold strategy of continuing to press governments for unilateral measures and working in regional contexts to secure mine-free zones. The seeds of an alternative process, however, had already been planted. During the January session of the conference, eight pro-ban states – Austria, Belgium, Canada, Denmark, Ireland, Mexico, Norway and Switzerland – met with the ICBL to discuss a concerted strategy. Two further meetings were held during the negotiations in April and May, resulting in an offer by Canada to hold a small strategy meeting for NGOs, pro-ban governments and international organizations.

Although not apparent at the time, a profound change in the nature of the campaign was underway. To this point, the principal pro-ban actors – the ICBL, the ICRC and the UN agencies – had engaged in a relatively typical, if extremely successful, advocacy campaign. While some governments were more sympathetic than others, there is no doubt that the campaigners were lobbying from the outside. Within a matter of months, however, the principal dynamic of the campaign to ban landmines would be transformed into a strategic partnership between non-state actors and core pro-ban states.

The Ottawa Process

When the Ottawa meeting was first proposed, organizers hoped that as many as 20 states might ultimately gather to strategize with the ICBL and the ICRC. Yet over the summer months, there were indications that many more were interested. This raised the problem of the criteria on which states would be invited. The ICBL vigorously advocated a very high threshold, fearing that borderline states would attempt to undermine the overall objectives. The Canadian government, on the other hand, supported a lower threshold, hoping to bring on board marginal countries. The approach ultimately adopted was to circulate a draft final declaration that committed participants to "the earliest possible conclusion of a legally binding international agreement to ban anti-personnel mines." Those states that supported such an outcome were welcome to participate, others could come as observers. NGO participation was another matter to be decided. Consultations during the summer had alleviated some initial suspicions from ICBL members of Canada's sincerity in seeking a ban, concerns further allayed when the ICBL was offered a seat at the table as a full participant.

The conference, Towards a Global Ban on Anti-Personnel Mines, was held in Ottawa on October 3–5, 1996. Fifty states attended as full participants, including the United States, France and the United Kingdom, another 24 as observers, along with representatives from the ICRC, the UN and dozens of NGOs. During the course of the gathering, the full range of issues relating to the global landmines crisis was addressed both in formal sessions and in a series of thematic workshops. Yet by the second day concerns were being raised by pro-ban activists that the discussions were not leading to clear conclusions and that political momentum was being lost. Support for the UN Conference on Disarmament, proposed by several delegations as the appropriate venue for further multilateral negotiations, appeared to be growing.

Behind the scenes, however, government statements were being carefully monitored by Canadian officials in order to gauge the depth of support for rapid negotiations leading to a comprehensive ban. As originally designed, the Ottawa conference was to yield two products, a revised final declaration, and a plan of action setting out a series of events and objectives. By early morning of the third day, both documents had been finalized by Canadian officials and key ICBL members. In his closing remarks, however, Canadian Foreign Minister Lloyd Axworthy shocked the conference by calling for stand-alone negotiations leading to a comprehensive treaty banning landmines, and inviting participants to return to Ottawa in December 1997 for a treaty-signing conference. The challenge was greeted with applause from the campaigners and chagrin from many diplomats.

Almost everyone was caught completely off-guard, as only the ICBL leadership and the ICRC were informed in advance.

This was the launch of the so-called Ottawa Process, a "fast-track" diplomatic initiative to negotiate in less than 14 months an international convention to ban the use, stockpiling, production and transfer of anti-personnel mines. Although considerable support clearly existed for greater restrictions on the use of mines, at the outset the success of the Ottawa Process was far from certain. At a steering group meeting immediately following the Conference, the ICBL decided to support the initiative fully, but the enthusiasm of states was much harder to read. Most pro-ban states were initially hostile due to the lack of consultation in the lead-up to Axworthy's announcement. More problematic, however, was the insistence by a number of prominent states that the Conference on Disarmament (CD) remained the appropriate venue for addressing the mines crisis. Even modest success within the CD was sure to draw vital support away from the Ottawa Process.

The Conference on Disarmament

Throughout the autumn of 1996, the debate over the suitability of the CD as a venue for landmine negotiations remained entirely theoretical. Supporters of the CD approach, including Australia, France, Britain, Germany, Spain, Finland and the United States, argued that a ban on production, transfer, stockpiles and use of anti-personnel mines was self-evidently a disarmament treaty and should therefore be taken up by the already existing multilateral disarmament negotiating body. Additional advantages included the presence in the CD of the major producers and users of landmines, the legitimacy conferred by working through established UN channels, and the CD's recent successes on chemical weapons and nuclear testing.

Most supporters of the Ottawa Process, however, lacked confidence that the CD would be an effective negotiating venue. First, as the Conference on Disarmament operates on the basis of consensus, it was widely believed that resistant states would revert to their CCW negotiating tactics and simply block any serious effort to ban the weapon. Second, while supporters claimed that the 64-member CD engaged the major producers and users, opponents countered that the CD was not universal and excluded most severely mine-affected states. Furthermore, while acknowledging recent CD successes, campaigners were quick to point out the glacial pace of the process; both recent conventions had been under negotiation for decades. Finally, ban advocates argued that landmines should be addressed as a humanitarian crisis rather than a security issue. As such, an arms control venue with its emphasis on intrusive verification measures was inappropriate.

Interesting though the debate was, it became moot when the Conference on Disarmament was unable to agree to include the subject on its 1997 agenda. On January 17 the United States, backed by France and Britain, proposed that the CD take up the issue of anti-personnel mines. Supporters of the "fast-track" were in the difficult position of opposing its inclusion while not wishing to undermine the CD itself. The compromise for most was to accept complementary action by the CD as long as it did not undermine the Ottawa Process. Mexico, supported by countries such as India and Indonesia, took a much more aggressive stance arguing that the CD should not be diverted from its core responsibilities for nuclear disarmament. A strong pro-ban state, Mexico also argued that the landmines crisis demanded urgent action, noting that "swiftness is not this Conference's main virtue."[2] By June 1997, the CD had appointed a Special Coordinator for Landmines to canvass the views of the 60 delegations. Characterized as "talks about talks," the appointment was a clear signal that consensus was unachievable. For the foreseeable future, the Ottawa Process was the only viable forum.

From Ottawa to Oslo

In essence, the Ottawa process was defined by three characteristics: a close partnership between states and NGOs, a like-minded coalition comprising a core group of small and medium-sized states, and a set of negotiations undertaken outside normal multilateral channels. The "core group" was a particularly important element. Of the eleven members, eight had attended the original meeting between the ICBL and pro-ban states in January 1996 – Austria, Belgium, Canada, Denmark, Ireland, Mexico, Norway and Switzerland. In the interests of strengthening the group, and ensuring better regional representation, South Africa, Germany, Philippines and Netherlands were also included. Although they worked together informally in the period leading up to the Ottawa Conference, the first official meeting of the group occurred only in February 1997.

From that point on, these countries routinely shared information, strategized together, and carefully coordinated activities. The division of labor among the core group broke down along functional lines: South Africa, Mexico and the Philippines were regional champions; the Netherlands and Ireland played key roles while holding the EU presidency; Austria was responsible for drafting the treaty; Belgium was to host a major conference in June; and Norway was to host the Convention negotiations in September.

In practice, the Ottawa Process involved two tracks: a series of meetings and conferences to prepare and consult on the text of the treaty, and an intense schedule of conferences, consultations, lobbying and campaigning to build political support for a comprehensive ban.

An early outline of a treaty had already been prepared by Austria and circulated during the Ottawa Conference. In the wake of the conference and with a treaty-signing ceremony just over a year away, the ICBL also produced a draft text. On the basis of consultations with governments and

NGOs, Austria developed its outline into a concise text of only 13 articles and held a meeting in Vienna, February 12–14, 1997, to solicit views. The Experts Meeting on the Text for a Total Ban Convention was designed to appeal to states supporting both the Ottawa Process and the CD. While opponents of the "fast-track" process involved themselves only grudgingly, it was an indication of the powerful momentum behind the Ottawa Process that 111 states participated.

Following the first round of consultations, the core group met in March and again in April to consolidate a second draft. A second major meeting of 120 countries was held in Bonn in April to address the thorny questions of verification and compliance. Competing perspectives were clearly visible in those discussions, with pro-ban states arguing that humanitarian law does not require the intrusive verification measures commonly associated with arms control agreements. By late spring, the Austrian text had been carefully revised and widely disseminated and the conditions for its acceptance as the principal text for the Oslo negotiations appeared favorable.

The first step in marshalling political support for the "fast-track" treaty was the annual UN General Assembly resolution, "An International Agreement to Ban Anti-personnel Landmines." Although the United States had been its principal sponsor since the early 1990s, Canada had been circulating a strongly worded alternative during the final stages of the CCW review conference. Under pressure, Canada allowed the United States to continue to lead on the resolution on the condition that there was no reference to the Conference on Disarmament. The final text of Resolution 51/45/S, put before the General Assembly on December 10, 1996, welcomed the conclusions of the recent Ottawa Conference and called on states to "pursue vigorously an effective, legally-binding international agreement to ban the use, stockpiling, production and transfer of anti-personnel mines with a view to completing negotiations as soon as possible." The resolution was passed 156–0 with ten abstentions.

Having secured this key global endorsement for "fast-track" negotiations, the effort to build political will shifted to regional initiatives. Through a series of closely coordinated meetings and conferences sponsored by the ICBL, the ICRC, governments and regional organizations, clear commitments in favour of the ban treaty were secured. Of the conferences held over that six month period, the 4th International NGO Conference to Ban Landmines in Maputo, Mozambique, February 25–28, 1997, was perhaps the most significant. In preparation, the ICBL followed its normal approach of capacity-building for local campaigns. Building on strong ban organizations in South Africa and Mozambique, additional national campaigns were launched in Zambia, Zimbabwe, Angola and Somalia. The conference itself attracted more than 450 NGO participants from 60 countries and the final declaration expressed unqualified support for the Ottawa Process. The profile of the conference also resulted in a series of commitments from key regional states. South Africa and Mozambique announced unilateral landmine bans, while Malawi and Swaziland indicated support for a comprehensive ban treaty.

In the weeks leading up to the Brussels Conference on Anti-Personnel Mines in late June 1997, it was clear that the flurry of diplomatic consultations and NGO campaigning had been remarkably successful. In early January, only 30 countries had committed to the Ottawa Process, but by late May the number had risen to more than 70. The regional conferences had been particularly successful, especially in Africa, as a majority of African states had agreed to support a comprehensive ban. In addition, shifts in policy accompanied new governments in the United Kingdom and France, resulting in support for a comprehensive ban from two of the permanent five of the UN Security Council. The prospects for a signing ceremony in December appeared excellent, yet a negotiated text did not yet exist and prominent governments, including the United States, continued to hold out.

The international conference in Brussels from June 24–27, 1997, the last major stop on the road to Oslo, was designed to lock in support for the treaty among the 155 participating states. In many respects the meeting was a watershed. The NGO community was out in force, with more than 130 representatives from 40 countries. In her closing statement, ICBL coordinator Jody Williams coined the phrase that was to be the NGO rallying cry to the end of the Oslo negotiations: "No exceptions, no reservations and no loop-holes." While the United States did not participate in the meeting, officials summoned other delegations to their hotel in Brussels for bilateral consultations. In a sign of things to come, these heavy-handed tactics did not yield the desired results. The ICBL briefed delegations going in and debriefed them coming out. Judging from official statements, few seemed swayed by United States pressure. Due to complete lack of progress in the Conference on Disarmament, states previously supporting the US stance began to switch sides. France, the United Kingdom, Italy, Spain, the Czech Republic, Hungary and Bosnia all supported the Ottawa Process for the first time. The Brussels Declaration, signed by 97 countries, welcomed the convening of a Diplomatic Conference in September by the government of Norway to negotiate a ban treaty and identified the Austrian draft treaty as the text to be discussed.

The Oslo negotiations and the ban treaty

The dynamics of the Oslo negotiations were fundamentally altered by the US decision on August 18, 1997 to sign the Brussels Declaration and participate in the Conference. While the decision was hailed by some as a major concession, ICBL members were unconvinced that the Americans were genuinely "like-minded." The shift in US policy was the result of a compromise between Secretary of State Albright, encouraging participation for political and diplomatic reasons, and the Joint Chiefs of Staff, who fundamentally opposed key provisions of the Austrian text. Consequently, the US strategy was to press for a series of "non-negotiable" amendments, including a geographical exemption for the use of landmines in Korea, a definitional change allowing the use of US mixed-system anti-tank mines, a nine-year deferral period for compliance with key provisions, a substantial delay in the entry-into-force provisions, strengthened verification measures and the right to withdraw when "supreme national interests are threatened" (Wareham 1998: 230–3).

Full participation at the Oslo Conference was limited to countries supporting the Brussels Declaration. When it opened on September 2, 90 states were registered. Also in attendance were 32 observer states, representatives of the ICRC and UN agencies, and scores of NGO campaigners. Electing the president and setting out conference rules of procedures was the first order of business (Dolan and Hunt 1998: 408–10). Behind the scenes, core group members had been preparing Jacob Selebi, South Africa's Ambassador to the UN in Geneva, for the job of president. In addition to solid African National Congress credentials that would carry weight among African delegates, Selebi was also known for his direct approach to managing negotiations. Draft rules of procedure, based on the UN principle that decisions could be taken by two-thirds majority vote, had also been circulated in advance. Pro-ban states and campaigners were greatly relieved when both were adopted without debate. In addition, the ICBL was granted observer status, giving it access to all meetings and the right to intervene.

Selebi began immediately to set out a bold work plan. The first week was designed to proceed quickly though the Austrian text to identify problem areas and demonstrate broad consensus for the existing language. The second week was scheduled for detailed negotiations to resolve contentious issues, leaving the third week for finalizing the text and translation. No time was allocated to lengthy opening statements. Instead, the president requested that all proposed texts be tabled in the first three days.

Had the United States not been present, a range of potentially divisive issues might have occupied the delegates. Indeed, substantive disagreement over key articles of the Austrian text led to the creation of five working groups, each chaired by a member of the core group. But it was the "non-negotiable" US demands that dominated the early discussions. While some support existed for specific American amendments, particularly from Australia, Japan, Poland and Ecuador, strong objections from core group members inevitably followed. By adopting the position that "nothing was agreed until everything was agreed," Selebi was able to simply note the scale of the opposition to particular proposals and proceed. At the end of the second week, the US had still not gained agreement on any of its proposals with the exception of strengthening the verification and compliance provisions.

Over the three-day weekend the Americans attempted to revise their proposals while lobbying hard in key foreign capitals. When the conference reconvened on Tuesday 16 September, the United States requested a further 24-hour extension to finalize its alternative text and, much to the surprise of the ICBL, Canada supported the request. Fearing a compromise that would undermine the treaty, activists publicly denouced the Canadian decision. It was the first public break in the relationship between NGOs and the Canadian government since they had joined forces in the summer of 1996. In spite of intense negotiations, however, including two late-night calls between President Clinton and Prime Minister Chrétien, the distance between the two governments proved unbridgeable. The Americans were simply unwilling to move on three fundamental issues: the right of withdrawal, the nine-year deferral and an exemption for their anti-tank systems. On September 17, the United States withdrew its amendments, the revised Austrian text was approved by delegates without a vote, and the conference was over.

Contrary to expectations, the Convention became stronger over the course of the negotiations. In addition to improvement on compliance and verification, the important word "primarily," inserted into the definition of a mine during the 1996 CCW negotiations, was removed. Five years after the formation of the ICBL and less than twelve months after Axworthy's call for the stand-alone negotiations, a simple, unambiguous and comprehensive ban on anti-personnel mines had been agreed.

With the treaty negotiated, the only remaining question was how many states would return to Ottawa to sign. The drive to ensure that existing commitments were converted into signatures received a welcome boost on November 10, 1997 with the awarding of the Nobel Prize to the ICBL and its coordinator Jody Williams. Over the course of the next three months, several key states including Japan, Greece and Australia declared their intention to sign. Ultimately, 122 states signed the Convention in Ottawa at a conference attended by 2,400 representatives from the signatory governments, 35 observer governments, international organizations and NGOs. Three countries ratified the convention during the signing ceremony and the 40th ratification, the key to triggering entry-into-force, was deposited with the Secretary-General in New York by Burkina Faso on September 17, 1998.

The success of the campaign: an analysis

The negotiation of a treaty banning landmines less than five years after the ICBL's founding represents a remarkably successful example of humanitarian advocacy. The essence of the campaign, from start to finish, was that the human costs exacted by anti-personnel mines far outweighed their military utility. Their banning means that for the first time a weapon widely employed by militaries has been prohibited. Securing the 40 ratifications necessary for entry into force in just over nine months was also unprecedented. As of September 2000, 148 countries had signed and

136 had ratified. Even those prominent states unwilling to sign have modified their behavior as a result of the campaign. The United States complies with several of the Convention's provisions while both Russia and China have ceased exporting anti-personnel mines. This section identifies key factors in the success of the advocacy campaign; the following section assesses the broader significance of banning landmines.

The post-Cold War context

Factors outside the control of the advocates contributed to the campaign's success. The significance of the geopolitical environment within which the campaign developed must be addressed first. While efforts to restrict the use of mines began in the 1970s, only after the fall of the Berlin Wall and the end of the Cold War did a prohibition became a possibility. Two aspects of the post-Cold War environment are important. First, the end of the Cold War resulted in the break-up or weakening of rigid superpower blocs. As noted earlier, unilateral actions by states helped transform the campaign from raising public awareness to adopting concrete measures. Key turning points for the campaign – the US export moratorium and the Belgian legislation banning mines – were undertaken by NATO members outside of NATO decision-making structures. Neither decision would have been conceivable during the Cold War.

Second, with the end of the Cold War, conflict in the developing world was no longer viewed simply through the lens of global competition. Attention to these conflicts in their own right resulted in increased recognition of the human toll exacted by light weapons, including landmines. Furthermore, the resolution of long-standing conflicts and the reconstruction of war-torn societies became a prominent objective of the international community. It was in this context that landmines were discussed in Boutros-Ghali's 'An agenda for peace' (1992). A series of UN-mandated missions in Cambodia, Angola, Mozambique and Bosnia drew further attention to the scale of the landmine crisis. The vulnerability of UN peacekeepers added urgency to finding a solution.

Fortuitous circumstances

The success of the campaign was not simply a matter of what the pro-ban forces did right or the conducive geopolitical environment; they benefited from favorable developments beyond their control. Four other factors were of particular importance. First, landmines were not a highly profitable industry. As the producers of landmines were small munitions companies unconnected with the major defense contractors, a major potential advocate for the continued use of mines did not materialize. Second, military leaders did not have evidence to support their claims for the military utility of mines. There is little doubt that mines can be effective in certain circumstances, and had comprehensive studies on the military utility of mines existed, the split between ministries of defense and foreign affairs that was critical to the success of the campaign would have been less easily achieved. Third, changes in government in both France and Britain in the late spring of 1997 resulted in critical policy shifts that brought two powerful states into the pro-ban camp and for the first time split the strident opposition of the permanent five members of the UN Security Council to the early elimination of landmines. Finally, the hesitancy of the United States to engage in the Ottawa Process was a crucial factor in the success of the campaign. Throughout early 1997 the United States continued to promote the CD as venue for addressing the landmines crisis. Under-estimating the momentum behind the Ottawa Process and the cohesiveness of pro-ban states, the United States then pursued heavy-handed tactics both in Brussels and in Oslo leaving their remaining allies in an untenable position.

The International Campaign to Ban Landmines

The first key step taken by the ICBL was to define anti-personnel landmines as a discrete problem within the general context of the human costs of violent conflict. The landmine crisis exploded during the 1970s and 1980s, and mines were commonly cited simply as one of a number of challenges facing war-ravaged societies. The campaign effectively isolated landmines as a discrete problem amenable to the identifiable solution of a compre-hensive ban. From the outset, clear distinctions were drawn between those mines targeted by the campaign (all anti-personnel mines including self-neutralizing devices) and those that were not (command-detonated devices and anti-tank mines). In the case of the 1980 CCW, the catalyst for the negotiations was the widespread use of napalm, but the scope of the Convention was broadened to include a wide range of anti-personnel weapons. In the case of the landmines, the initial focus on a single weapon was maintained throughout the negotiating process.

The enduring focus on landmines can be attributed in large measure to the field-based origins of the campaign. Support from the non-govern-mental sector for previous attempts to restrict anti-personnel weapons had been led by peace and disarmament groups one step removed from the battlefields. In contrast, the core of the ICBL was composed of organizations focusing on assisting victims and clearing mines, while most of the pro-minent individuals had years of experience working in mine-infested countries and included mine victims, deminers and medical staff. For activists, these weapons were no abstract threat but rather a daily menace in the drive to assist victims and rebuild war-torn societies. The field-based orientation was maintained even as the coalition expanded, with most of the organizations representing humanitarian, development and human rights perspectives. This formidable expertise laid the foundations for the production and dissemination of compelling evidence backing ICBL claims. Effective use was made of the visual media including travelling photograph exhibits, videos highlighting the impact of landmines and televised documentaries.

To assess the ICBL as an organization, it is important to draw a distinction between the Steering Committee that gave global strategic direction and the broad-based coalition that provided the foundation for national level campaigns and links to grassroots activism. The Committee was responsible for establishing broad policy directions, including defining the core objectives, setting out strategy for the various negotiating sessions, and targeting key regions and countries for capacity-building efforts. Composed initially of the six early partners in the campaign, the Committee was loosely organized with no formal structure, budget or secretariat. It is difficult to assess whether this informality, while offering great flexibility, was an important factor in the success of the campaign. It was certainly a major point of contention for European members who consistently advocated a more structured approach. In time, formal Committee membership was expanded from the six founding members to include representatives of the Afghan, Cambodian, Kenyan and South African campaigns and Rädda Barnen (Save the Children, Sweden). In practice, key individuals and organizations were regularly included in Steering Committee meetings. In contrast to its prominent public profile the core of the ICBL was constructed around no more than two dozen full-time activists and total expenditures of $1–2 million per year in later stages (Goose 1998).

Among the hundreds of organizations that made up the broader coalition, several dozen were sufficiently engaged in the campaign to send representatives to key international meetings. As a result, more than 100 NGO activists participated in the major conferences and negotiations. The strength and cohesiveness of this diverse set of NGOs was a key factor in the success of the campaign. Significant differences of opinion were evident behind the scenes, particularly between those lobbying government officials intensively and those with closer links to victim assistance and mine clearance efforts. Yet, in spite of these disagreements, all NGOs attending worked within the coalition framework. Major statements were agreed by consensus and circulated on ICBL letterhead. This public posture of consensus was maintained throughout the campaign, even when severe tensions existed within the US campaign over how to address US military opposition to the proposed ban.

The greatest strength of the campaign, however, lay in the dozens of well-coordinated country campaigns. The model for the national campaigns was remarkably consistent. In most cases, they were coordinated by umbrella groups linking existing organizations and networks. By mobilizing already existing capacity, campaigns were managed with minimal formal infrastructure. In this way, hundreds of organizations became integral parts of the campaign without devoting substantial human or financial resources.

Close links between country campaigns and the ICBL were critical in ensuring consistent and coordinated lobbying. The importance of e-mail to the success of the campaign has, however, often been overstated. While there is no doubt that it facilitated the cheap dissemination of information, e-mail was not widely used until 1995, by which time the campaign was already well underway.

In all cases, national campaigns began with the twin objectives of raising public awareness of the mines crisis and lobbying government officials to commit to a comprehensive ban. In some countries (e.g. United States, Australia and Japan), these objectives remained unchanged throughout the campaign. In others (e.g. Canada, Norway, Belgium, Netherlands), shifts in government policy led to close working relationships between NGOs and government officials.

Venues

The success of ICBL advocacy efforts can be examined in the context of the four key arenas where landmines were discussed: the CCW review conference, the proposed US/UK control regime, the Conference on Disarmament, and the Ottawa Process. In the first of these, ICBL efforts were devoted to consciousness-raising at the expense of focused lobbying on the text of the Protocols. Recognizing that the prospects for swift action were slim, the ICBL effectively used the CCW conference to draw attention to the human costs of mines. The campaign was also extremely successful in encouraging countries to offer rhetorical support for the eventual banning of mines. Far less attention was paid, however, to negotiations of the revised Protocols, including the important change in the definition of an anti-personnel mine. While the word "primarily" was ultimately removed from the Ottawa Convention definition, aggressive campaigning might have avoided this setback entirely.

The debates surrounding the proposed US/UK control regime have been under-analyzed in discussions of the successes of the ICBL. In the early stages, with strong leadership from the United States and United Kingdom, prospects appeared promising. Although the proposed regime to prohibit regular mines while allowing self-neutralizing mines was challenged by less industrialized countries as establishing a double standard, it was supported by most highly industrialized countries, including many states that were to become key supporters of the Ottawa Process. The failure of the so-called smart mine regime to become the principal international response to the landmine crisis can be attributed largely to effective ICBL campaigning. By challenging the reliability of the technology and highlighting the indiscriminate nature of these high-tech mines, the campaign made support for this approach untenable for key European governments.

In the case of the Conference on Disarmament, both the ICBL and the core group opposed adding landmines to the agenda. However, neither was forced into the awkward position of campaigning against the CD taking up the issue since several members of the Conference were adamant that nuclear weapons be the focus of attention. It is unlikely, however, that the NGO coalition would have been effective advocates at the Conference in Geneva. Rules of procedure including decision-making by consensus and limited access for NGOs would have been similar to the CCW negotiations, and the composition of most delegations would have been comparatively conservative. There is no doubt that the prevailing structure and mind-set at the Conference on Disarmament in Geneva favored those opposed to an early ban.

The nature of ICBL advocacy changed fundamentally between the end of the CCW review conference and the start of the Ottawa Process in the autumn of 1996. For the remainder of the campaign, advocacy was undertaken through close collaboration between the ICBL and the core group of states. As a result, it becomes more difficult to assess the distinct contributions of the NGO campaign. It is clear, however, that the NGO coalition continued to be the key player in countries and geographic regions with hesitant or intransigent governments. The greatest successes for the ICBL during this period were in Southern Africa. Beginning with the Mozambique Conference, the ICBL with the support of the full range of pro-ban partners turned sub-Saharan Africa into a formidable bloc in favor of the Ottawa Process. Members of the coalition were also instrumental in laying the groundwork for shifts in policy in key countries such as the UK and France, and later Japan and Australia. The campaign was also extraordinarily effective in locking in wavering support from countries committed to the Ottawa Process. Concessions may well have been made during the Oslo negotiations without the aggressive campaigning of the NGOs.

The ICRC and UN agencies

Fundamental to the success of the landmines campaign was the effective working relationship between the ICBL and other key non-state actors. In most other analyses, the importance of the ICRC and UN agencies as key partners in the campaign has received insufficient attention. Information from Red Cross doctors provided critical empirical evidence of the scale of the humanitarian crisis and the excessively injurious nature of the weapon. From a policy perspective, early activity by the ICRC was consistent with its activities in the lead-up to the 1980 Conventional Weapons Convention. Although the first meetings of military experts concluded that the utility of the weapon was high and that only modest restrictions were achievable, the meetings did raise the profile of landmines. They also began an engagement with dissenting military personnel and ultimately worked closely with individuals who would have been unwilling to be closely associated with the ICBL. This was ultimately to prove extremely effective in challenging the accepted wisdom on the utility of mines. Though not "unprecedented" as the ICRC's early publications claimed, the launch of a media campaign added credibility to the campaign bridging the early demands of the ICBL and the development of the core group of states. The UN Secretary-General and key humanitarian agencies, most prominently DHA and UNICEF, were also critical partners adding credibility in the early going. In the latter stages of the campaign, the United Nations and the ICRC filled important gaps in ICBL capability. Both were particularly active in geographical regions such as Asia where the NGO campaign was weak.

The core group

Once the emphasis of the campaign had shifted from raising public awareness to negotiating a comprehensive treaty banning mines, the core group of states became a central player. Two factors are critical in their success: the composition of the group itself and the structuring of the Ottawa Convention negotiations. By design, core group members included regional champions tasked with bringing other states into the Ottawa Process. The cross-regional representation in the group also undercut traditional UN negotiating blocs. Including members of the European Union, the Non-Aligned Movement, the OAS, the OAU and ASEAN ensured both that these bodies could not categorically oppose a ban, and facilitated the building of regional support.

Equally important was the way in which the core group managed the series of meetings leading up to the negotiating session in Oslo. Pursuing the negotiations in a "stand-alone" format, rather than as part of an existing process such as the CCW or the CD, was critical to the success of the Ottawa Process. By taking the negotiations outside traditional disarmament forums, the core group managed to avoid the entrenched logic of arms control measures such as the need for agreement from all major military powers and the emphasis on intrusive verification. The core group also took great care to ensure that the issue of landmines was not raised in inhospitable multilateral environments such as NATO and, at times, even the European Union.

By pursuing a free-standing negotiating forum, the core group was able to determine the appropriate timing and procedures for meetings and negotiations. Throughout the Ottawa Process, participation in formal meetings was based on the process of self-selection. Those countries agreeing with the stated objectives of the conference were accepted as official participants; others were welcome as observers. Even more important was the ability of the core group to create favorable negotiating conditions in Oslo, including the two-thirds majority vote for decisions, the selection of Selebi as president, and the full participation of the ICBL.

The wider meaning

Assessments of the significance of the campaign to ban mines tend to be divided on the question of whether the campaign is replicable. On the one hand, it is argued that its success can be attributed to the characteristics of the weapon. From this perspective, landmines was an "easy" case with little transferable significance. On the other hand, it is suggested that the campaign represented an unprecedented break with traditional diplomacy and established a model for aggressive campaigns on a host of other pressing international issues. While there is an element of truth in both interpretations, assessing the significance of the campaign requires more nuanced interpretation.

To the degree that it was easy at all, the campaign to ban landmines was easy only in retrospect. When the idea of an initiative to ban mines was first proposed in the early 1990s, seasoned NGO campaigners were convinced that there was simply no chance for success. Three years into the campaign, one expert on humanitarian law and a champion of citizen-based movements wrote that weapons will be banned only if they are perceived to have limited utility and to be at odds with the dignity of military profession. Concluding that neither of those conditions applied to landmines, he argued that the prospects for a comprehensive ban were bleak and that more limited restrictions should be pursued (Falk 1995).

During the campaign, the nature of the landmine problem was characterized in stark terms and a comprehensive ban was commonly identified as the only effective response. But this strategy was not due simply to the characteristics of the weapon. Rather, it was the product of painstaking research, broadly disseminated documentation and a carefully orchestrated grassroots campaigning undertaken by the ICBL, the ICRC and key UN agencies. Similarly, numerous pitfalls lay in the path of the core group as they attempted to construct support for a comprehensive ban treaty. Again, irrespective of the characteristics of the weapon, there was nothing predetermined about the final outcome.

The claim that the campaign has represented an unprecedented break with diplomatic and civil society practice also needs to be tempered. Stark parallels can be found in the roles and effectiveness of civil society advocacy efforts during the 1899 Hague Peace Conference banning dum-dum bullets and the campaign to ban landmines (Hubert 2000: 1–3). As with the campaign against landmines, the opposition to the dum-dum bullet came first from doctors with direct experience in the field and was subsequently picked up by a range of peace organizations. Furthermore, the dissemination of authoritative studies, media and publicity work, and the lobbying of delegates during the negotiations, are all common features of the roles of non-state actors. The publicity campaign launched by the ICRC as "unprecedented" has more similarities than differences with its crusade against chemical weapons in the 1920s. The approaches of states to these respective disarmament negotiations also have strong similarities. Progress was made on the basis of unilateral actions of states as part of stand-alone negotiations that did not depend on consensus among the participants. In addition, major powers in the first instance refused to sign. These examples suggest that the novelty commonly attributed to the landmine campaign is somewhat overstated.

This is not to suggest that there was nothing innovative about the campaign to ban landmines. There is no doubt that NGOs played a far more significant role in raising the international profile of landmines than was the case with the dum-dum bullet. Furthermore, the strategic cooperation among the core group far exceeded the cooperation among like-minded states in the 1890s. The close working partnership between the ICBL and the core group is also a important difference. Finally, although the influence of NGO advocacy on security issues stretches back more than a century, the landmines case seems to suggest a strengthening of national and grassroots support. In large measure, however, the landmine campaign can be seen as revitalizing a pre-World War II style of disarmament negotiations rather than establishing an entirely new approach to international diplomacy. From this perspective, it is the Cold War years rather that the 1990s that diverge from the longer-term patterns in humanitarian advocacy.

Notes

1 For a more extensive analysis, including a review of the campaign to ban dum-dum bullets and a comparison with campaigns on the International Criminal Court, child soldiers and small arms, see Hubert 2000.
2 "Statements for the CD," *Disarmament Diplomacy*, Issue 13, February–March 1997.

Bibliography

Arms Project, The, a division of Human Rights Watch, and Physicians for Human Rights (1993) *Landmines: a deadly legacy,* New York: Human Rights Watch.
Aubert, M. (1990) "The ICRC and the problem of excessively injurious weapons," *International Review of the Red Cross* 279: 477–97.
Blagden, P. (1996) *Anti-personnel Landmines: friend or foe? A study of the military use and effectiveness of anti-personnel mines,* Geneva: ICRC.
Boutros-Ghali, B. (1995) "Foreword," in K. Cahill (ed.) *Clearing the Fields: solutions to the global land mines crisis,* New York: Basic Books and the Council on Foreign Relations: xii–xiii.
—— (1994) "The landmines crisis: a global disaster," *Foreign Affairs* LXXIII (5) 8–13.
—— (1992) "An agenda for peace," A/47/277.
Coupland, R. (1989) "Amputations from antipersonnel mine injuries of the leg," *Annals Royal College of Surgeons of England* 71: 405–8.

Coupland, R. and Korver, A. (1991) "Injuries from antipersonnel mines: the experience of the ICRC," *British Medical Journal* 303: 1509–12.

Dolan, M. and Hunt, C. (1998) "Negotiating in the Ottawa Process: the new multilateralism," in M. Cameron, R. Lawson and B. Tomlin (eds) *To Walk without Fear: the global movement to ban landmines,* Toronto: Oxford University Press: 392–423.

Falk, R. (1995) "Walking the tightrope of international humanitarian law: meeting the challenge of land mines," in K. Cahill (ed.) *Clearing the Fields: solutions to the global land mines crisis,* New York: Basic Books and the Council on Foreign Relations: 69–86.

Goose, S. (1998) "Strategizing about international citizens campaigns," *The Progressive Response* II (8).

Hays Park, W. (1995) "The humanitarian law outlook," in K. Cahill (ed.) *Clearing the Fields: solutions to the global land mines crisis,* New York: Basic Books and the Council on Foreign Relations: 45–59.

Hubert, D. (2000) *The Landmine Ban: a case study in humanitarian advocacy,* Providence, RI: Watson Institute.

ICRC (1995) *Landmines: time for action,* Geneva: ICRC.

—— (1995a) *ICRC campaign against antipersonnel landmines,* Geneva: ICRC.

—— (1992) *Mines: a perverse use of technology,* Geneva: ICRC.

James, B. (1996) "50 nations agree to make landmines easier to find," *International Herald Tribune,* May 3.

McGrath, R. and Stover, E. (1991) "Injuries from land mines," *British Medical Journal* 303: 1492.

New York Times (1996) "An open letter to President Clinton," April 3.

Stover, E. and McGrath, R. (1991) *Landmines in Cambodia: the coward's war,* New York: Human Rights Watch and Physicians for Human Rights.

UNICEF (1994) *Landmines: a scourge on children,* Geneva: UNICEF.

US State Department (1993) *Hidden Killers: the global problem with uncleared mines – a report on international demining,* Implementation of Section 1364, National Defense Authorization Act for Fiscal Year 1993.

VVAF (1995) *After the Guns Fall Silent: the enduring legacy of landmines,* Washington, DC: VVAF.

Wareham, M. (1998) "Rhetoric and policy realities in the US," in M. Cameron, R. Lawson and B. Tomlin (eds) *To Walk without Fear: the global movement to ban landmines,* Toronto: Oxford University Press: 212–43.

4 "International lawmaking of historic proportions"

Civil society and the International Criminal Court

William Pace and Jennifer Schense

> Make no mistake about it, this is international lawmaking of historic proportions.
>
> (*Times of India* 1998, on the process that produced the Rome Statute)

The International Criminal Court (ICC) is one of the most significant achievements of the twentieth century. It represents a renewed commitment of the majority of the world's nations to putting an end to impunity through coordinated efforts of strengthened national judicial systems and a new international criminal jurisdiction. For the first time, international law will be applicable directly to the actions of individuals on a systematic and permanent basis.

The ICC is a permanent, independent institution, established to investigate and prosecute individual perpetrators for the worst crimes: genocide, crimes against humanity and war crimes. The Rome Statute, the basis for the creation of the Court, also includes the crime of aggression, which can only be adjudicated once it has been defined by the Court's governing Assembly of States Parties. The statute does not recognize any immunities for officials or others, but does not prosecute individuals under the age of 18 nor does it prosecute acts that took place before the Rome Statute's entry into force on July 1, 2002.

The Rome Statute was adopted at the conclusion of a diplomatic conference held in Rome, Italy in June–July 1998 and represents the culmination of a process that originally began after World War II but which was substantially revitalized at the United Nations (UN) at the end of the Cold War. In this respect, the ICC is a product of the time period in which the project came to fruition: the decade between the conclusion of the Cold War and the September 2001 attacks in the United States. This decade saw the emergence of the concept of human security, backed by middle-power states and by non-governmental organizations (NGOs) of civil society. The ICC is a flagship institution of the human security agenda, and is representative as well of what is described as the "new diplomacy," a pragmatic and methodological approach to the development of international law. The

ICC community faces increasing challenges in light of efforts by major world powers in recent years to undermine the role of international law and to disrupt lines of cooperation between the UN and other international organizations and the ICC.

The birth of the ICC provides interesting insights into the constructive interplay between law and democracy at the international level. It is important foremost to recognize the role of the UN as a potent forum for the development of the Rome Statute and its subsidiary instruments. The procedural framework provided by the UN within which work on the ICC progressed fostered the growth of a constructive and practical partnership between like-minded governments and members of the NGO Coalition for the International Criminal Court (CICC or Coalition), known in many quarters as the "new diplomacy." This procedural framework and NGO–government partnership together empowered hundreds and eventually thousands of NGOs from around the world to input their experience and expertise into what otherwise could have been a distant and inaccessible process. The involvement of civil society acted as an accountability mechanism, pushing to ensure that the process adhered to the highest possible legal standards. At the same time, the continual involvement of the CICC and its members and their focus on distributing public information about the process worldwide lent the ICC process a greater transparency worldwide.

This framework and partnership also empowered small and middle-sized states to engage in the process as an informal coalition or Like-Minded Group (LMG). The use of LMGs is not uncommon at the UN; what is uncommon is how long the LMG in the ICC process has engaged in and largely directed the ICC process.

This chapter will briefly explore the relevant UN procedures that have fostered the ICC process. It will also examine the nature of the NGO–government partnership and how it functioned. Finally, it will contemplate the impact that the success of the ICC process continues to have on the role of NGOs at the national level and what that may bode for greater accountability and transparency at that level.

UN procedures and the work of NGOs at the UN

The UN Charter creates a framework whereby the primary actors in the international legal order are governments, international organizations and NGOs. Civil society enters into international, intergovernmental fora and negotiations as representatives of "accredited" NGOs. NGOs do not have a formal negotiating or voting role, but a consultative role.[1]

It is notable that – setting aside the rather popular phenomenon of UN global conferences, which are already being phased out – relatively few NGOs are consistently active at the UN, as compared to advocacy or special interest groups at the regional, national or local level (this is especially true in comparison with special interest activism in the United States). At most, only a handful of NGOs regularly monitor the General Assembly's Sixth (Legal) Committee,[2] compared with the tens of thousands that follow lawmaking in capitals around the world. Given the importance of the legal standards and lawmaking processes arising from Sixth Committee deliberations, the impact of effective NGO action at this level can be disproportionately effective. The same can be said for the deliberations of the UN Security Council, which is monitored by 20 or fewer NGOs on a regular basis.

The World Federalist Movement–Institute for Global Policy (WFM–IGP or WFM), the host organization of the CICC Secretariat, was one of the few NGOs active at the UN to recognize that procedural issues governing NGO participation, such as NGO accreditation, were fundamental. WFM paid special attention to the basic needs that Coalition member organizations would have if they were going to be effective participants. Among these needs were access to intergovernmental meetings, in particular access to the meeting floor and to delegates before and after meetings; access to meeting documentation; and the right to present their own documents to delegates. Frequently, NGOs at the UN focus on obtaining the right to make oral statements at such meetings. However, WFM recognized that obtaining such a right was highly overrated and would likely foreclose the right to any other kind of interaction. Simply put, prepared oral statements from NGOs have not generally facilitated or fostered the kind of ongoing dialogue between NGOs and governments which is essential for NGO input to be effective.

WFM has been strategic in its efforts to facilitate and fund the participation of NGO experts, especially from developing countries: securing badges for NGO participants to allow them access to the UN and to key meetings; reserving rooms for NGO meetings and for meetings between NGOs and delegations; and arranging for meeting documentation to be delivered, in bulk to the NGO meeting room, where WFM interns undertook the onerous task of sorting them into folders for participating NGOs.

In addition, WFM has been careful to instruct participating NGOs, especially those new to the process, regarding the rules of procedure and decorum of the UN. This was important, so as to be certain that NGO behavior was in conformity with UN rules and to ensure that there would be no excuse for excluding NGOs from proceedings. Especially in the early years, given that NGOs did not have automatic access to meetings of the UN General Assembly, NGO participation was as reliant on good practice as on legal right.

Despite some of the procedural challenges that faced NGOs desirous of making a contribution to work on the ICC, the UN at the same time provided an ideal forum for NGO–state interaction on such cutting-edge questions of international law as the ICC. Despite the tremendous criticism of the UN in the world's media, the UN is increasingly recognized as a forum for pushing progressive issues globally. The human security agenda has received a substantial boost through discussions – among other subjects – on protection of civilians, in particular women and children, in armed conflict, the proliferation of small arms and weapons of mass destruction, as well as on the ICC. Discussions especially in the committees of the General Assembly have been able to avoid to some degree the power politics of a body like the Security Council, so dominated by states focused on the maintenance and progression of military and intelligence-based superiority in order to protect only their sovereignty and their national interests. It is in the General Assembly that middle-power states have been able to focus more effectively and consistently on root-cause issues, in part as a reaction to the perception that the efforts of the UN are purely reactive to crises and act only as band-aids to cover but not cure serious and systemic problems.

The NGO–state partnership

> I have worked with non-governmental organizations for 15 years, and I have never encountered the degree of efficiency, capacity and collaboration that the Coalition has been able to generate.
>
> (Luis Moreno Ocampo, ICC Prosecutor, letter dated September 3, 2003)

The partnership between the Coalition and the LMG of states traces its roots back to the early days of renewed discussion of the ICC, which took place in the UN General Assembly's (GA's) Sixth Committee. A number of states seized the opportunity in the more open post-Cold War environment at the UN to encourage the GA to take up the ICC project, an initiative which began in the early days of the UN's history but which foundered on Cold War antagonisms. The GA called upon the UN's International Law Commission to produce a draft statute for an ICC, and the Sixth Committee undertook to examine that draft in 1994.

A few states and NGOs observing the Sixth Committee supported the idea of finalizing this draft at a diplomatic conference, but due in large part to opposition from the permanent members of the Security Council, the Sixth Committee, on receipt of the International Law Commission's draft, decided instead to refer the draft for further discussion to an Ad Hoc Committee of the GA. NGOs and a number of states following the Sixth Committee were dismayed with this result, certain that further, unfocused discussion would lead nowhere. They decided separately that they would each have to be more organized and efficient if they wanted to have a hand in setting the agenda for the ICC process. They also decided that it would be necessary for NGOs and states to work in coordination.

In early 1995, NGOs founded the Coalition, in the recognition that NGOs would have to pool their political strength and expertise, share the substantial work ahead and find worldwide support if the obstacles facing the creation of the ICC were to be overcome. At that point, the Coalition boasted around 30 members, including several NGOs that had followed the Sixth Committee deliberations. At the same time, the six or seven key supportive states participating in the Ad Hoc Committee discussions had already begun to form the LMG during the Sixth Committee negotiations and undertook to do so now in earnest.[3] As already mentioned, this is a common strategy through which groups of states can informally caucus and otherwise coordinate their efforts to reach a shared goal. Such caucuses can be very effective, although they are often short-lived, disbanding the moment the goal is achieved or even before, where emerging differences among members cannot be reconciled.

Early coordination between NGOs and states was naturally framed and facilitated by the UN and by its procedures, as discussions were centered in the GA and in the conference rooms and halls of the UN Secretariat's basement. Coordination between the Coalition and the LMG evolved through small steps taken together; for example, the Coalition was unable to secure on its own a meeting space within the UN Secretariat building for use during the GA's ICC-dedicated meetings. The Coalition solicited and received support from a number of like-minded states, who regularly reserved rooms on the Coalition's behalf. Indeed, even basic access for NGOs to the meetings was dependent upon supportive states. As NGOs do not have regular access to meetings of the GA, states must adopt meeting-specific resolutions that grant NGOs the right to observe, distribute materials and to make statements. The LMG consulted closely with the Coalition each year on the language of the resolution for ICC-related meetings, to ensure NGO access to the meetings.[4]

The Coalition and its members made use of the space the LMG helped to secure in the UN building among other things to organize meetings between NGOs and states and other experts. These meetings provided a forum in which the Coalition and the LMG could begin to explore the substantive issues being discussed by the Ad Hoc Committee and the Preparatory Committee that followed. These continuous interactions also cemented the working relations between NGO and government represent-atives, who maintained contacts between sessions of the various committees. These regular NGO–government meetings in turn relied on the timetable of regular UN ICC meetings, set jointly by the UN Secretariat and by states. This timetable helped to keep states focused on the ICC, and provided a framework to which the Coalition and the LMG could peg key goals and around which they could strategize.

The LMG also benefited from discussions in the Ad Hoc Committee and Preparatory Committee and with NGOs, in that these interactions helped to identify what would become the core membership of the LMG. The original LMG members, coordinated by Canada, informally recruited new members, inviting delegations to meetings at the Canadian mission to discuss the substance of the draft statute, based on the interventions of those delegations at committee meetings. Other interested delegations approached the LMG directly and asked to be included. By the time of the diplomatic conference, the membership of the LMG was nearly 70 states, representing all regions of the world. Discussions also helped to foster a growing sense of consensus within the LMG.

In fact, many of the early goals shared by the Coalition and the LMG were at least partly procedural in nature. Both were eager to see the draft statute moved eventually onto a track towards completion, which would mean convening a diplomatic conference. Therefore, the LMG and the Coalition shared the goal of setting a date for that conference, as well as finding a state to host it. The move from the Ad Hoc Committee to the Preparatory Committee, which met in 1996 and 1997, was also an achievement, as the Preparatory Committee had a mandate to engage in drafting a convention text, while the Ad Hoc Committee did not. Finally, in approaching the diplomatic conference, held in Rome, Italy, in June–July 1998, the LMG and the Coalition shared the goal of completing the draft statute by the end of the conference, in accordance with a number of key principles that both shared.

Success in achieving procedural goals in turn created the space for progress on the substance of the discussions themselves, the further development of what would become the Rome Statute. The Ad Hoc Committee provided the framework for free and open-ended discussion of key issues underpinning the creation of the ICC. States and NGOs alike realized that substantial and detailed technical research would have to be conducted in order to properly frame and evaluate the issues facing the ICC statute's drafters. The LMG looked to the Coalition and its members in part to provide this research, as NGO representatives could often dedicate more time to such efforts than government delegates at the UN or in capitals, who always had to juggle many different portfolios at once, moving from meetings on the ICC to meetings on terrorism, law of the sea, economic development, or peace and security, to name only a few. NGOs – like Human Rights Watch, Amnesty International, FIDH (International Federation of Human Rights Leagues) and the Lawyers' Committee for Human Rights – often had the mandate to develop a level of expertise which government delegates did not. The value that delegates placed on this research, and the esteem and professional respect towards their NGO counterparts that this generated, cannot be overestimated. This symbiosis has come to characterize the working relations between NGOs and states in the ICC process.

The strong working relations between governments and NGOs, as well as the nature of the LMG, cutting as it did across regional and traditional government grouping lines, often had the effect of undermining the power of any individual regional or other governmental grouping to control the process. In a prominent example, towards the end of the Rome Conference, India attempted to activate the Non-Aligned Movement (NAM) to scuttle the treaty, disingenuously invoking a high principle of the NAM and demanding the inclusion of nuclear weapons in the statute. This effort failed, in part because so many members of the NAM were in the LMG, and in part because of the closeness in timing between the Rome Conference and India's first testing of a nuclear weapon. The LMG was able to positively engage traditional groupings, including the NAM. The European Union was, of course, the most prominent such example.

This symbiosis has generated a phenomenon upon which a number of actors have commented. More than one conversation between delegates and NGOs has led observers to query, half in jest, which is the government and which the NGO? In part, such queries reflect a basic misunderstanding, an oversimplification of the nature of these two roles which are fundamentally more complex in reality. At the same time, constructive interactions between states and NGOs over time can and have led to a greater awareness and appreciation of the skills that each brings to the table and the challenges that each faces in its work. In this way, NGO representatives learned about the political obstacles that state delegates may face in pushing for constructive decisions or awaiting clear instructions from superiors in distant capitals, and honed their own advocacy skills, in identifying when quiet diplomacy would be more effective than public protestations. State delegates gained greater respect for their NGO colleagues, based on years of working together, and came to respect and rely upon broader and more transparent consultative processes to support their intergovernmental negotiations. Delegates also drew on their own personal and professional expertise in relevant areas of international law, as well as the more open political space for dialogue created by the UN process and the "new diplomacy," to take bolder positions and make stronger efforts to stick to them, reaching across traditional divisions to find support from other states where before there might have been deadlock.

These working relations between NGOs, states and international organizations characterize the "new diplomacy." This phrase reflects a new approach to international negotiations in which the strengths of very different actors coalesce to create an influence greater than that of any of the individual actors themselves. That strength is applied to the development and implementation of strategic campaigns to achieve treaties or intergovernmental outcomes, in processes that might otherwise yield to the lowest common denominator logic of the search for consensus. The impact of the "new diplomacy" is that no individual actor, regardless its power, may undercut or wreck a process which the majority of other actors support.[5] The "new diplomacy" arose in particular in response to the excruciating process that led to adoption of the treaty on the Law of the Sea, which a single state held up and weakened through constant watering down, only to refuse to support it after its adoption. The "new diplomacy" addresses what could be described as idealistic areas of law and development, if idealism can be described as the pursuit of basic human decency through the protection by the law of those vulnerable, for example, to the fallout from the trafficking of small arms and landmines, or the perpetration of the most heinous known crimes. However, the "new diplomacy" approaches these goals in a level-headed way, recognizing that watered-down treaties are not effective and may be worse than nothing, but that in order to achieve a regime worth supporting – both politically and financially – states sometimes have to take strong stands and step away from the consensus process that they otherwise prefer. Supportive states know that leaving powerful states out is a risk, but they move forward hoping and planning that over time and with the gradual establishment of the treaty regime, objections of the few states left out of consensus can be addressed and overcome, or that governments will change and the new governments will choose to join the treaty.

This level of coordination, reflecting the unique roles of each of the actors, has made it possible for the NGO community and more importantly for small and middle-power states, to play a serious role in the development of international law. What is surprising for many, but what should also be evident, is that the procedural framework within which these actors have proceeded has had an impact on the capacity of the "new diplomacy" to achieve its goals as well.

Finally, the Coalition has developed strong working relations with the UN Secretariat itself through the medium of procedure. At the start of the ICC process and at times throughout, the UN Secretariat and the Coalition have been at odds, in part because UN Secretariat officials were skeptical about the prospects of the ICC negotiations generally and about whether NGOs in particular could play a constructive role. The Office of Legal Affairs of the UN Secretariat was particularly unaccustomed to working directly with NGOs, especially in the forum of the General Assembly, which does not allow regular NGO access to its work. However, the UN Secretariat and the Coalition Secretariat shared something very important in common: a responsibility to remain neutral and to provide basic services to their members, each seeking through its own role to facilitate the smooth functioning of the negotiation process. Once the states agreed to include NGOs in the ICC meetings, through passage of yearly resolutions, the UN Secretariat also had responsibilities for procedures to manage the involvement of NGOs. The Coalition became a natural ally to the UN Secretariat, and eventually the UN Secretariat passed key responsibilities in this area directly to the Coalition. In particular, the UN Secretariat requested the Coalition to undertake in large part the process of registering NGOs for the Rome Diplomatic Conference. In addition, during the meetings of the Preparatory Commission that followed Rome, the UN Secretariat relied on the Coalition to facilitate NGO registration for the Preparatory Commission, to distribute documents to NGOs present, and otherwise to inform NGOs about the working methods and environment of the UN, so that they could constitute a constructive presence in the ICC process. In the end, the working relations between the Coalition Secretariat and the UN Secretariat were strengthened to the point where even the intercession of states to secure meeting space in the building for NGOs was no longer necessary; the Coalition was able to secure its own space directly from the UN Secretariat.

The link to the national level

By the time of the Rome Conference, nearly 800 NGOs were members of the CICC, representing the full spectrum of NGO activity, including NGOs focusing on human rights, the rights and concerns specifically of women and children, disarmament, the development of the legal professions, victims, peace, faith-based NGOs and many others. More than 300 NGOs were in attendance at the conference. It is remarkable to note that almost all of the NGOs participating in the ICC process participated within the Coalition umbrella. This remains true, eight years later. There were only a handful of mostly extreme nationalist, right-to-life groups which opposed the Rome Statute and so did not work within the Coalition, but who continued to benefit from the documentation services of the CICC.

Work on the ICC could not have been so successful if it were conducted on the international level alone. Developments at the national level, even those external to the ICC process, have also played a key role. To cite a few positive examples, the election of the Labour government in the United Kingdom and the appointment of Robin Cook as Foreign Secretary resulted in a demonstrable shift of that government towards an ethical foreign policy. In addition, the leadership of Lloyd Axworthy as Canadian Foreign Minister provided a nexus around which the LMG drew additional strength, as it did with the landmines process. In contrast, the election of the Bush administration in the US has galvanized the organization of an anti-ICC campaign, whereas the Clinton administration was critical of the ICC but remained constructively engaged in the process.

From the days of the Ad Hoc Committee, the Coalition has engaged in efforts to raise awareness of the ICC at the national level. Efforts to educate key stakeholders and to raise awareness generally about the ICC continue to be the foundational element of the Coalition's mandate and work. It is this effort to raise basic awareness that has allowed the Coalition to develop such a large membership base; as of 2003, the Coalition comprises nearly 2,000 NGOs. This membership base has supported work in many crucial areas at the national level, including the campaign to achieve 60 ratifications of the Rome Statute, the number necessary for the Statute to enter into force, and efforts to promote the development of strong implementing legislation in as many countries as possible.

The Coalition goes beyond the strictures of traditional networks in that it engages not only in comprehensive information-sharing, but also in the development and implementation of joint strategies to address complex problems, such as the development of national implementing legislation or combating the US government's worldwide anti-ICC campaign. These campaigns are of a nature that even the largest Coalition members could not undertake them on their own; instead, they required the sustained coordination of NGOs of all sizes and mandates, from all over the world.

But it is important to emphasize that more than 95 percent of the Coalition's work focused on the provision of vital education, communication and other services to Coalition members, the UN and governments, as opposed to issue-oriented advocacy. Advocacy is the highly publicized and controversial "tip of the iceberg." In this, the work of the Coalition Secretariat and the activities of Coalition's members should be distinguished.

The Coalition's approach – to decentralize the substantive work, to maintain a low-profile, service-based Secretariat and to maximize the independence of the members to act – has been undertaken in recognition of the fact that local and national NGOs are much better placed to assess political conditions in their own countries, to identify key stakeholders, to assess how best to motivate political will to ratify and to evaluate existing national laws and legislative processes with an eye towards implementation. To facilitate this work, the Coalition Secretariat plays a more neutral role, only taking positions on fundamental issues where it is clear that the membership supports it. The focus of the Secretariat instead is to provide information and other essential coordination services to Coalition members, to facilitate their constructive involvement in the ICC process. In this, the Coalition Secretariat bears some resemblance to the key coordinating secretariats of the International Campaign to Ban Landmines.

The Coalition Secretariat also plays an essential role in helping to level the playing field between smaller national NGOs and larger international NGOs, in essence empowering smaller NGOs to make a substantial contribution to the ICC process at the international level. The Coalition Secretariat accomplished this by maintaining a steady stream of updates and information about the ICC process to the members, through its website and through information listservs in English, French, Spanish and now Portuguese. In addition, the Coalition Secretariat funds the participation of active Coalition members in the UN meetings on the ICC, to provide them with the opportunity to build further their own substantial expertise and to make further professional contacts.

The Coalition's work, however, rests on the development of strong national networks and local coalitions in each region, such as the Mexican Coalition, which includes around 25 members, maintains a Technical Secretariat that is elected by member organizations and serves for a six month term, and whose activities have contributed to the supportive position of the Mexican government. The US networks, Washington Working Group on the ICC and American Coalition for the ICC, to mention only two – involve more than 100 US groups. The Canadian, UK, and French networks have made crucial and timely political contributions. Scores of NGOs in Asia have participated in national and regional meetings and initiatives. Other networks or national coalitions, such as the Mongolian Coalition, are younger, smaller or more informal. Each is, in some way, unique. It is likely that there are national networks or branches, for example in Africa, that are operating almost independently of the international CICC. And very often the international secretariat of CICC knows the name of only a few members of a national network. While some aspects of the ICC campaign are naturally more short-term, as with the campaign to promote signature of the Rome Statute, others require a sustained commitment to ensure their success. The development of national networks and coalitions is intended to provide a kind of continuity that fosters and facilitates this long-term commitment of resources and expertise.

In this regard, the work of local and national NGOs will prove most crucial, perhaps, when it comes to the development of strong implementing legislation given their expertise, based on years of engagement in their own national systems. Implementing legislation is one of the most fundamental and most complex areas of work on the Rome Statute; it is fundamental because the ICC's system of complementarity relies on national judicial systems to make the first efforts to investigate and prosecute war crimes, crimes against humanity and genocide. It is complex because in order for states to successfully address such crimes, they must make substantial alterations to their criminal laws, as well as addressing areas of the law that facilitate cooperation with other states and with the ICC. It is a somewhat shocking fact that 50 years after the Holocaust, the Nuremberg trials, and the adoption of the Geneva and Genocide Conventions, most nations have never codified these crimes in their national laws. Generally, states must modify a range of laws, including their criminal codes, their mutual cooperation laws and even sometimes their constitutions.[6] Again, this will be one of the major legacies of the Rome Statute.

There are particular challenges at the national level where the need for transparency and the participation of civil society in the development of legislation is not recognized. For example, in many countries, the development of new laws implementing international obligations are not subject to a public or transparent process, meaning that the input of outside experts is simply not considered. However, it is also true that national networks can more systematically challenge government processes that are closed to outside input. In many countries, such as in France, the United Kingdom, Brazil, Canada and Ghana, to name a few, governments have been receptive to requests from civil society to have the opportunity, either informally or formally, to provide substantive expert input into drafts before they are enacted. The Coalition Secretariat endeavors to connect local and national networks to each other and to provide technical guidance to encourage efforts to achieve greater transparency in the national legislative processes.

It will be interesting to evaluate in the long term the role that such national networks may be able to play in affecting the policies of their governments *vis-à-vis* war crimes and other crimes of concern to the international community. It is hoped that support from the international level will provide them crucial leverage to open up processes that might otherwise have been closed and thereby to create a precedent for deeper civil society involvement in national legislative processes in general.

Conclusion

The accomplishments of establishing the ICC have been multiple and profound, in terms of contributions to the globalization of the cause of human rights, democracy, justice and the rule of law as an alternative or counter-balance to economic globalization or the subsumation of the rule of law to the use of force. The Rome Statute also embodies a powerful tribute to the power of civil society to have an impact on the development and practice of international law. It presages the strengthening of international law, and in particular, the ideal of universal equality before the law.

The ICC process continues to be a landmark process in which civil society remains involved, not just in the drafting of a treaty, but in the day-by-day building of a potentially revolutionary new institution on the basis of that treaty. In this regard, the ICC process will take in its stride the actual establishment of the Court and look forward to the difficult first years of this new institution as yet another challenge to be welcomed and embraced. Nothing less than the long-term success of the ICC process, the long-term stability of the ICC community (nationally, regionally and internationally) and the long-term impact of these developments on the face of international law, remain to be won.

Notes

1 There is no single definition of civil society, but it is generally understood that civil society represents a broad spectrum, among which NGOs are only one element. The Center for Civil Society of the London School of Economics (2003) has posed an initial working definition of civil society as follows: "Civil society refers to the set of institutions, organizations and behavior situated between the state, the business world, and the family. Specifically, this includes voluntary and non-profit organizations of many different kinds, philanthropic institutions, social and political movements, other forms of social participation and engagement and the values and cultural patterns associated with them." Non-governmental organizations is a name practically invented in the UN Charter. It is easier to classify states and treaty organizations and their represent-atives, but NGOs are an extremely diverse sector. The term NGO has historic-ally described mostly not-for-profit organizations working in intergovernmental forums; these organizations are usually known by other terms at the national and local community levels.

2 "The General Assembly's structure includes six Main Committees, which correspond to the major fields of responsibility of the General Assembly. They consider agenda items referred to them by the General Assembly and prepare recommendations and draft resolutions for submission to the General Assembly plenary. . . . All UN members have the right to be represented on each of these committees. Each committee elects its own officers. Decisions are made by a majority of the members present and voting, a majority of the committee constituting a quorum." The Sixth Committee, otherwise known as the Legal Committee, addresses issues of a legal nature (New Zealand Ministry of Foreign Affairs and Trade 2001: 24).

3 The small group of supportive states continued to work together. This group grew to include over 20 like-minded states by the end of the year, including Argentina, Australia, Austria, Canada, Denmark, Egypt, Finland, Germany, Greece, Italy, Lesotho, the Netherlands, New Zealand, Norway, Portugal, Samoa, Singapore, South Africa, Sweden, Switzerland and Trinidad and Tobago.

4 It is important to note that if individual states, such as the China, India, the United Kingdom or the United States, had decided to exclude NGOs, they could certainly have done so, as they had almost always before. It is not clear why powerful governments with serious reservations about the ICC negotiations allowed NGOs access to this process in the Sixth Committee of the GA. The authors of this chapter believe that even these nations had powerful hopes for the process and recognized the importance of NGOs if any progress was to be achieved. Further, the decade of 1989–99 at the UN, the post-Cold War decade, was characterized by a tremendous increase of democracy at every level of political society. More research on this issue should be conducted.

5 It is arguable that the Bush administration has understood much more directly the impact and implications of the "new diplomacy" than did the Clinton administration. The Bush administration's campaign to undermine the ICC and to weaken state support for the institution is consonant with the desire to retain and heighten the capacity of the United States to effectively and unilaterally veto any international action with which it does not agree. It is not clear whether the Bush administration, if it secures a second term, will continue to seek to destroy the new international organization or will attempt to terminate, severely weaken or modify the treaty when it is opened at the review conference scheduled to occur in 2009.

6 A range of completed implementing legislation is available on the Coalition's website at http://www.iccnow.org/resourcestools/ratimptoolkit/nationalregional tools/legislationdebates.html.

Bibliography

Center for Civil Society, London School of Economics (2003) "What is civil society," http://www.lse.ac.uk/collections/CCS/what_is_civil_society.htm (accessed on 7 November 2003).

New Zealand Ministry of Foreign Affairs and Trade (2001) *United Nations Handbook*, Wellington, New Zealand: New Zealand Ministry of Foreign Affairs and Trade.

Times of India (1998) "Editorial," August 1.

5 The Pinochet case

The catalyst for deepening democracy in Chile?

Ann Matear

Introduction

The military *coup d'etat* of September 11, 1973 which overthrew the democratically elected government of Salvador Allende Gossens represented a dramatic break with Chile's long-standing democratic political tradition. On assuming power, the military regime embarked on a radical restructuring of the Chilean state and society which transformed political, economic and social relations. The state was converted into an authoritarian bureaucracy, whereby the military, supported by right-wing civilian groups, assumed the administrative and legislative functions of the state for the next 17 years. Political parties were banned, the parliament was put into recess, trade unions and other social organizations of popular participation were repressed as the military junta attempted to eradicate the support base of the left-wing parties. Since the return to democracy in 1990, Chile has enjoyed many of the characteristics of a liberal democracy, yet the legacy of military rule casts a shadow over the quality of democracy.

Transitions never leave a blank slate and governments often face formidable political, social and legal constraints which severely restrict the choices available (Pridham 2000). In the Chilean case, the armed forces continued to enjoy legal prerogatives which gave them substantial influence over decision-making. The continued application of the 1978 Amnesty Law exempted the military from prosecution for human rights violations committed between 1973 and 1978. This weakened the principle of equality before the law, one of the basic requirements of a liberal democracy. The apparent inability or unwillingness of civilian governments to respond to the demands for justice denied individuals their civil rights and left the process of democratization in Chile stunted and truncated. It was clear that Chile had not progressed in linear fashion from transition to fully consolidated democracy. The human rights question remained unresolved and the disappeared were still unaccounted for; the military remained unrepentant and unpunished and continued to evade civilian control.

The relationship between democracy and justice is complex and is based on a series of political, institutional and legal requirements. These include the protection of the rights and liberties of citizens; respect for the rights of minorities; the independence of the judiciary; and the rule of law. Given that these legal requisites underpin democracy, no individual, group or institution can be deemed beyond the law, for without the equal application of the law democracy cannot be substantive or meaningful. From this perspective, human rights organizations in Latin America and elsewhere have consistently argued that the defense of human rights is integral to the process of democratization. Under democracy, it is the responsibility of government – morally and legally – to protect its citizens from those elements who would violate even the most basic human rights. Moreover, human rights lawyers and non-governmental organizations have argued that justice requires democratically elected governments to punish crimes committed by former regimes. Theirs is essentially an ethical position, which proposes that prosecution is a moral obligation to the victims and their families (Huntington 1991). This perspective is supported by international law which opposes amnesties on the grounds that they promote impunity, fail to deter such abuses happening again and that, rather than promoting reconciliation, they forge deep divisions in civil society (Albon 1995). If, as occurred during the Chilean transition, a government fails to prosecute because of pressure from the military and their supporters, then it is apparent that authoritarian enclaves remain; the military is not subordinate to civilian rule and therefore the transition will be incomplete and democratization will be slowed or even halted (Garretón 1996). If prosecution does not occur because of a lack of political will among elites, the rule of law is again undermined and the new democracy is de-legitimized before the citizens and the international community (Benomar 1995).

The important relationship between justice and democracy was apparent from the beginning of the transition in Chile but, faced with the threat of a return to military rule, a pragmatic justice prevailed. Following the handing over of power to a center-left coalition government in March 1990, substantial reforms of the Chilean judicial system were initiated which emphasized greater independence and accountability. The impact of these changes was evidenced by the mid-1990s, as organizations and individuals sought justice through the national courts for human rights abuses. The human rights movement's unrelenting struggle for justice challenged the limits of the restricted democracy negotiated between the military and civilian elites and played a key role in deepening the process of democratization.

Drawing on cross-class support, social movements, the Church and the non-governmental sector had all contributed to building a viable opposition to the military regime during the 1980s. Active both within and beyond national borders in defense of universal human rights, the human rights movement has developed the capacity to operate transnationally (Cohen and Rai 2000). Central to the emergence of transnational movements is the identification of shared goals, the development and exchange of strategic information, and the ability to coordinate activities despite geographical distance. Such movements are likely to draw on collaboration from a range of formal and informal political actors, who are able to mobilize resources at national and international levels (Smith 1998). Similarly, Kumar (2000) emphasizes the importance of access to and sharing of information as a vital part of networking activity among transnational movements and their ability to move rapidly and flexibly to make use of the information at their disposal.

While human rights cases were being presented in Chilean courts in the mid-1990s, a parallel process was underway in Spain. These developments would subsequently demonstrate the potentially global reach of the human rights movement and the importance of key individuals within it. Charges of genocide were filed against Pinochet and the three other members of the ruling junta in a Valencia court on 4 July 1996. The Spanish criminal process was set in train by Miguel Miravet Hombrados, the chief prosecutor of the High Court of Valencia and the president of the Union of Progressive Prosecutors in Spain (Unión Progresista de Fiscales). This was the result of collaboration between human rights organizations, non-governmental organizations and lawyers in order to compile evidence in support of these charges (Wilson 1999). The groundwork was laid through the coordination of various organizations including the Salvador Allende Foundation in Spain. This organization was headed by Joan Garcés, a lawyer and former Allende advisor who coordinated the action on human rights abuses in Chile.[1] Other key actors in Spain included the Human Rights Secretariat of the United Left Party and the Spanish section of Amnesty International; the ecumenical organization Justice and Peace (Servicio de Paz y Justicia – SERPAJ) which operates in a number of Latin American countries; and in Chile, the Corporation for the Promotion and Defence of People's Rights (CODEPU) (Davis 2000). Although these high-profile legal initiatives received scant coverage in the English-speaking media, they attracted considerable publicity in Spain and Latin America, thereby encouraging witnesses to come forward and undoubtedly signaling to the perpetrators of human rights abuses that their impunity might be short-lived.

Pinochet's detention in a London clinic on October 16, 1998 was not an audacious stunt but was the result of lengthy and sustained campaigning, coordination and painstaking investigation by human rights organizations in Chile and around the world. The transnational network was spurred into action when Spain's United Left became aware of his whereabouts and requested a judicial order for his arrest in relation to his role in Operation Condor, a cross-border campaign of terror, kidnapping and disappearance of named individuals. The Spanish judge Baltasar Garzón, of the National Court (Audiencia Nacional)[2] complied with the request and Pinochet was detained on a provisional warrant signed by a London magistrate on his behalf (Davis 2000).

This initial stage emphasized universal principles of human rights and the universal jurisdiction which could achieve justice for the families of victims which they had been denied in Chilean courts. Subsequent developments in the case revealed the complexity of translating the principle of universality into practice, as it became clear that the pursuit of justice would have to take place within a sovereign national jurisdiction, whether in Britain, Spain or in Chile. Bringing Pinochet to trial in a British or Spanish court could have been justified on the basis that the Chilean courts had failed to challenge his claims of immunity as a former head of state. In doing so, it could have been argued that the Chilean courts had endorsed impunity and forced citizens to seek justice outside of national borders (Golob 2002a). However, this would be a partial view of political and judicial developments in Chile during the 1990s, for substantial reforms of the judicial system emphasizing independence and accountability had already begun in 1990. Furthermore, several high-profile individuals from the military regime were brought to trial in Chile from the mid-1990s onwards and, by the time of his arrest in 1998, judges were also investigating charges filed against Pinochet himself in the Chilean courts.

While this case may have broken new ground in the investigations of human rights abuses at international level, it is still too early to determine what will be the legacy of this case for international justice and human rights law. The impact of Pinochet's arrest can be more clearly identified within the national context. This chapter examines how the former general's detention and progressive isolation from political life rapidly became a catalyst for wide-ranging political and legal developments in Chile which have significantly deepened and strengthened democracy. As Golob (2002b: 24) points out, the issues raised by this case "are as much about national and popular sovereignty as they are about transcended borders, globalised justice or universal rights." Pinochet's arrest provided the impetus required for the human rights issue to be re-examined when many in Chile and abroad had hoped that it was a closed chapter. Reopening the human rights question forced the government to acknowledge publicly that democracy in Chile was seriously flawed by the Constitution and the non-application of the law. Pinochet may have been under arrest, but Chilean justice and democracy were on trial.

The struggle for democracy in Chile, 1973–90

Following the military coup in 1973, new forms of popular association rapidly emerged in response to the regime's violations of human rights. Throughout the 17 years of military rule, the Church operated as an umbrella organization for many social organizations, provided vital linkages with the international ecumenical community, and acted as a legitimating force in negotiations with the state. Human rights organizations were set up with the support of the Church, to provide legal and medical assistance, food and refuge to victims of state repression and their families.[3] Under the Christian Humanist Academy, the Church provided an important space for independent research centers and many academics who had been purged from their posts in the universities. Diverse organizations sprang up in low-income neighborhoods in response to the deteriorating economic and social condition which resulted from the regime's neoliberal policies. Social movements developed self-help projects for low-cost housing, popular education, community health care and consumer-producer cooperatives, often in collaboration with national and international non-governmental organizations (Lehmann 1990). In addition, new social actors emerged in response to the violence of the state and challenged the existing social structures in defense of their rights. For example, women from the popular sectors[4] developed support networks for those with relatives in prison or who had disappeared. Many of these women's organizations progressively moved beyond the specific issues of human rights and economic survival, which had characterized the years immediately after the *coup*, to increasingly gender-based demands and to establish links between women's oppression and the global issues of inequality and democratization (Matear 1999). In contrast to those social movements which had existed before the 1973 military *coup*, these new movements involved a wider range of social actors who operated sectorally or territorially, were oriented towards specific needs and who were less tied to the political parties (Foweraker 1995).

The experiences of the social movements under the military regime had emphasized different ways of decision-making which would directly affect those involved, bringing about greater representation and accountability. The challenge was to envisage how these experiences could be translated into post-dictatorship politics at local, regional and national levels, and to construct a more inclusive, participatory and representative democracy than had existed prior to the *coup* (Matear 1996). However, it became apparent during the transition period that many social movements were harboring unrealistic expectations. From the mid-1980s until the transition to democracy, the social movements' objective of removing the military regime appeared to coincide with the re-emerging political elites' aim of reconstructing democracy. The elites emphasized the technical perspective of the new democracy – the mechanics of government, establishing channels of communication and institutions – and arguably were less concerned with the quality of the democracy they hoped to create. For the popular sectors represented through the social movements, there were hopes that the new democracy *per se* would facilitate justice, equality of opportunity, representation and participation in which a wide range of social actors could be involved.

The transition to democracy began with the plebiscite of 1988. The plebiscite offered the people of Chile the opportunity to express their support for eight more years of Pinochet rule (vote "Yes") or their desire for a return to democracy (vote "No"). The voting went against Pinochet and was considered fair and fraud-proof, with foreign observers present to monitor every transparent ballot box. But the dynamic of the transition to democracy rapidly moved away from the mobilization of the social movements towards the political parties. The political elites deemed the contraction of civil society to be a prerequisite for establishing and consolidating democracy. As the opposition moved into government, their enthusiasm for social movements, alternative grassroots politics and popular mobilization quickly evaporated. The same channels which had contributed to ending the dictatorship could easily lead to civil unrest if not demobilized. The memories of the social movements' destabilizing role towards the end of the Allende government (1970–3) continued to weigh heavily on the political class. Consequently, the emphasis was on the return to institutional politics and required the contraction of civil society; politicians and many trade union leaders encouraged consensus on the political and economic models rather than debate.

Arguably, a free and lively civil society and a relatively autonomous political society are among the conditions considered essential for democracy to flourish (Linz and Stepan 1996). Indeed, an active and resourceful civil society can effectively counter-balance the power of the state and thus play an important role in constructing and defending democracy (Diamond 1994). However, during the transition to democracy in Chile, the danger was that the fragile, emergent party system would not be able to channel a range of diverse, competing and conflicting interests effectively if civil society were "over-active" and excessively politicized. Consequently, by the early 1990s, civil society was not perceived as an essential component of Chilean democracy but as a potential threat to its survival, in sharp contrast to the high levels of popular mobilization and grassroots politics which had flourished during the military regime. The process of formal representation in an increasingly complex society was an alienating experience for many and led to a profound sense of disempowerment, particularly among the popular sectors. However, the pursuit of justice continued beyond the transition, for the human rights movement did not abandon or restrain its demands for justice; nor did it quietly withdraw from public life and allow the human rights issue to disappear from the political agenda.

Democratization and human rights in the 1990s

The Constitution of 1980, which was approved in a plebiscite, institutionalized the concept of an "authoritarian democracy" and elevated the political role of the armed forces by giving military officers permanent legislative and administrative positions. The Constitution outlined a timetable for the return to a restricted democracy and by working within this framework, successive governments since 1990 have seen their scope for reform extremely limited. When the military regime handed over power to an elected civilian government in March 1990, it still commanded significant support among the population. Moreover, it was handing over a strong and successful economy and it had secured substantial influence for the military and their supporters through the "binding laws" (Loveman 1995).[5] Consequently, the armed forces were in a strong position to guide the transition and secure important advantages for themselves under the new civilian government. It might have been expected, therefore, that a negotiated transition between civilian elites and the military would result in a restricted democracy, in which the armed forces would remain immune from prosecution for human rights violations (Huntington 1991). In such circumstances, it was argued, the manner in which those accused of human rights violations were dealt with could potentially destabilize the transition process. General Pinochet had threatened dire consequences if any of his men were brought to trial.

Yet, the military's attempts to silence the debate on human rights in Chile and abroad was futile, for throughout the period of military rule, the international community had been aware of the widespread and systematic policy of human rights violations committed in the aftermath of the *coup*. Beginning in 1974, the United Nations prepared a series of special reports on human rights abuses in Chile, and throughout the decade a number of resolutions were passed in the General Assembly and the Human Rights Commission. During the 1980s the international community also maintained a critical position towards the government of Chile due to the human rights situation (Chilean Human Rights Commission 1991).[6] The criticism of the regime from civil society has been no less forceful. The human rights movement in Chile and abroad has argued consistently that without justice, there could be no meaningful democracy in Chile. They have called upon successive elected governments to seek justice for the human rights abuses committed during the military regime. Yet, despite the pressure from the human rights movement and the support of the UN to achieve justice through a legal solution, the politics of pragmatism prevailed between elites and the military.

Within the limits of the pacted transition, the Aylwin government opted for a pragmatic response of compromise and reform whereby the human rights abuses would be investigated, the truth would be known but the government would stop short of prosecutions on the basis that they would be divisive. Human rights would best be dealt with under the dominant paradigm of democracy as the "greater good"; the maintenance of a democratic regime was perceived as the best hope for resolving the human rights issue in the future and for preventing such abuses happening again. The more radical demands from the families of victims and human rights organizations, which required that the truth be known, the victims be compensated and the guilty be punished, were rejected as risking subordinating democracy to human rights (Garretón 1996).

A human rights policy which provides mechanisms to establish the truth surrounding human rights violations is likely to enjoy greater legitimacy and consensus thereby avoiding accusations of partiality at national and international levels. By making the truth officially and publicly known, the violations and their eventual resolution are framed, not only as the concern of those individuals directly affected, but of society as a whole (Zalaquett 1995). It was to this end that President Patricio Aylwin set up the Commission for Truth and Reconciliation in 1990. Headed by Senator Raul Rettig, its remit was to investigate and establish the truth about the nature and extent of the political repression committed during the dictatorship. The composition of the Commission allowed for the participation of human rights groups, the victims of abuses and their families, but the Commission received no cooperation from the police or the armed forces.

The report issued by the National Commission for Truth and Reconciliation was a significant step forward since through this report, the Chilean state officially and publicly acknowledged that between September 11, 1973 and March 11, 1990 there had been serious, systematic and mass violations of human rights, resulting in the deaths or disappearance of 3,197 people (Chilean Human Rights Commission 1991). Moreover, the report played another important function by challenging the military regime's version of Chilean history as it provided, for the first time, hard evidence confirming that human rights violations had occurred during the dictatorship (Acuña and Smulovitz 1996). Despite criticism from the political right of the investigation conducting a witch-hunt, the veracity of the report was recognized and the abuses documented therein were condemned by the United Nations and the Organization of American States. Furthermore, the Commission went some way to advancing the process of social reparation as it provided a forum in which the veracity of the victims' experiences could be acknowledged. The report detailed recommendations for legal, institutional and educational reforms to prevent such abuses happening again, and reparations for the families of victims.

Clearly there are limits to how much can be achieved by such Commissions for, as Claus Offe has observed, "some of the traces of the old regime cannot be removed or compensated for at all, as one cannot 'undo' the past" (Offe 1996: 82). Individuals accused of atrocities were not named by the report and instead, information implicating individuals was submitted to the courts. However, most cases were prevented from coming to trial by the 1978 Amnesty Law and demands for justice at the level of civil society went largely unanswered. Legal action was limited to those families directly affected by human rights abuses bringing cases against individual military officers in civil proceedings. As a result, the human rights question was not excluded from public debate, but it was "privatized" in the sense that individuals stood accused of crimes for which the military as an institution was not held responsible. Moreover, the civil proceedings failed to make fully explicit the relationship between the crimes committed, the trauma suffered by individuals and by society, and the repressive political situation in the nation (Becker *et al.* 1995).

However, by the mid-1990s, a different strategy to achieve justice for the human rights violations committed by the military regime began to gather force. The Chilean judicial system had been tainted by its associations with the former military regime and the forces of reaction, for, following the military *coup* in 1973, the Supreme Court handed over responsibility for trying political cases to the military courts. The judiciary had been largely uncritical of the emergency legal powers which the junta gave itself, and either supported or ignored the extra-legal repression and abuses committed by the armed forces (Fruhling 1997). The political bias of the judges appointed to the Supreme Court by the military was evidenced by those cases when military personnel accused of human rights abuses stood trial but were not convicted despite overwhelming evidence; in other instances, the Supreme Court discouraged the Appeal Courts from pursuing investigations into human rights violations (Garretón 1996). Even after the transition to democracy, Pinochet continued to wield undue influence over the judiciary through his representative in the Supreme Court who effectively blocked many human rights trials from the outset (Brett 2000).

Not surprisingly therefore, in the immediate aftermath of the military regime there was little public confidence in the legal system. Yet, over time new Supreme Court judges were appointed under democratic governments and a number of high-profile trials resulted in prosecutions. So, a full three years before Pinochet's arrest in London, faced with pressure from the human rights movement, the Chilean state began to assume its responsibility by defending the rights of its citizens and challenging the authoritarian enclaves. The first step was the judges' acknowledgement that Chile's ratification of international treaties on civil and political rights took precedence over national law and, consequently, the 1978 Amnesty Law could not cover acts of murder committed by the armed forces outside Chile. The impact of this reinterpretation was first felt when General Manuel Contreras stood trial for the murder of Chilean ambassador Orlando Letelier and his assistant Ronni Moffit, in Washington DC in 1976. A request for extradition to the United States had previously been refused by the Supreme Court and, in order to see justice done, the Letelier family began legal proceedings against Contreras in Chile in 1995. Despite protests and threats from the military, the government headed by Eduardo Frei Montalva did not back down when the Supreme Court convicted Contreras and his second-in-command, Colonel Pedro Espinoza. After five months of wrangling between the government and the upper echelons of the military command, the court's decision was enforced and Contreras and Espinoza were sentenced to terms of imprisonment (Hunter 1998).[7] Subsequent reinterpretation of the Amnesty Law led to the conclusion that it only applied to human rights abuses committed between 1973 and 1978. Consequently, acts resulting in murder committed after 1978 could also be pursued through the courts. This resulted in the successful prosecution of military officers and DINA personnel in a number of high-profile cases and sent a clear indication that, by in the mid-1990s, it was actually possible to seek justice for human rights cases through the courts in Chile.[8]

Pinochet under arrest: justice, democracy and reconciliation

The first legal challenge to General Pinochet in Chile actually preceded his arrest in London in October 1998 by ten months. It was presented by Gladys Marín, the leader of the Communist Party, for the kidnapping and murder of her husband. By the time of Pinochet's arrest in London, a further number of cases had been brought against him in Chile by human rights lawyers, associations of the families of the disappeared, and professional bodies representing teachers and health professionals whose members had been kidnapped or murdered. From this point onwards, the legal machine swung into operation and further charges were subsequently brought against the former general even while he remained in the United Kingdom.

The order for Pinochet's arrest in London was issued by the Central Court Number 5 of the Audiencia Nacional in Spain, driven by the co-ordinated efforts of the already mentioned international network of organizations working on human rights. The judicial process began with the Spanish authorities issuing warrants through Interpol to the British magistrate, which meant that the arrest was not a political but a legal question.

His detention shattered any illusion that Chile had come to terms with the legacy of 17 years of military rule – on the surface, the nation appeared to have made peace with its past, but it became immediately apparent that wounds had not healed nor was the transition to democracy complete. Chilean society was polarized into two equal camps as a MORI poll revealed, showing that 44 percent welcomed his arrest while 45 percent viewed it negatively. However, it is notable that the majority of the population did not fear a return to the dark days of the dictatorship. According to the survey, 66 percent considered that the stability of the political system was not in danger, compared to 22 percent who perceived it to be under threat. Only 8 percent feared there might be a military *coup*.[9] The events in London forced the Chilean government to confront the reality of the situation, that the image of democracy and justice at home and abroad would be irreparably damaged if it were seen to condone impunity for the armed forces.

Pinochet's arrest also presented a serious challenge to the status quo on human rights at international level and highlighted the potential to develop new roles for international law. The pursuit of justice became framed at international level as the defense of universal human rights and the pursuit of the perpetrators of crimes against humanity. At the same time, however, it became immediately apparent that there were few precedents as no former head of state visiting another country had ever been brought to account by its criminal process due to the immunity from prosecution assumed to be conferred by head of state/diplomatic immunity (Robertson 1999).

Yet, while the international aspects of the Pinochet case attracted a great deal of interest in the international media, the case had serious implications for national sovereignty and how the search for justice might impact on Chilean democracy. The right was able to exploit nationalist sentiment in Chile and portray the center-left government as caving in to Spain and Britain, neo-imperialist powers meddling in the internal affairs of a sovereign state. The issue of national sovereignty proved particularly complex as, for different reasons, the right-wing parties and the center-left government argued that Pinochet should not stand trial abroad. The government was at pains to emphasize that it was defending the jurisdiction of the Chilean courts and the sovereignty of the Chilean state; it was not defending Pinochet or the crimes of which he stood accused. The right saw no reason why he should stand trial at all.

The questions of sovereignty and the role of international law were hotly debated at the Iberoamerican Summit in 1999, when those Heads of State present declared that the imposition of laws in third-party states was "a violation of the principles which govern the international community; [such actions] weaken multilateralism and are contrary to the spirit of cooperation and friendship which should exist between our people" (*El Mercurio*, Wednesday, November 17, 1999). The case highlighted the complexity of the issue as, from the perspective of less powerful nations, the judicial aspects of globalization, like the political and economic aspects, could prove to be a double-edged sword. It could risk undermining the sovereignty of weaker nations, placing their often fragile democracies under pressure. More positively, it might be concluded that the "coercive power of the cosmopolitan liberal consensus" effectively strengthened the hand of the Chilean government, when faced with internal opposition to seeking justice through the national courts (Golob 2002b: 25). Viewed from this perspective, Pinochet's arrest was a catalyst for subsequent wide-ranging political and legal developments in Chile which deepened and strengthened democracy.

In June 1999, the former Minister of Defense, Edmundo Perez Yoma, proposed the setting up of the Mesa de Diálogo (Round Table for Dialogue) which was composed of representatives from the government, the armed forces, human rights lawyers, religious communities, the cultural sphere and the world of science (Aguilar 2002). The organizations representing the families of the disappeared did not participate on the grounds that knowing the truth was not sufficient – they continued to demand that those responsible be brought to justice. The various participants approached the Mesa with different aims and objectives. The government's priority was to bring about national unity through the official recognition that agents of the state had indeed violated human rights and by establishing the whereabouts of the disappeared. The human rights lawyers aimed to demonstrate publicly that the abuses were not isolated cases committed by individual military officers against individual civilians, but that they were systematic and institutional abuses which had formed part of state policy. According to Commander-in-Chief of the Armed Forces, Ricardo Izurieta, the military aimed to finally draw the transition to a close through participating in this dialogue.

Many months passed while the military, government and human rights lawyers engaged in frank and tense discussion in the Mesa de Diálogo. Agreement was finally reached on June 13, 2000 when the military agreed to cooperate in the investigations into the whereabouts of the disappeared, thereby, in their view, furthering the cause of national unity. However, even this came with strings attached for, in order to secure the collaboration of the military, a mechanism was devised whereby information could be given in strict anonymity. In May 2000, President Lagos proposed legislation to Congress that would protect those who wished to reveal information about the location of the disappeared (Aguilar 2002). The legislation providing for professional secrecy was approved in 33 hours by a large cross-party majority in both Congress and Senate, indicating the high levels of commitment from all political parties to seize the moment. Despite the broad political consensus, the arrangement was strongly opposed by human rights organizations who feared that its provisions for anonymity would obstruct criminal investigations and result in impunity.

In any case, a legal loophole meant that the military ran little risk of prosecution by revealing the whereabouts of the disappeared, particularly in those cases which occurred in the days and months immediately after the *coup d'état*. During the 1990s, human rights groups had exploited the fact that the 1978 Amnesty Law covered murder but did not apply to kidnappings. Since the disappeared were officially "missing" rather than murdered, charges could be brought against military officers for the crime of aggravated kidnapping. However, once the remains of the bodies were located, the charge would be murder; if the crime had been committed before 1978, it would fall under the provisions of the Amnesty Law.

The Mesa's deliberations concluded with a public broadcast in January 2001 by President Ricardo Lagos, which revealed the whereabouts of 180 of the disappeared. However, there was little solace for the families who learned that, in the majority of these cases, the bodies of their loved ones had been thrown into lakes, rivers and the sea (Barton and Murray 2002: 336). For them, there could be no final closure. The anonymity assured by the legislation passed in 2000 and the continued application of the Amnesty Law for crimes committed between 1973 and 1978 meant that there was little likelihood of those responsible being identified and brought to trial.

It is doubtful that increased criminal investigations into human rights abuses and the collaboration of the military in locating the remains of the disappeared could have been achieved if Pinochet were at liberty in Chile. His arrest in London in October 1998 effectively signaled the beginning of his progressive marginalization from political and military affairs. As his detention continued, his traditional supporters on the right, including the business class and many within the armed forces, began to publicly distance themselves from him. This was particularly marked during the 1999 presidential election campaign, when the right-wing candidate Joaquín Lavín was at pains to emphasize the distance between the current political right and the former military regime. On returning to Chile from Britain on health grounds, the remaining barrier to bringing an effective prosecution against Pinochet was his senatorial immunity which could only be removed by the Chilean courts. Initially unthinkable, he was stripped of his immunity in June 2000 and, for more than a year, the charges against Pinochet continued to grow as the prosecution focused its efforts on establishing his direct involvement in the notorious Caravan of Death. Yet, almost three years after his arrest in London, the charges against Pinochet were finally dropped on July 10, 2001. The Court of Appeal ruled, with a vote of 2–1 in favor, that the former general was suffering from dementia and was unable to defend himself in a court of law, and thereby effectively extinguished Pinochet as a political force in Chile.

Conclusion

While this was far from the outcome which the human rights organizations had hoped for, the pursuit of justice for human rights violations has impacted positively on the process of democratization in Chile in several respects. It has demonstrated that, while the question of human rights and justice remains unresolved, the transition to democracy will remain incomplete. The role and institutional identity of the military under democracy were sorely challenged by Pinochet's arrest. Yet, prosecutions have been brought against members of the armed forces and the military have engaged in frank and open dialogue with human rights lawyers and representatives of the government. They have demonstrated their adherence to the democratic rules even when they perceived the interests and reputation of their institution to be under threat. The political right has repositioned itself in relation to the electorate as a result of Pinochet's arrest. Although in the initial stages, the right retained its "atavistic link" to the military regime and came out in staunch support of the general (Garretón 2000: 66), as the process became more prolonged the right correctly perceived that a strong association with Pinochet would be viewed negatively by the electorate. The process has enabled the right-wing parties to release themselves from their *Pinochetista* past and to modernize politically. The fact that Joaquín Lavín, the right-wing presidential candidate, came within a whisker of winning the election, seems to vindicate the strategy of "*de-pinochetization*" for the right in Chile.

It might be concluded that as a result of the legal, attitudinal and institutional changes which followed Pinochet's arrest in 1998, democracy in Chile has been found to be stronger and more resilient than many had suspected. However, it would be difficult to conclude that justice has been done in the case of Pinochet as doubts must linger over the decision to drop the charges on medical grounds. Chilean law specifies that the only medical grounds acceptable are dementia or madness; no other illness or affliction can be accepted. However, pressure from political elites and the armed forces clearly cannot be ruled out, leaving the relationship between justice and democracy uncomfortably opaque even at the end of this lengthy process. Throughout the criminal investigations and legal challenges of recent years, the premise that under democracy all citizens are equal before the law and that no-one is above the law was being tested in Chile. While the civilian authorities have indeed forced many military officers to answer to the law, the same principle has not, in the end, been extended to Pinochet himself.

Notes

1 A personal communication from the late Sola Sierra, founding member of the Association of Families of those Executed for Political Reasons (Agrupación de Familiares de Ejecutados Políticos), Portsmouth, November 17, 1999, highlighted the role played by individuals such as the Spanish lawyer Joan Garcés who, having been an advisor to the Allende government in Chile, following the *coup* continued to work for justice on human rights from Spain and played a key role in bringing the charges against Pinochet in Spain during the 1990s.

2 The choice of the Audiencia Nacional was highly appropriate as it is a special criminal court created to deal with transnational crimes including drug trafficking and terrorism.

3 Religious groups from several denominations established the National Committee for Aid to Refugees (Comité Nacional de Ayuda a los Refugiados, CONAR) in September 1973, the Chilean Committee for Cooperation for Peace (Comité de Cooperación para la Paz de Chile, COPACHI) one month later and, following its dissolution in 1975, the Catholic Church formed the Vicariate of Solidarity (Vicaría de la Solidaridad) to carry on the work.

4 In a Latin American context, the term "popular sectors" refers to the urban poor, the working class and lower middle class.

5 The binding laws were a series of decrees issued by the military government between the elections in December 1989 and the handing over of power to the elected civilian government in March 1990. They prevented the incoming government from dismantling key aspects of the political and economic restructuring which had occurred under military rule.

6 In 1976, the UN Ad Hoc Working Group on Chile was designated and it concluded that cases of torture committed by the military government should

be prosecuted by the international community as crimes against humanity. Resolution No. 5 of the General Assembly of the United Nations in 1979 called for investigations in Chile to establish the whereabouts of people who had disappeared for political reasons. Subsequently, under Resolution No. 11 of the General Assembly of the United Nations in 1987, it was proposed that the findings of these investigations should be made known to the families of victims and those responsible should be brought to justice regardless of the Amnesty Law of 1978.

7 Contreras and Espinoza were sentenced to seven and six years' imprisonment respectively in the special prison at Punta de Peuco. Further charges were brought against Contreras for the attempted murder of Bernardo Leighton and his wife in Rome 1975; in October 1999 the Supreme Court granted his extradition to Italy to face charges.

8 These included the murder of the trade union leader, Tucapel Jimenez, in 1982, and the prosecution of ten officers for the *caso degollados* in 1985 (the murder of three professionals by slashing their throats). The DINA (Dirección Nacional de Inteligencia) was the secret police responsible for the "dirty war" which resulted in the disappearance and death of many individuals during the military regime. The DINA was involved in terror activities abroad including the assassination of General Carlos Prats in Argentina in 1974 and Orlando Letelier in Washington in 1976.

9 The MORI poll was conducted in 29 cities in Chile, between 17 and 24 November 1998. It was based on interviews with 1,190 Chileans across all social strata over the age of 18, resident in cities with a population of more than 40,000 inhabitants. The margin of error was 3 percent. This was the first public opinion survey to openly consult on the perceptions of guilt or innocence of the former dictator.

Bibliography

Acuña, C. H. and Smulovitz, C. (1996) "Adjusting the armed forces to democracy: successes, failures, and ambiguities in the Southern Cone," in E. Jelin and E. Hershberg (eds) *Constructing Democracy: human rights, citizenship, and society in Latin America*, Boulder, CO: Westview Press.

Aguilar, M. I. (2002) "The disappeared and the Mesa de Diálogo in Chile 1999–2001: searching for those who never grew old," *Bulletin of Latin American Research* 21 (3): 413–24.

Albon, M. (1995) "Project on justice in times of transition (report of the inaugural meeting)," in N. J. Kritz (ed.) *Transitional Justice: how emerging democracies reckon with former regimes. Volume 1: General Considerations*, Washington, DC: United States Institute for Peace.

Barton, J. and Murray, W. (2002) "The end of transition? Chile 1990–2000," *Bulletin of Latin American Research* 21 (3): 329–38.

Becker, D., Lira, E., Castillo, M. I., Gómez, E. and Kovalskys, J. (1995) "Therapy with victims of political repression in Chile: the challenge of social reparation," in N. J. Kritz (ed.) *Transitional Justice: how emerging democracies reckon with former regimes. Volume 1: General Considerations*, Washington, DC: United States Institute for Peace.

Benomar, J. (1995) "Justice after transitions," in N. J. Kritz (ed.) *Transitional Justice: how emerging democracies reckon with former regimes. Volume 1: General Considerations*, Washington, DC: United States Institute for Peace.

Brett, S. (2000) "Impunity on trial in Chile," in *Rethinking Human Rights, NACLA Report on the Americas* XXXIV (1) (July/August): 34–6.

Chilean Human Rights Commission/Centro IDEAS, Ministry of Foreign Affairs of Chile (eds) (1991) *Summary of the Truth and Reconciliation Commission Report* (in Spanish), Santiago de Chile: Bobenrieth and Brintrup; English translation published 1992, Santiago de Chile: Gráfica CeBe Ltda.

Cohen, R. and Rai, S. (2000). "Global social movements: towards a cosmopolitan politics," in R. Cohen and S. Rai (eds) *Global Social Movements*, London and New Jersey: Athlone Press.

Davis, M. (2000). "The Pinochet case," London: University of London, Institute of Latin American Studies Research Papers.

Diamond, L. (1994) "Rethinking civil society: toward democratic consolidation," *Journal of Democracy* 5 (3): 4–17.

El Mercurio, various editions, Santiago de Chile, October 1998–July 2001.

Foweraker, J. (1995) *Theorising Social Movements*, London: Pluto Press.

Fruhling, H. (1997) "Judicial reform and democratization in Latin America," in F. Aguero and J. Stark (eds) *Fault Lines of Democracy in Post-Transition Latin America*, Boulder, CO: Lynne Rienner Publishers.

Garretón, M. A. (2000). "The Chilean right," in K. Middlebrook (ed.) *Conservative Parties, the Right, and Democracy in Latin America*, Baltimore, MD: The Johns Hopkins University Press.

—— (1996) "Human rights in democratization processes," in E. Jelin and E. Hershberg (eds) *Constructing Democracy: human rights, citizenship, and society in Latin America*, Boulder, CO: Westview Press.

Golob, S. (2002a) "The Pinochet case: 'Forced to be free': abroad and at home," *Democratization* 9 (4): 25–57.

—— (2002b) "'Forced to be free': globalized justice, pacted democracy, and the Pinochet case," *Democratization* 9 (2): 21–42.

Hunter, W. (1998). "Civil–military relations in Argentina, Brazil and Chile: present trends, future prospects," in F. Agüero and J. Stark (eds) *Fault Lines of Democracy in Post-Transition Latin America*, Miami, FL: North-South Center Press.

Huntington, S. P. (1991) *The Third Wave: democratization in the late twentieth century*. Norman, OK: University of Oklahoma Press.

Kumar, C. (2000). "Transnational networks and campaigns for democracy," in A. Florini (ed.) *The Third Force: the rise of transnational civil society*, Tokyo: Japan Center for International Exchange; Washington, DC: Carnegie Endowment for International Peace.

Lehmann, D. (1990) *Democracy and Development in Latin America*, Cambridge: Cambridge University Press.

Linz, J. and Stepan, A. (1996) "Towards consolidated democracies," *Journal of Democracy* 7 (2): 14–33.

Loveman, B. (1995) "The transition to civilian government in Chile, 1990–94," in P. Drake and I. Jaksic (eds) *The Struggle for Democracy in Chile*, revised edn, Lincoln, NE and London: University of Nebraska Press.

Matear, A. (1999) "Gender relations, authoritarianism and democratization in Chile," *Democratization* 6 (3): 100–17.

—— (1996) "Desde la protesta a la propuesta: gender politics in transition in Chile," *Democratization* 3 (3): 246–63.

Offe, C. (1996) *Varieties of Transition: the East European and German experience*, Cambridge, UK: Polity Press.

Pridham, G. (2000) "Confining conditions and breaking with the past: historical legacies and political learning in transitions to democracy," *Democratization* 7 (2): 36–64.

Robertson, G. (1999). *Crimes Against Humanity: the struggle for global justice*, London: Penguin Press.

Smith, J. (1998) "Global civil society? Transnational social movement organizations and social capital," *American Behavioral Scientist* 42 (1): 93–107.

Wilson, R. (1999). "Prosecuting Pinochet: international crimes in Spanish domestic law," *Human Rights Quarterly* 21 (4): 927–79.

Zalaquett, J. (1995) "Confronting human rights violations committed by former governments: principles applicable and political constraints," in N. J. Kritz (ed.) *Transitional Justice: how emerging democracies reckon with former regimes. Volume 1: General Considerations*, Washington, DC: United States Institute for Peace.

6 Civil society and environmental justice

Carolyn Stephens and Simon Bullock[1]

Introduction

This chapter discusses the link between environmental rights, health and social justice, and development, articulated through the concept of "environmental justice." At its simplest, this idea states that "all people have the right to live in a healthy environment."

But the simplicity of the concept of environmental justice conceals an enormous scope and challenge. The focus on *all people* means that actions to secure environmental justice for one group of people must not deny others – such as those in other countries or in future generations – their equal right to a healthy environment. Is this a new idea? The idea of equal rights to health has been debated since the first writings of the early philosophers. "Health for All" was a mantra coined by the World Health Organization (WHO) and upheld by public health practitioners for decades. But there is a new aspect to environmental justice today: it is the international and temporal scope of the concept *all people* that makes the new ideas of environmental justice so challenging. Overall, environmental justice offers a fresh perspective. Its two basic premises are, first, that everyone should have the right and be able to live in a healthy environment, with access to enough environmental resources for a healthy life, and second, that it is predominantly the poorest and least powerful people who are missing these conditions. Taking these two premises together suggests that a priority is to ensure that the adverse conditions faced by the least powerful people are tackled first. As well as implying environmental rights, it implies environmental responsibilities. These responsibilities are on this current generation to ensure a healthy environment exists for future generations, and on countries, organizations and individuals in this generation to ensure that development does not create environmental problems or distribute environmental resources in ways which damage other people's health. It is only in the last decade that such a rights- and equity-based formulation has been developed that clearly articulates the link between the social and environmental aspects of sustainable development.

As well as introducing the idea of environmental justice, this chapter also outlines the extent of current environmental injustices, and suggests some of the main actions that local and international civil society networks can and are taking to tackle them.

Origins of environmental justice

The idea of environmental justice in its current form was developed in the United States. Its development was almost exclusively driven by civil society organizations (CSOs), many from a civil rights background. Since the late 1970s, a civil society network of over 5,000 black, Hispanic and indigenous grassroots communities has organized strong political opposition to the siting of environmentally hazardous industrial facilities in predominantly black neighborhoods and indigenous people's reservations in the United States. This movement has made substantial progress nationally and internationally. By 1994, President Clinton ordered that "each Federal agency shall make achieving environmental justice part of its mission" (Clay 1999: A308). The United States Environmental Protection Agency defines environmental justice as:

> The fair treatment and meaningful involvement of all people, regardless of race, ethnicity, income, national origin or educational level with respect to the development, implementation and enforcement of environmental laws, regulation and policies. Fair treatment means that no population, due to policy or economic disempowerment, is forced to bear a disproportionate burden of the negative human health or environmental impacts of pollution or other environmental consequences resulting from industrial, municipal and commercial operations or the execution of federal, state, local and tribal programs and policies.
>
> (United States Environmental Protection Agency 2003)

This has led to various positive policy responses. For example by 2003, the United States Environmental Protection Agency had begun piloting new methods of risk assessment to apply to environmental exposures, based on criticisms from environmental justice groups of the conventional means used to assess such risks.

What are environmental rights?

The US definition of environmental justice implies both "substantive" and "procedural" rights to a healthy environment. Thus, environmental justice can include both the right to a healthy environment (substantive) and the right to participate in the decision-making process to obtain that right (procedural). Internationally, since the 1992 UN Global Conference on

Sustainable Development in Rio human rights law has been modified along the same lines to reflect principles of substantive and procedural environmental rights and thus, potentially, environmental justice. For example, Box 6.1 shows relevant draft principles (drafted in 1995 but still in draft form today) of the UN Sub Commission on Human Rights and the Environment (Boyle 1996).

The principles currently developed at international level draw heavily on existing human rights law and international environmental law (ibid.).

Box 6.1 UN Sub-Commission on Human Rights and the Environment, draft principles

International substantive rights

- Freedom from pollution, environmental degradation and activities that adversely affect the environment or threaten life, health, livelihood, well-being or sustainable development;
- Protection and preservation of the air, soil, water, sea-ice, flora and fauna and the essential processes and areas that are necessary to maintain biological diversity and ecosystems;
- The highest attainable standard of health;
- Safe and healthy food, water and working environments;
- Adequate housing, land tenure and living conditions in a secure, healthy and ecologically sound environment;
- Ecologically sound access to nature and the conservation and sustainable use of nature and natural resources;
- Preservation of unique sites;
- Enjoyment of traditional life and subsistence for indigenous peoples.

International procedural rights

- The right to information concerning the environment;
- The right to receive and disseminate ideas and information;
- The right to participation in planning and decision-making processes, including prior environmental impact assessment;
- The right of freedom of association for the purpose of protecting the environment or the rights of persons affected by environmental harm;
- The right to effective remedies and redress for environmental harm in administrative or judicial proceedings.

(Boyle 1996: 48)

Thus, although the United States now has the clearest legal definition of environmental justice, European countries often have constitutions that could be used for the protection of environmental and human rights. For example, the Spanish Constitution contains a right for people to enjoy an "environment suitable for the development of the person," and the Portuguese Constitution states that "everyone shall have the right to a healthy and ecologically balanced human environment and the duty to protect it" (Douglas-Scott 1996: 110). In addition, Europe also has several region-wide treaties that deal with environment and health protection at the level of rights, including the European Convention on Human Rights dating from 1950.

From policy and procedural perspectives, there are advances in the way that state-level actors have shifted policy towards more transparent and equity-led information systems – which can provide information on injustice and support civil society towards equity. For example, the United Kingdom's Independent Inquiry into Inequalities in Health in 1998 made the following statement one of its major recommendation:

> As part of all health impact assessment, all policies likely to have a direct or indirect effect on health should be evaluated in terms of their impacts on health inequalities, and should be formulated in a way that by favouring the less well off they will, where possible, reduce inequalities.
>
> (Acheson *et al.* 1998)

Furthermore in October 2001, European states ratified the Aarhus Convention, which guarantees rights to information and access to decision-making at a regional level (United Nations Economic Commission for Europe (UNECE) 2003).

But despite these apparent shifts forward, millions of people within developed countries – and billions of people globally – still live in environments that damage their health. Even in countries such as the United Kingdom, despite a raft of laws, regulations and policies controlling air pollution emissions and imposing air quality standards, emissions of nitrogen dioxide and particulates are killing over 12,000 people prematurely every year, according to the government's own health advisors. This has led campaigners from civil society-based environmental NGOs to shift the definition of environmental justice – broadening its scope to international and intergenerational injustice and to push for changes in European and international legislation (ibid.).

Until now, citizens have had little redress over routine health-damaging exposures related to the citing of hazardous waste dumps, roads or industries. In addition, past and recent environmental crises such as Chernobyl, the BSE affair and dioxin contamination have all occurred despite Europe's well-developed constitutional, environmental and human rights frameworks (Lang 1999; Ryder 1999). Alongside these difficulties for current generations is a more long-term problem: at present, there is no binding legislation that could be used by civil society groups to protect future generations. As Dobson has pointed out, "no theory of justice can henceforth be regarded as complete it if does not take into account the possibility of extending the community of justice beyond the realm of present generation human beings" (Dobson 1998: 244–5). Finally, many of these exposures occur in a international context of military conflicts between states, which continue to occur with little attention to the short- or long-term impacts they may have on current or future generations, or on the environment.

Environmental justice – broadening the scope

Within the United Kingdom, environmental justice has grown in importance since the mid-1990s. Initial analyses by academics and NGOs of the distribution of environmental exposures have shown that it is the poorest and powerless sections of society who are affected worst by problems of air pollution (McLaren and Bullock 1999). Other analyses for different environmental impacts are starting to show similar results. These analyses have been linked by CSO groups to sustainability discourses and their focus on future generations – a completely powerless group – and equity between countries. This broadens the United States's focus on environ- mental justices solely within countries. This is providing a framework for CSOs within and between countries – who are all campaigning in various ways and on different issues for a healthy environment – to find common cause.

It is the complex nature and scale of environmental harms that has pushed local CSOs to realize that they must not act parochially: solutions are not sustainable or just if they displace or create problems elsewhere. For example, current levels of greenhouse gas emissions are higher than the planet can tolerate – as has been agreed legally and internationally in the Kyoto Protocol (United Nations Environment Program (UNEP) 1999) – imposing environmental injustices on future generations. Other issues which reinforce the same point include the disposal of nuclear waste, control of water resources and production of bio-accumulative and persistent chemicals. The climate change issue also highlights intragenerational equity concerns: the majority of climate change gases are produced by Western countries, while the majority of the negative impacts will be felt by people in Southern countries – for example 99 percent of all the 605,000 people who have died in climate disasters between 1990 and 2000 lived in developing countries (UNEP 2002). Increasing awareness of these issues has affected the development of environmental and social campaigns by civil society groups across Europe. For example, tackling the problem of "cold homes" in the United Kingdom by making fuel cheaper would have contributed to climate change. An environmental justice perspective, pushed by environmental CSOs, has led the UK government to a focus on energy efficiency, as a means to tackle the cold homes problem while reducing adverse effects on other countries and generations (Department for Food and Rural Affairs 2003).

At a policy level, Europe has accepted the US premise that the current disproportionate impacts of environmental hazards must be addressed (although in Europe these impacts appear to be determined by income more than by race). But for European civil society groups, environmental justice analysis and action has taken a more international and generational stance. It also focuses on the availability and use of environmental resources, not just on impacts of environmental hazards. For example, in response to the difficult problem of how environmental resources should be distributed in a world of ecological limits, member groups of the environmental CSO Friends of the Earth in Europe, and now in Southern America and Asia, have advocated the use of "equal distribution of sustainable resource consumption between countries on a per capita basis" (Carley and Spapens 1997). This formulation sets a limit to the consumption of environmental resources by individual countries, bounded by equity considerations to future generations and other countries. Friends of the Earth, Scotland, have launched a campaign for environmental justice on these lines. They argue that:

> Our conception of environmental justice therefore brings together the need for global and intergenerational equity in resource consumption and ecological health, with a priority to act with those who are the victims of that inequality in the present. No less than a decent environment for all, no more than our fair share of the Earth's resources.
>
> (Scandrett *et al.* 2000)

There are therefore three spatial/temporal aspects of environmental justice on which CSOs take action

- *National:* related to the state of environmental injustice within a country, local region or city.
- *International:* related to the extent to which a region imposes injustice on other countries.
- *Generational:* related to the extent to which we as a species impose injustices on future generations, regionally and globally.

And there are also four types of environmental injustices – the distribution of exposure to environmental impacts (costs), the distribution of access to environmental resources (access), the differential ability of different groups to influence decisions affecting the environment, and whether policies have a distributional impact (see Table 6.1).

Table 6.1 Scales and types of environmental injustice

Examples of existing environmental injustices	Environmental costs	Environmental access	Participation in decision making	Inequitable policies
National (UK)	Pollution from industry located in mainly poorer areas	Low use of national parks by ethnic minorities	Lack of third party rights on planning decisions	Flood defense allocation based on value of property
International	Mining in developing countries for developed country consumption	Limited access to healthy foods for the farmers who supply most of the supermarkets of the North	Disproportionate lobbying power of Western governments on bodies such as the WTO	Valuation techniques which value people's lives differently – USA v. developing countries
Inter-generational	Production of bio-accumulative, persistent chemicals	No access to the consumer goods for those who experience the disbenefits of overcon-sumption	Failure to use precautionary approaches for chemicals policy	Risk assessment models which do not take into account extra vulnerability of embryos

The next sections looks at the trends in these areas and common themes. The final sections look at responses.

Environmental justice within industrialized countries

Even in rich countries within Europe and the United States, there are major environmental impacts on people. These impacts are borne disproportion-ately. There is a lack of information, but the available evidence strongly suggests that it is poorer people who suffer from the worst environmental conditions. Box 6.2 documents some examples of substantive environ-mental injustice in the United Kingdom – a comparatively rich country within Europe.

There are gross health inequalities in the United Kingdom (Acheson *et al.* 1998). The UK government's Health Strategy states that "During the 1980s and 1990s the gap between rich and poor widened and the health gap grew wider" (Her Majesty's Government 1999). These health inequalities are the result of complex factors including environmental impacts. The type of environmental inequalities highlighted in Box 6.2 exacerbate the other inequalities faced by poorer people, and add to the burden of health inequalities.

Similar income and health inequalities exist elsewhere. Children in poorer countries, and of poorer families within wealthier countries, experience less

---

Box 6.2 Environmental justice in the United Kingdom

Pollution

Factories emitting toxic pollutants are disproportionately located in poorer communities. Research comparing the government's data on polluting factories with income data for postcodes, showed that:

- There are 662 polluting factories in the United Kingdom in areas with average household income of less than £15,000, and only five in postcode areas where average household income is £30,000 or more.

- The more factories in an area, the lower the average income. In Teesside, one area has 17 large factories. Average income in the area is £6,200 – 64 percent less than the national average.

- In London, over 90 percent of polluting factories are in areas with below-average income, and in the North East, the figure is over 80 percent (McLaren and Bullock 1999).

- A follow-up study in 2001 found that 82 percent of carcinogen emissions from industry come from factories in the most deprived 20 percent of wards (Friends of the Earth 2001).

Transport

The recent UK government inquiry into Inequalities in Health notes that "The burden of air pollution tends to fall on people experiencing disadvantage, who do not enjoy the benefits of the private motorised transport which causes the pollution." As well as pollution, road accidents also affect the poorest people worst (Acheson *et al.* 1998).

Housing

Nearly 9 million households in the United Kingdom suffer from fuel poverty – the lack of affordable warmth. Fuel poverty exacerbates ill-health and is a major contributor to the 32,000 extra winter deaths in the United Kingdom each year. The main cause of fuel poverty is poor-quality housing, homes with terrible levels of energy efficiency, and it is poorer people who live in the worst-quality housing. Seventy six percent of all households earning less than £4,500 are not able to heat their homes to minimum health-based heating standards (Department of the Environment 1996).

healthy living and learning environments. Children go on to experience reinforcement of this cycle in their adulthood, with less access to remunerated, secure and rewarding employment. There is a further issue highlighted by recent work in the United States – this cycle links to a cumulative exposure to environmental risks by poorer communities (Corborn 2000; Evans and Kantrowitz 2002; Faber and Krieg 2002). Cumulative exposure means that individuals and communities, often the least economically powerful, experience the environment as a complex of harmful exposures both at one time and over time. Thus, evidence in the United States and United Kingdom shows that poorer communities are more likely to live near hazardous waste sites and busy roads, they have poor-quality housing, and limited access to transport, or affordable and uncontaminated food and water – sometimes all at the same time. These exposures often combine with more hazardous employment and lower incomes for families. These cumulative exposures can link to long-term illnesses, which in turn affects family incomes, and further perpetuates a cycle of environmental and social injustice.

Policies as well as impacts can also be deeply unjust. Substantive injustices are caused, in part, by procedural injustices (see Box 6.3).

For example, waste disposal policies are not designed to hurt poorer communities, but they can, through the decision-making process, if wealthier groups can access decisions more easily and avoid perceived harm. For example in 1998, residents of Greengairs – a relatively poor community in Scotland – found that a local landfill operator was accepting toxic PCB waste from Hertfordshire in England – a comparatively much richer area.[2] Dumping of this waste is illegal in England, but regulations are less strict in Scotland. CSO campaigning brought an end to the dumping and also secured other environmental and safety improvements (Scandrett *et al.* 2000), but inadequate enforcement of regulations, derisory fines and poor identification of pollution levels are still major national problems (McBride 1999).

Box 6.3 The procedural injustices that lead to substantive environmental injustice

"When you say that it (incineration) is acceptable, it is acceptable to the more articulate sections of the population. From what you have said, the incinerator ends up in the less articulate sections of society. I do think we ought to make that quite clear."

Lord Judd questioning Richard Mills of the UK National Society for Clean Air and Environmental Protection (Ryder 1999: 372).

Environmental justice internationally

The world has never seen the scale of concentration of wealth and power that we witness today, nor the scale of difference in life chances between those who will live over 75 years and those who will die before their first birthday. For the tiny minority (less than 10 percent of the world's population) who live to over 75 years, sustainability continues to be about recycling domestic garbage, saving home energy and/or buying organic. Meanwhile, these lucky people continue flying, driving – and Christmas shopping – around the planet, as if there really were no tomorrow. For the enormous majority of 5 billion people on less than US $1 a day, sustainability is still mostly about surviving until tomorrow, and hoping that there will be a tomorrow. For many children, our future generations, prospects are bleak. The WHO reports that diarrheal diseases kill around 2 million children under the age of five every year, and are almost entirely related to unsafe drinking water and the lack of sanitation. Air pollution from combustion of fossil fuels for cooking and heating causes respiratory infections which are responsible for up to 20 percent mortality in children under five years of age (WHO 2001).

International environmental injustice occurs at three levels. First, through certain countries' appropriation of the overwhelming share of the world's environmental resources. Second, by means of richer countries causing adverse environmental and social impacts in poorer countries through their demand for exported consumer products. And third, through international structures, such as the IMF or World Bank – dominated by Western governments – that impose policies on poorer countries which exacerbate the first two problems, or prevent them from investing in public health infrastructures.

Human health and the environment in Latin America, Asia and Africa is affected by what could be described as environmentally unjust consume and waste societies of industrialized Northern countries. For example, Europe produces 31 percent of the world's carbon dioxide emissions, with only 13 percent of the world's population (World Resources Institute 1997). Further, in per capita energy, the people of the United States consume five times more than the people of Europe (UNEP 1999, 2002).

This consume and waste society also involves considerable appropriation of environmental resources of poorer countries by richer countries. Southern wood, land, minerals and metals are still being used predominately for further Western development, not Southern development, and raw commodity prices remain low (Dobson 1998; Latouche 1993). Southern countries also suffer from the imposition of outdated or dangerous Western technologies, processes and by-products. Waste too toxic for disposal in the West is routinely reported entering the South despite the Basel Convention.[3] Pesticides produced in the West and banned for health and environmental reasons at home are exported to and used in the South.

Leaded petrol accounts for over 95 percent of sales in Africa – in Europe, Sweden has completely phased out this neuro-toxin (WHO 1997).

Finally, it is also important to note that poorer people in Africa, Asia and Latin America are not the main beneficiaries of the use of their country's resources, which is driven by a development model which is dominated and run by Northern hemisphere countries. Increases in inequality over the last 130 years are gross: the ratio of income per capita in the richest countries over that in the poorest countries has increased from 11 in 1870 to 38 in 1960, and to 52 in 1985. More importantly, there has been a more profound concentration of resources to fewer individuals. Thus, the ratio between the average income of the world's top 5 percent of people and the world's bottom 5 percent increased from 78 to 1 in 1988, to 123 to 1 in 1993 (Buckley 1999).

One root of these asymmetries of access to resources lies in unequal educational and work opportunities. The International Labour Organization (ILO) report that 500 million workers earn less than $1 per day and 160 million people internationally are unemployed, of which 50 million are now in industrialized countries (ILO 2001). Those who do enter work find themselves trapped in production at any cost for the consume and waste economy. WHO's occupational health group report their concern that in the context of globalized production processes:

> There is a development of free trade zones, where occupational health and environmental legislation may be poor and where hazardous or strenuous production processes are concentrated. . . . Of particular concern is increasing flexibility in labor policies that may lead to a weakening of commitment to occupational health and safety programs. The stress of global competition may lead employers to view the prevention of occupational injuries and protection of workers' health not as an integral part of quality management, but as a barrier to trade. Freer trade as part of globalization has already led to a number of adverse occupational health impacts.
>
> (WHO 2003)

Sometimes, if not often, examples of environmental injustice in one country are closely meshed to the lifestyles of individual members of civil society in another: particularly lifestyles of citizens in Northern countries with their complex links to impacts on the poor in Southern countries. The sustainable consumption movement argues that these impacts can only be halted when individual consumer choices change. And perhaps they will change as civil society groups network internationally to provide more concrete information on the environmental and social impacts of Northern consumption patterns. Take, for example, the popular shrimp – which has moved from luxury to healthy food choice in many Northern diets. Net imports of shrimp into the European Union have increased by more than four times from 1981 to 1998. Western Europe consumed 400 million lb of shrimp in 1993. The amount of shrimp consumed in the United States has doubled in the last decade to some 1 billion lb a year, making it the one of the most popular seafoods in the country. Seven countries produced about 86 percent of the farmed shrimp production in 1995 – six Asian and one Latin American. Shrimp farms throughout Asia harvested 558,000 tons in 1995, accounting for 78 percent of the world's farmed shrimp production (Food and Agriculture Organization 2003). Yet shrimp farming has devastated traditional rural communities in these regions through intensive farming practices, overuse of antibiotics and changes to aquatic ecosystems. Loss of mangroves has increased risks for coastal communities from tidal waves and cyclones, and the industry has led to the displacement of hundreds of thousands of people from lands used traditionally and sustainably for generations.

> I say to those who eat shrimp – and only the rich people from industrialised countries eat shrimp – I say they are eating the blood, sweat and livelihood of the poor people of the third world.
>
> (Shri Banke Behary Das, India, in Environmental Justice Foundation 2003)

From this single example, it is perhaps clear that huge political will and CSO pressure will be required to tackle the unjust distribution of resources and opportunities that can be traced through example after example. The extent of this crisis in international environmental justice was highlighted in the Johannesburg World Summit on Sustainable Development in 2002 when Venezuelan President Hugo Chavez, Chairman of the Group of 77 – which represents 132 developing countries – articulated the views of many when he said that "the generalities that had been set out could be seen as retrograde. I would have preferred emphasis on human rights, such as the right to housing, health, drinking water, life." He concluded: "The world is standing on its head" (UN 2002).

Intergenerational environmental justice

In addition to these gross issues of environmental injustice in the current generation, current economic activities also tend to heavily undervalue the rights of future generations (Attfield and Wilkins 1992; Belsey 1992; Dobson 1998; McMichael 1993; McMichael *et al.* 1994; Smil 1993).

A clear example is in the field of chemicals policy. Through heavily polluting industrial activities the global environment is now contaminated by persistent and bio-accumulative chemicals. The effects of this are uncertain, but many of these chemicals have now been found to have subtle and unanticipated adverse effects on wildlife. One class of chemicals – Endocrine Disrupting Chemicals (EDCs) – is known to affect the reproductive and developmental function of a wide range of creatures. The effects on humans are uncertain, but what is clear is that their and other chemicals' routine dispersal into the environment is an enormous and probably irreversible gamble with the health of children and future generations (Fur 1999; UNEP 2002; Williams 1998). In the face of grave uncertainties, the main current policy response by governments is to wait for more evidence – this approach places the burden of proof of safety onto civil society actors, rather than onto the chemical itself. It ensures that the concerns of those who benefit from the use of a process are weighted far higher than those who potentially suffer – particularly children and future generations. This has been described as "toxic trespass," and this situation in effect means that "there is a lack of consent among those who suffer the burden of 'acceptable risks.' This differs widely from medical ethics, where testing should only occur with the express permission of those involved and only where these is no alternative" (Steingraber 1999).

Chemical policy does not provide the only example of intergenerational injustice. Nuclear power is another technology where the benefits accrue to the current generation, but the majority of costs (through waste management) will have to be borne – perhaps in perpetuity – by future generations. Part of the problem is that decisions are routinely made such that costs in the future – beyond 30 years – have almost negligible impact on policy. But perhaps more important is the use of risk assessment models which consistently undervalue and often completely ignore uncertainties. Uncertainty is an unavoidable component of decisions involving environmental and public health harm (ibid.). Decisions must be based on what is *not* known, as well as what is known.

Participants at the Wingspread Conference on the Precautionary Principle in the United States in January 1998 argued that "decisions about toxic chemicals should ask the basic question of whether exposure is safe for a six week old embryo; if not, then the activity should not occur" (ibid.). Civil society groups have targeted conventional risk assessment as a particular problem, in that, as an important method to identify environmental health impacts, it perpetuates an impression that risk exposures are independent of each other, and it underestimates or discounts uncertain, long-term harms.

State responses and civil society

Every person's right to a healthy environment is a good guiding principle for environmentally just policies – it sets the bottom line for substantive rights. However, implementation and enforcement of rights principles is difficult. For example, Boyle (1996) and several others note that states in Europe and elsewhere have constitutions that maintain the right to health and "sufficient" environments. Some include procedural rights also. Yet articulation of these rights within current legal frameworks proves difficult, partly because current legal systems often operate to protect more powerful interests against the claims of less powerful ones (UNECE 1999). Powerful actors within governments often resist calls to environmental justice for similar reasons of powerful agency.

The UNEP argues that globalization, characterized by rapid movement of capital, skills, employment, ideas and technologies, "is a concern at a number of levels. From a purely practical point of view, it drives global demand for an unsustainable level of consumption." Further, "the shift towards corporate globalization means that decision-making at transnational companies levels is often more influential than local and regional decision-making" (UNEP 2002). Finally, correlating with trends in social polarization, globalization is leading towards an "attitude of survival in a declared context of inevitable economic war" between states, regions, communities and individuals. Globalization is weakening the power of the state to regulate and increasing economic and social fragmentation, particularly of peripheral communities (UNEP 1999, 2002).

The current effects of globalization are a strong counter-weight to any attempts to reduce inequalities or environmental injustices. Also, the continuing actions of organizations such as the World Trade Organization appear to be exacerbating rather than reducing inequalities by prioritizing trade and economic concerns far higher than environmental or social issues. Strong policies will be required to ensure that globalization does not further exacerbate inequalities and damage the environment (Dower 1992; Stephens *et al.* 2000).

In the face of these powerful interests a strong and coherent CSO voice is imperative. It needs to be grounded in local experience, as this is where effects are being felt. It is for this reason that very local community-based CSOs have become such important players in the environmental justice movement and have widened their remit and their ambitions over time. CSOs and actors thinking about environmental justice include academics in professional bodies such as the International Society for Environmental Epidemiology, the UK Chartered Institute of Environmental Health and the European Public Health Association. They join grassroots thematic networks linked by themes such as chemical policy and its impacts on women and children – for example, the Women's Environmental Network, the Women's Caucus for Sustainable Development or Women in Europe for a Common Future. Add to this the environmental NGO community with their local and international remit, and an increasing focus on the links between social and environmental concerns. There are also professional NGOs such as the Environmental Law Foundation, the Foundation for International Law and Development, and International Doctors for the Environment, and finally they are joined by the many single-issue campaign CSOs who come together around their local problems or around a single issue of burning concern. Together this loose coalition is pushing on three doors: shifting science and policy towards precaution and prevention;

changing access to information and pushing on the right to know; and pushing towards increased participation and accountability. Effectively these three doors are the doors to procedural justice – which link to substantive justice through their effect on quality of and access to information, and through their impact on access to decision-making.

Civil society and information for the future

CSOs and individuals may be working more together, and with an ever strengthening and coherent case. However, it has been suggested that individuals and groups in civil society are gradually losing any rights they may have had to participate in the development, implementation and enforcement of environmental laws, regulation and policies (Lang 1999). Social exclusion internationally from decision-making processes is a procedural injustice, when whole sections of the society cannot access a space in policy decisions (Cameron and Mackenzie 1996). It could be argued, for example, that people are losing their procedural rights as governments cede power to organizations such as the World Trade Organization (Koivusalo 1999).

People should have the power to affect the decisions that affect them. The "toxic trespass" of all our bodies, mentioned above, is a clear example of the current lack of control people exercise over decision-makers. And broadening decision-making is not only necessary – both from a rights and a precautionary perspective – it should also lead to better decisions. Currently, though, people have little control. Where participation is offered, it is most often in the context of extremely unbalanced power arrangements. In some countries, like the United Kingdom, there is a presumption in favor of development, with little accountability of developers to local people.

Good Neighbor Agreements, used in the United States, could be one way to improve accountability – these are both legally binding and voluntary agreements between industry and community which can include clauses on community access to information, negotiated improvements in pollution prevention, and guarantees of good unionized jobs going to local people or other local economic benefits. This is not local economic democracy, but is a certain improvement in the accountability of industry to other stakeholders as well as the traditional shareholders (Scandrett *et al.* 2000).

However, whatever processes are developed a key way to increase the capacity of local people to influence the decisions that affect them is to improve the quality of information they are able to access. This is an area where academics working in collaboration with local communities can make a major difference.

Another key but more conventional role for academics is to improve the quantity and quality of analysis of the distributional effects of policy. Risk assessment models and policy evaluation tool kits have only rudimentary distributional analyses even for the United Kingdom. Coverage of potential distributional effects across continents or generations are barely considered. Principles of environmental justice should be an integral part of policy. There is a clear role for the academic community first to assess policy tools to see whether they are causing or reducing environmental injustices (at all levels), and second to show how these policy tools can be revised, or by what they can be replaced, in order to achieve environmental justice.

Finally, perhaps one of the most interesting pieces of civil society action in recent years has been to pull all these threads of information, participation and justice together. The Aarhus Convention is a new policy tool, developed by civil society groups in Eastern Europe and the former Soviet Union, and is the new participatory legislation on environmental harm developed for Europe. The Aarhus Convention is a new kind of environmental agreement. It links environmental rights and human rights. It acknowledges that we owe an obligation to future generations. It establishes that sustainable development can be achieved only through the involvement of all stakeholders. It links government accountability and environmental protection. It focuses on interactions between the public and public authorities in a democratic context and it is forging a new process for public participation in the negotiation and implementation of international agreements.

The subject of the Aarhus Convention goes to the heart of the relationship between people and governments. The Convention is not only an environmental agreement, it is also a Convention about government accountability, transparency and responsiveness. The Aarhus Convention grants the public rights and imposes on state parties and public authorities obligations regarding access to information and public participation and access to justice (UNECE 2003). Kofi Annan has hailed this as the entry to a new democracy:

> Although regional in scope, the significance of the Aarhus Convention is global. It is by far the most impressive elaboration of principle 10 of the Rio Declaration, which stresses the need for citizens' participation in environmental issues and for access to information on the environment held by public authorities. As such it is the most ambitious venture in the area of "environmental democracy" so far undertaken under the auspices of the United Nations.
>
> (UNECE 2003)

The Aarhus Convention entered into force on October 30, 2001. States are still ratifying it and civil society groups are still working out how to make it work for justice. We have yet to see if such ambitious legislation can make a real difference to local or international environmental justice. But it is at least increasingly clear that a network of civil society actors will be pushing for change all over the world – with or without legislative support.

Notes

1 The authors acknowledge the assistance of Alister Scott of the Science and Policy Research Unit SPRU, University of Sussex, who in his former role of Assistant Director of the Global Environmental Change Program (GECP) helped to shape this chapter and a GECP Special Briefing on which it is partly based. We gratefully acknowledge the support of the UK Economic and Social Research Council, GECP, Friends of the Earth and the World Health Organization (WHO) in work contributing to this chapter.

2 PCB (Polychlorinated biphenyls) are highly toxic and durable synthetic organic compounds that accumulate in the tissue of organisms. Health effects that have been associated with exposure to PCBs include acne-like skin conditions in adults and neurobehavioral and immunological changes in children. PCBs are known to cause cancer in animals. PCBs have been found in at least 500 of the 1,598 National Priorities List sites identified by the Environmental Protection Agency (EPA).

3 In 1994, a unique coalition of developing countries, environmental groups and European countries succeeded in achieving within that Convention, the Basel Ban, a decision to end the most abusive forms of hazardous waste trade. In 1995, the Basel Ban was turned into an amendment to the Convention which, when ratified by member states, will enter into force.

Bibliography

Acheson, D., Barker, D., Chambers, J., Graham, H., Marmot, M. and Whitehead, M. (1998). *Independent Inquiry into Inequalities in Health Report*, London: HMSO.

Attfield, R. and Wilkins, B. (eds) (1992) *International Justice and the Third World*, London: Routledge.

Belsey, A. (1992) "World poverty, justice and equality," in R. Attfield and B. Wilkins (eds) *International Justice and the Third World*, London, Routledge: 35–50.

Boyle, A. (1996) "The role of international human rights law in the protection of the environment," in A. Boyle and M. Anderson (eds) *Human Rights Approaches to Environmental Protection*, Oxford: Clarendon Press: 43–71.

Buckley, R. (1999) *1998 Annual Review of Development Effectiveness*, Washington, DC: The International Bank for Reconstruction and Development.

Cameron, J. and Mackenzie, R. (1996) "Access to environmental justice and procedural rights in international institutions," in A. Boyle and M. Anderson (eds) *Human Rights Approaches to Environmental Protection*, Oxford: Clarendon Press: 129–53.

Carley, M. and Spapens, P. (1997) *Sharing Our World*, London: Earthscan.

Clay, R. (1999) "Still moving toward environmental justice," *Environ. Health Perspect.* 107 (6): A308–10.

Corborn, J. (2000) "Shifting the discourse of risk through cumulative risk assessment," Towards Sustainability: Social and Environmental Justice Conference, June 2000, Tufts University, Boston.

Department for Food and Rural Affairs (2003) *Sustainable Energy: fuel poverty*, DEFRA. 2003, at http://www.defra.gov.uk/environment/energy/fuelpov/ (accessed November 4, 2003).

Department of the Environment (1996) *English House Condition Survey: energy report*, London: HMSO.

Dobson, A. (1998) *Justice and the Environment*, Oxford: Oxford University Press.

Douglas-Scott, S. (1996) "Environmental rights in the European Union: participatory democracy or democratic deficit?," in A. Boyle and M. Anderson (eds) *Human Rights Approaches to Environmental Protection*, Oxford: Clarendon Press: 109–29.

Dower, N. (1992) "Sustainability and the right to development," in R. Attfield and B. Wilkins (eds) *International Justice and the Third World*, London: Routledge: 93–117.

Environmental Justice Foundation (2003) *Smash and Grab: conflict, corruption and human rights abuses in the shrimp farm industry*, London: Environmental Justice Foundation.

Evans, G. W. and Kantrowitz, E. (2002) "Socioeconomic status and health: the potential role of environmental risk exposure," *Annu. Rev. Public Health* 23: 303–31.

Faber, D. R. and Krieg, E. J. (2002) "Unequal exposure to ecological hazards: environmental injustices in the Commonwealth of Massachusetts," *Environ. Health Perspect.* 110 (Suppl. 2): 277–88.

Food and Agriculture Organization (2003) *European Shrimp Markets*, GLOBEFISH Research program, Volume 60, at http://www.globefish.org/publications/researchprogram/vols/vol60.htm (accessed on November 4, 2003).

Friends of the Earth (2001) *Pollution and Poverty: breaking the link*, London: Friends of the Earth.

Fur, P. D. (1999) "The precautionary principle: applications to policies regarding endocrine-disrupting chemicals," in C. Raffensperger and J. Tickner (eds) *Protecting Public Health and the Environment. Implementing the precautionary principle*, Washington, DC: Island Press.

Her Majesty's Government (1999) *Saving Lives: our healthier nation*, London: HMSO.

International Labour Organization (ILO) (2001) *International Labour Report*, Geneva: ILO.

Koivusalo, M. (1999) *World Trade Organisation and Trade-Creep in Health and Social Policies*, Geneva: GASSP, STAKES.

Lang, T. (1999) "The new Gatt Round: Whose development? Whose health?" *Journal of Epidemiology and Community Health* 53 (11): 681–2.

Latouche, S. (1993) *In the Wake of the Affluent Society: an exploration of post-development*, London: Zed Books.

McBride, G. (1999) *Scottish Applications of Environmental Justice*, Edinburgh: University of Edinburgh.

McLaren, D. and Bullock, S. (1999) *The Geographic Relation between Household Income and Polluting Factories*, London: Friends of the Earth.

McMichael, A. (1993) *Planetary Overload: global environmental change and the health of the human species*, Cambridge, UK: Cambridge University Press.

McMichael, A., Woodward, A. and van Leeuwen, R. (1994) "The impact of energy use in industrialised countries upon global population health," *Medicine and Global Survival* 1 (1): 23–32.

Ryder, R. (1999) "'No-one ever died from dioxin': the dioxin problem in Britain," *The Ecologist* 29 (6): 369–74.

Scandrett, E., McBride, G. and Dunion, K. (2000) *The Campaign for Environmental Justice in Scotland*, Edinburgh: Friends of the Earth Scotland.

Smil, V. (1993) *Global Ecology: environmental change and social flexibility*, London: Routledge.

Steingraber, S. (1999) "Lessons from Wingspread," in C. Raffensperger and J. Tickner (eds) *Protecting Public Health and the Environment. Implementing the precautionary principle*, Washington, DC: Island Press.

Stephens, C., Bullock, S., Lullo, R. D. and Giobellino, B. (2000) "Our view. Act local, think global? Or act local, act global? How international environmental and social justice can be achieved if local governments reach out to each other," *EG – Local Environment News* 4.

United Nations (2002) "The Johannesburg summit test: what will change?" http://www.johannesburgsummit.org/html/whats_new/feature_story41. html (accessed on November 7, 2003).

United Nations Economic Commission for Europe (UNECE) (2003) *Convention on Access to Information, Public Participation in Decision-Making and Access to Justice in Environmental Matters*, Geneva: UNECE, at http://www.unece.org/ env/pp/. (accessed on November 4, 2003).

—— (1999) *Convention on Access to Information, Public Participation in Decision-Making and Access to Justice in Environmental Matters*, Geneva: UNECE.

United Nations Environment Program (UNEP) (2002) *Global Environmental Outlook 2003*, Nairobi, Kenya: UNEP.

—— (1999) *Global Environment Outlook Geo2000*, Nairobi, Kenya: Earthscan Publications.

United States Environmental Protection Agency (2003) *Environmental Justice*, US EPA, at http://www.epa.gov/compliance/environmentaljustice/.30/10/2003 (accessed on November 4, 2003).

Williams, C. (1998) *Environmental Victims: new risks, new injustice*, London: Earthscan.

World Health Organization (WHO) (2003) *Globalization and occupational health: some problems*, Geneva: WHO, at http://www.who.int/oeh/OCHweb/OCH web/OSHpages/Globalisation/GlobalisationOH.htm.21/082003 (accessed on November 4, 2003).

—— (2001) *World Health Report 2000*, Geneva: WHO.

—— (1997) *Health and Environment in Sustainable Development: five years after the Earth Summit*, Geneva: WHO.

World Resources Institute (1997) *World Resources 1996–1997*, Washington, DC: Oxford University Press.

7 "The most debilitating discrimination of all"

Civil society's campaign for access to treatment for AIDS

Bridget Sleap

Introduction

> You violate a person's humanity by testing him or her for HIV without consent, or by improperly divulging information about his or her health status. But the deepest violation of another person's humanity is to deprive that person of the means to remain healthy, to fight off illness and to live – or die – in reasonable comfort and dignity. ... Discrimination in the allocation of resources is the most debilitating discrimination of all.
>
> (Justice Edwin Cameron[1])

In December 2002 only 5 percent of the estimated five and a half million people living with HIV and AIDS in less developed countries were getting the antiretroviral drugs (ARVs) they needed to save their lives (ITAC 2002). This is despite the fact that drug prices had fallen by an average of 85 percent since 2000 (WHO 2002). Of the 70 low-income countries surveyed by the World Health Organization (WHO) in 2001, half had virtually no access to ARVs and only one pregnant woman in 30 had access to services for the prevention of parent-to-child transmission of HIV (ibid.).

This chapter looks at the role of civil society involvement in human rights protection around issues of access to treatment for HIV and AIDS. It examines the international intellectual property rights protection system at the heart of disputes over domestic legislation and the power of the pharmaceutical industry in protecting its own interests. Against this background it assesses three civil society campaigns that are at once local and global, in Brazil, South Africa and Kenya, and their relative successes and failures to secure access to treatment for HIV and AIDS.

The right to health

The appointment for the first time of a UN Special Rapporteur on the Right to Health in September 2002 demonstrates the growing recognition of the importance of the right to health. Although not all civil society groups concerned with access to treatment have campaigned under the slogan of a "right to health," it is important to have a clear definition of what this right entails. The term right to health has been used as somewhat confusing shorthand for a number of provisions in international treaties and declarations that focus on the enjoyment of the highest attainable standard of health[2] and have been ratified or acceded to by the majority of countries. However, as with other economic, social and cultural rights, this right to health has suffered from questions over its justicability and feasibility of implementation in poorly resourced countries. Carl Wellmann has gone as far as saying that its lack of definition makes it useless in determining any moral duties that arise from it (1999: 155). General Comment 14 on Article 12 of the International Covenant on Economic, Social and Cultural Rights (the ICESCR) from the Committee on Economic, Social and Cultural Rights attempts to clarify some of these issues.

What is made clear in the General Comment is that the right to health is not a right to be healthy but to have equality of opportunity within the health system. This principle of equity is reiterated in the need for both availability of, and accessibility to, health services on the basis of non-discrimination and affordability, and for health services to be acceptable in terms of medical ethics and cultural appropriacy as well as in terms of quality of care. Obligation to ensure this rests with both the state party and the international community. Equity and non-discrimination are therefore at the heart of the right to health, two main areas of concern in the case of antiretrovirals, access to which at present is based on wealth, place of birth, international trade regulations and the policies of pharmaceuticals, rather than need. Article 12 is not the only human right provision that is concerned with access to treatment, but it is the most important.

Box 7.1 What are antiretrovirals (ARVs)?

There are three types of ARV drugs available that attack the virus at different stages in its life cycle. In December 2002 there were 33 new ARVs in the development pipeline. The aim of ARV treatment is to inhibit replication of HIV, the virus that causes AIDS, and boost the immune system's ability to fight infection. ARVs are usually taken in a combination of three or more drugs of two different types (combination therapy). This has only been used on a large scale in developed countries since 1996. Development of new pills containing more than one drug is reducing the number of tablets needing to be taken on a daily basis.

The first ARV, AZT or zidovudine, was approved in the United States in 1987. ARVs have not, however, been available in the majority of less developed countries mainly due to the high prices. Cost has also been a factor in the global North. In 1989, after a vigorous two-year campaign, the US NGO ACT-UP got the producers, Glaxo Wellcome, to lower the price by

20 percent in the United States. As will be illustrated in the case studies later in this chapter, whilst there has been an awareness of their availability in Central and South American countries since the early 1990s, it is only in the last four years that treatment has been considered a possibility in sub-Saharan Africa and Asia. Despite the overriding message of the 14th International AIDS Conference in Barcelona in July 2002 being the necessity of both prevention and treatment, there is still a body of opinion that thinks that the emphasis in less developed countries should be on prevention.

As with any complicated drug regimen, there are fears about the development of drug resistance, of patients not taking their drugs on a regular basis (non-compliance), of side effects and of lack of training amongst health personnel to monitor and administer the drugs effectively. However a Médecins Sans Frontières pilot project in Khayelitsha in South Africa has shown that such regimens can be successfully delivered in resource-poor settings with minimal health infrastructure.

Whilst ARVs in themselves do not prevent transmission, they do reduce the amount of virus in the blood and this is thought to make transmission less likely. Their availability may make people more willing to go for testing as, when treatment is available, the health benefits of knowing whether you are HIV positive or negative are more likely to outweigh the pressures that encourage not knowing.

However, access to ARVs is not going to stop the epidemic by itself and is only one part of an effective response. According to a recent study of 12,000 people living with HIV and AIDS in the United States, 44 percent were not diagnosed until they presented symptoms attributed to AIDS (Garrett 2001). In other words, the fact that late diagnosis is only due to poverty and lack of access to healthcare can no longer be assumed. There are other issues such as denial, shame, fear and stigma that also affect access to treatment, as well as the availability of drugs.

Human rights, HIV and AIDS

The focus on HIV and AIDS and human rights is not a new one. HIV/AIDS is the first new pandemic in the post-war era of global human rights. Since the early 1980s the rights paradigm in this field has shifted from a focus on individual rights violations in developed countries as a result of being HIV-positive, to prioritizing existing violation of rights increasing the vulnerability to infection amongst already marginalized groups, particularly in less developed countries, in the late 1990s. There is still a reluctance amongst some sections of civil society in less developed countries to use a human rights framework or discourse for issues so sensitive and taboo as who is having sex with whom, where and how and the consequences of this. The use of the language of human rights in the private sphere is no more universal amongst HIV and AIDS activists than it is amongst other sections of society.

The present rights debate around access to treatment for HIV and AIDS is, however, more subject to criticism on the question of practicality than the inappropriacy of universal rights ideals. The right to equal access to healthcare exists in the public sphere, with the state and increasingly pharmaceuticals and large corporate employers the accountable actors. What this right does not do is question the very sexual relationships dictated by established social constructs that put so many people at risk of HIV infection. It does not threaten the political and social status quo in the same way that reproductive and sexual health rights do, but instead challenges both global and local inequities within healthcare systems. Perhaps it is for these reasons that campaigns for this right have met with so much support and acceptance, whilst attempts to empower women to negotiate and control their sexual relationships have had such little success. As recently as 2001, the United Nations member states could still not agree to use language such as "commercial sex workers" and "men who have sex with men" in their General Assembly Special Session Declaration on HIV and AIDS.

With recent developments around access to treatment so prominent in the media, the rights debate around the disparities and inequities in global health is becoming more prominent. Although court cases in South Africa, for example those brought against the government by 39 pharmaceutical companies and by the Treatment Action Campaign, have gained the most media attention, there have been other successful legal precedents around access to treatment. In Costa Rica in 1997, the Constitutional Supreme Court of Justice found that refusal of the national health care system to provide free antiretrovirals was an illegal violation of the right to life and with it, the right to health (Matoros 1999). In another example ACCSI, a Venezuelan NGO campaigning for access to treatment for HIV and AIDS, used lawsuits and advocacy initiatives to force the Venezuelan government to recognize that people living with HIV and AIDS have the right of access to healthcare and the benefits of science and technology (Carrusco 2000). Whilst it may not be appropriate in every setting, the use of law as a strategy for securing access to treatment for HIV has been central to the more successful campaigns.

The role of civil society

Civil society groups have played an active role throughout the 20 years of the epidemic. Civil society is here seen to be non-governmental organizations (NGOs), faith-based organizations, trade unions, consumer groups, academic institutions, but does not include the private commercial sector. In less developed countries civil society groups have been significant in service provision, ranging from testing, counseling and home-based care to information services. With weak state health infrastructures, NGOs have been essential in providing care and services that the state system is unable or unwilling to offer. The very nature of HIV and AIDS and the taboos surrounding sex and some traditional practices often make it easier for NGOs than for governments to address these issues and work within the affected communities. However, in terms of drug distribution and monitoring, governments are presently reluctant to hand this activity over to civil society, despite the successful example of Brazil, which will be discussed in more detail later. Some countries have a more developed HIV and AIDS civil society than others. In Uganda, for example, with a long history of NGO interventions, there is a feeling that it would take little to train lay people, already providing other services such as counseling, to administer and monitor ARVs once standards of care have been established.[3]

The civil society campaigns for access to treatment in less developed countries are often also in confrontation with their own governments who may lack the political will to make HIV and AIDS treatment a priority, have a poor human rights record and have few resources available to them for reasons including debt repayments and various structural adjustment conditions attached to loans, which render them unable to invest adequately in their health systems. This chapter will look at the role of civil society in campaigning for equal access to treatment but not at its role in delivering that treatment. The three countries discussed, Brazil, South Africa and Kenya, are all at different stages in terms of how long these campaigns have been running, which ARVs are presently available and the political will amongst the respective governments in delivering them. What is similar with all of them is that part of each of the civil society campaigns revolves around domestic legislation that will ensure that the right to access to treatment is protected by law.

The WTO and TRIPS

Central to access to treatment is the question of patent rules and who owns the patent on a drug. Since a new medicine is an invention, it is subject to a patent. This patent can be on the medicine itself, the product or on the process of making it. Patent protection is designed to ensure that the inventor is rewarded for his/her efforts, and that profits are made to pay back the money spent on research and development. Until recently governments could decide themselves how long patent protection would last under their jurisdiction, or whether protection extends to the product, the process or both. Once patent protection has ended, other companies are free to manufacture the same drug. These copies of the original patented drugs are known as generics. Because generic manufacturers have not had to invest the same amounts of money in research and development, generics can be produced and sold at a much lower price.

The new international rules that standardize the use of patents are known as TRIPS, Trade-Related Intellectual Property. All the World Trade Organization (WTO) members must make their national legislation compliant to TRIPS, which includes the granting of patents for both processes and products for a period of 20 years. TRIPS came into force for developed countries in 1995. Less developed countries have until 2005 and 30 least developed countries until 2016 to make their national legislation compliant. But the latter provision does not include countries such as India that have a generic industry and could export generics cheaply to countries most affected by HIV, which is key to making ARVs available to those who need them. The two agendas that require some kind of balancing here are public health needs and intellectual property rights. The main provisions that enable governments to get cheaper drugs are compulsory licensing, parallel importing and Bolar provisions (see Box 7.2). These provisions must be written into domestic legislation in order for them to be used.

On paper it would seem that this standardization and globalization of intellectual property rights allows less developed countries enough leeway to import or produce low-cost versions of drugs, whilst affording patent holders the protection they require. However, given the political and economic power of the pharmaceutical industry relative to most less developed

Box 7.2 TRIPS provisions

Compulsory licensing allows the government to offer a license to a generic company to produce a patented drug without the permission of the original patent holder. Permission must first be sought, but if refused, generic manufacture can go ahead as long as the original company is given adequate renumeration and the length of generic production is limited. The company producing the generic drug pays a royalty, the level of which is set by a government agency. There are no limitations to when governments can issue a compulsory license, and in the case of a national emergency there is no need to seek permission from the owner of the patent.

Parallel importing is when a government looks for alternative, cheaper sources of a patented drug than that on sale in its own country. The cost of patented drugs can vary dramatically from country to country and the government does not need the patent holder's permission to shop around in this way. TRIPS states that governments permitting parallel importing cannot be challenged under the WTO dispute settlement system.

Bolar provisions allow generic companies to set up the necessary machinery for producing a generic before the 20-year patent expires so that they are ready to go into production as soon as the expiry date passes. If they do not do this, patent holders enjoy an extra extension of their patent exclusivity after the expiry date, since the generic company must register and test products before they can market them, which can take a number of years.

countries, few have been able to take advantage of these provisions. Doing so runs the risk of being taken to court by the pharmaceuticals or threatened with trade sanctions by the United States and other governments wishing to support their pharmaceutical industries. They also risk being taken through the WTO dispute settlement process.

It does seem, however, that the WTO is beginning to address the issues of access to treatment. The June 2001 special session of the WTO TRIPS Council, the monitoring body of TRIPS, was devoted to access to medicines and public health. The meeting was requested by 47 countries, including the Africa Group and countries from Asia, the Caribbean and Latin America, who asked the WTO to affirm that nothing in TRIPS prevents countries from taking measures to protect public health. In particular they asked for clarification on the flexibility of interpreting TRIPS, especially in relation to the use of compulsory licensing and parallel importing. In November 2001 a WTO ministerial working group approved the Doha Declaration allowing the overriding of patents on medicines in public emergencies. A year later in November 2002, a group of 25 WTO member states agreed to endorse the rules allowing for greater access to medicines but were unable to reach agreement on how to implement the rules. For example, whilst there was agreement on including medicines to treat HIV and AIDS, malaria and tuberculosis, there was still dispute as to whether to include those for cancer and diabetes.[4] In August 2003 an agreement before the WTO ministerial conference in Cancún in September allowed countries facing public health crises, such as HIV/AIDS, malaria or tuberculosis, to import the needed medicines from other countries authorized to manufacture generic drugs. However, the restrictions that came with this may in fact have prohibited any real importation of drugs (Médecins Sans Frontières, Campaign for Access to Essential Medicines 2003).

Most developed countries at the WTO special session in June 2001 expressed support for a clear WTO statement. The United States, however, takes the position that strong patents provide benefits for all countries, developed and less developed, and refuses to acknowledge less developed countries' concerns that TRIPS would have negative effects on access to affordable medicines. The United States has put obstacle after obstacle in the way of less developed countries trying to access affordable drugs. These obstacles include applying bilateral pressure on governments to prevent them from issuing compulsory licenses, for example in Thailand 1999–2000, and the US government exerts pressure by taking countries to WTO dispute procedures, for example Brazil, which will be discussed below. A further strategy is the annual publication of the Special 301 report. This provides an update on global intellectual property protection, including information on WTO disputes, the policies of various countries and placing countries on either the Priority Watch List or the regular Watch List. Countries are placed on these lists if the United States disapproves of their national policies or is trying to change them through bilateral pressure. As a result, being on these lists amounts to a de facto trade sanction as it indicates that the United States considers the country an investment risk (Love 1999). In November 2001 the Bush administration agreed to forego the use of blacklisting under 301 with regard to HIV and AIDS, malaria and tuberculosis treatment. However this did not extend to other essential medicines, and was seen by many activists as an empty gesture so soon after the administration had, by threatening to allow generic production, forced large price concessions from Bayer AG for its patented anthrax antibiotic in the wake of the September 11, 2001 terrorist attacks on New York and Washington.[5]

Civil society organizations, therefore, not only have to lobby their own governments to provide access to treatment but are also up against the US government, whose stance is influenced by the lobbying pressure of the pharmaceutical companies. In an era of globalization pharmaceuticals stand alongside oil and other multinationals in the enormous economies they control and the resulting political pressure that they wield. The global pharmaceutical market totalled US $364.2 billion in sales in 2001 (IMS Health 2002), 87 percent of which was in North America, Japan and Europe. Civil society is therefore up against the formidable combination of a vast economic market and the subsequent lobbying power of the pharmaceuticals.

Role of the pharmaceutical companies

There has been much in the media about the reduction of prices of ARVs by pharmaceutical companies, of offers of free donations and of public/private partnership projects for building clinics or providing care and support. Similarly, in October 2002 the Pharmaceutical Research and Manufacturers of America (PhRMA) endorsed requirements by the UN-sponsored Global Fund to Fight HIV/AIDS, TB and Malaria (the Fund) for those receiving grants from the Fund to buy the lowest-cost, quality-ensured drug available. However, the Fund itself had at this time yet to disburse any funds or draw in the amount of money it had predicted necessary to tackle the three diseases, thereby posing little threat to pharmaceutical markets. Whilst these efforts should not be dismissed, they are inadequate to address the scale of the crisis or to provide any degree of equity in health care and ensure access to treatment for those who need it. They are *ad hoc*, palliative measures that are no substitute for strong domestic legislation and systems that can provide long-term access to treatment.

What the campaigners for access to treatment for essential medicines and ARVs have done is call these companies to account, to question the ethics of putting patents and profits before the well-being of patients. Pharmaceuticals support patent legislation as they argue that this ensures that revenue is generated for research and development costs. However in

2001 Pfizer spent only 15 percent of its revenue on research and development and 35 percent on marketing, advertising and administration. In the same year, Merck spent 5 percent and 13 percent respectively (Families USA 2002 – see also Box 7.3).

Whilst access to treatment is only one aspect of the response to the HIV and AIDS pandemic, the international campaigns led by NGOs such as Médecins Sans Frontières and Oxfam and the national campaigns in South Africa, Brazil and Kenya are influencing a growing public opinion that sees as unacceptable the power of these companies and of the governments of developed countries, particularly the United States, in dictating whether someone lives or dies. Campaigns for access to treatment continue to grow in momentum, whilst social movements around the inequities of global capitalism have been less evident in the wake of the September 11, 2001 attacks on the United States. The rest of this chapter is devoted to three

---

Box 7.3 Two pharmaceutical giants – Pfizer and GlaxoSmithKline

The power of the pharmaceuticals is immense. In 1999 Pfizer, the largest company in the industry, spent US$3.8 million on external lobbyists in the United States. Warner-Lambert, with whom it merged in 2000, spent US$2.2 million. Finalization of a merger with Pharmacia Corporation in 2003 will make it the biggest pharmaceutical company in the world. According to an Oxfam report on the company, it has lobbied continuously and successfully to protect its commercial interests (Oxfam 2001a). Its chief executive, Henry McKinnell, is chairman of the PhRMA, the most powerful pharmaceutical lobby in the United States. Pfizer is a member of a number of other lobby groups and has sat on government advisory committees. It was influential in the setting up of TRIPS and makes suggestions on which countries the US government should place on the Special 301 report. The CEO of Pfizer UK is the vice-president of the Association of the British Pharmaceutical Industry (ABPI).

GlaxoSmithKline (GSK) is another pharmaceutical company producing ARVs that has immense influence in government and international policy. Before its merger with Smithkline Beecham in 2000, Glaxo Wellcome spent US$9.6 million between 1997 and 1999 on lobbying. In the same period Smithkline Beecham spent US$7.9 million. In the 2000 US election, Glaxo Wellcome donated over $1 million to the Republican Party, and was ranked number 35 in its top 50 contributors (Oxfam 2001b). As with Pfizer, GSK is also represented on a number of lobby groups including PhRMA and the International Chamber of Commerce.

Both companies provide examples of mergers of vast multinational corporations which command annual incomes larger than many less developed countries, with the resulting concentration of power in the hands of an influential, unaccountable few.

case studies. Although the process has not been without its problems, Brazil is often held up as the model of a less developed country being able to provide ARVs free of charge to all those who need them. South Africa has hit the headlines over both the government's defeat of 39 pharmaceutical companies in a court case concerning legislation on access to medicines, as well as over the defeat at Constitutional Court level of the government's attempt to limit provision of ARVs to pregnant women who are living with HIV. Despite this, the government has so far done little to improve access to ARVs. Kenya has received the least publicity and is in the early stages of its civil society campaign. Once again the focus has been around the passing of domestic legislation that will allow the government to exercise its rights under TRIPS. Access to the drugs themselves for the people living with HIV and AIDS is still a long way off.

Brazil

Access to treatment through the public health system is free and a fundamental right in Brazil, guaranteed in the Constitution and in the Sistema Unico de Saude (Unified Health System) legislation. WHO figures predicted that in 2000 there would be 1.2 million people living with HIV and AIDS in Brazil. In fact, in May 2001 the government estimated that there were only 536,000 Brazilians living with HIV (Ministry of Health 2001), although these estimates may be conservative. According to the National STD/AIDS Program, 358,000 AIDS-related hospital admissions were avoided between 1997 and 2001 (Vitoria 2002). In late 2001, Brazil agree to export its generic production technology to and train health care personnel from Lusophone countries and other countries affected by the epidemic. Brazil is seen as a success story: a less developed country able to provide the drugs only otherwise widely available in the rich countries of the West. Instead of paying up to US$12,000 a year in 2001 for a course of ARVs, Brazil paid US$3,000 and prices are still falling (Philadelphia Inquirer 2001). The government estimated that it had saved $500 million between 1998 and 2001 by producing generics locally (Kaiser Report, August 23, 2001). Brazil's success is due to a number of factors, not least the participation of an articulate, mobilized civil society movement working in close partnership with the Brazilian government.

The first NGO responses to the epidemic came in the early 1980s and, as in the United States, were linked to anti-discrimination and led by the gay movement. By 1989 there were more than 100 AIDS NGOs across Brazil. The National Sexually Transmitted Diseases/AIDS Program was launched in 1985, but did not really have a major impact until 1992 when the Brazilian Ministry of Health (MOH) set up the National AIDS and STD Control Program. This had an NGO Liaison Unit whose aim was to contract out HIV and AIDS services to NGOs. This government–NGO partnership was based on two performance-based contracting-out projects,

AIDS-1 and AIDS-2, co-financed by the Brazilian government and the World Bank. It did this through an annual competitive process, which resulted in a standardized contract including a system of regular NGO monitoring, evaluation and reporting to the MOH.

This system of partnership is considered to be central to the success of Brazil's response to the epidemic. Success was built on the existence of a strong, politicized social movement around HIV and AIDS; the involvement of NGOs in the design of the system; a national, coordinated strategy contracting NGO services; the running of the Liaison Unit by NGO staff; the quality of communication between the Unit and the NGOs; and, the provision of technical assistance by the MOH to NGOs in project design, monitoring and evaluation, and accounting. The MOH alone did not have the capacity to respond to the epidemic nor reach every level of society affected and so this system built on the existing capacity of both the MOH and the NGOs (Partnerships for Health Reform 2000).

However this partnership is not without its critics. As Ezio Tavora dos Santos Filho, Vice-President of the NGO Grupo Pela VIDDA, points out, whilst this has produced a close, cooperative partnership, it has also created NGO dependency on the government and a lack of distance that makes decentralization and long-term sustainability difficult.[6] The role of civil society as critic of the government is harder to carry out and the boundaries between the two are becoming increasingly blurred.

In 1991, the government made the decision to start buying medication for opportunistic infections (illnesses that people with a suppressed immune system, the result of HIV infection, are more likely to succumb to) and AZT, an antiretroviral. These would be distributed free of charge through the Unified Health System. Despite this legislation, distribution under the Unified System was irregular and inefficient in most of the states and municipalities, who along with the Union as a whole shared responsibility for the costs of health care. Even in Rio, a small state with a large network of health care centers and public hospitals, there were still distribution problems. The unusual political commitment to provision of free treatment was central to Brazil's ultimate success, but NGOs also played a key role in lobbying for the Sarney Law that came into force in 1997. This placed responsibility for the acquisition of AIDS drugs with the national government budget. NGOs were then able to lobby the states and municipalities for the acquisition of other drugs. As a result large-scale distribution of ARVs started in 1997. The lack of restrictive patent laws allowed the importation and production of generic drugs. This, coupled with an existing local pharmaceutical manufacturing industry, has enabled Brazil to provide generic equivalents of patented drugs for the majority of the ARVs that it distributes. The then government invoked the national emergency provision of TRIPS and started producing its own generic ARVs in the mid-1990s.

Lenient patent legislation, the constitutional right to free medication/treatment, legislation clarifying payment responsibilities and a strong civil society movement working in partnership with the government have all been key to Brazil's success in responding to the HIV and AIDS epidemic. The political will and commitment to provide access is rare in less developed countries and a key element to success. NGOs have used the media to put added pressure on the government to provide wider access to treatment; they have initiated legal proceedings against the government to ensure treatment for people living with HIV and AIDS in the face of delays in acquisition, unavailability of new drugs and delay in the enrollment of new cases. NGOs have not only raised awareness with the government but have also been instrumental in raising public awareness. Compared to other less developed countries, Brazilian society is well informed about the different issues surrounding HIV and AIDS, and the fact that free treatment is their right. In addition there are committed public health employees, judges and public laboratories which were producing and providing free generics, such as antibiotics, to public hospitals before the AIDS crisis developed.[7] There are still deficiencies and challenges in the system but Brazil has proved that it is possible for a less developed country, given the right circumstances, to provide the treatment its people need.

One such challenge to Brazil's policy was the recent dispute at the WTO over Brazil's generic production. The United States lodged a complaint with the WTO in May 2000 that Brazilian patent law violated TRIPS. The provision concerned states that a patent holder selling patented drugs in Brazil must forfeit its patent rights and be subject to compulsory licensing after three years if it does not manufacture those drugs within Brazil. In January 2001 the United States asked the WTO to review the law through its review panel, which is similar to a trade court, and to issue a ruling by June 2001. Under the provision, Brazil threatened to issue a compulsory license to start production of generic versions of nelfinavir and efavirenz, two patented drugs that alone make up 36 percent of Brazil's AIDS prevention budget. Efavirenz is patented and made by a US pharmaceutical. If the WTO had ruled in favor of the United States, not only would this have made continuation of Brazil's program unfeasible on price grounds, but it would also have created a precedent that may prevent other less developed countries from producing generics. However, on June 25, 2001, the first day of the United Nations General Assembly Special Session on HIV and AIDS in New York, the US Trade Representative, Robert Zoellick, announced that the United States would not be pursuing the complaint but would enter into discussions with Brazil to reach agreement. Brazil, in turn, agreed to inform US patent holders if it intended to make generic copies of their drugs.

In line with this agreement, in August 2001 the Brazilian government announced that it would issue a compulsory license for the manufacture of nelfinavir, manufactured by Roche under the brand name of Viracept, if Roche did not lower its prices any further. Pfizer is the patent holder. The Ministry of Health rejected Roche's 13 percent reduction in price offered at the beginning of 2001, seeking a 40 percent reduction which it estimated is the amount it would save by manufacturing the drug locally (Kaiser Report, August 23, 2001). The government said it would issue a compulsory license with or without Roche's permission and if without, this would have been the first time a less developed country had issued a compulsory license without the patent holder's consent and could have set an important precedent. Brazil would issue this compulsory license under the law that allows them to do so if they declare a national emergency. In September 2001, Roche reached an agreement with Brazil to reduce the price of Viracept by a further 40 percent. The bargaining power of the government over pharmaceuticals may have increased but pharmaceutical companies were said to have expressed relief at the decision (Kaiser Report, September 4, 2001). By not issuing a compulsory license, the Brazilian government committed themselves to this agreement and failed to set a precedent for other countries to issue similar licenses.

South Africa

Just as the US withdrawal of its complaint against Brazil was hailed as a victory for less developed countries against the strength of the United States and the pharmaceutical industry, so too was the dropping of the legal case in April 2001 brought by the Pharmaceutical Manufacturers Association (PMA) against South Africa. Just as Brazil is held up as a model for other less developed countries, so too events in South Africa have enormous influence on what happens not only in Southern Africa but also across sub-Saharan Africa. As in Brazil and Kenya, domestic legislation and its compliance with TRIPS is central to the calls to provide treatment for those who need it.

The suit against the South African government was first filed in the Pretoria High Court in February 1998. In question was Amendment 15(c) of the Medicines and Related Substances Control Amendment Act of 1997 which would allow both compulsory licensing and parallel imports of medicines into South Africa and establish a transparent pricing system through a pricing committee. On April 19, just days after the PMA was still attacking the legality of the Act, and after negotiations brokered by UN Secretary General Kofi Annan, attempts to reach an out of court settlement with the government failed and the PMA withdrew the case (Heywood 2001). Had it gone to court the case would probably have been a public relations disaster for the pharmaceuticals given the negative publicity they had already received in the run-up to the withdrawal.

Not least amongst the reasons for the South African victory was the role played by the Treatment Action Campaign (TAC), the civil society movement in South Africa around access to treatment for HIV and AIDS. In March Judge Bernard Ngoepe ruled that the TAC would be granted an *amicus curiae* brief, allowing them to make a submission to the court despite not being party to the case and ordered the PMA to respond to evidence and arguments made in the TAC's affidavits. According to Theodore Steele, COSATU Campaign Coordinator and an executive member of the TAC, it was this *amicus curiae* that raised human rights in the court case and was necessary to clarify the rights issues.[8] Affordability of treatment for HIV and AIDS became part of the case and the level of negative publicity for the pharmaceuticals increased. The TAC themselves believe that the government would not have won the case so quickly without global support and mobilization led by such NGOs as ACT-UP, Health Gap, Médecins Sans Frontières and Action for Southern Africa (ACTSA), the successor to the anti-apartheid movement in the United Kingdom (TAC 2001).

Just as significant as the legal implications of the South African victory is the fact that it showed that public opinion was not prepared to accept that these lifesaving drugs be priced out of the reach of those who need them most in order to ensure that pharmaceuticals maintain their profit margins. When the suit was filed very few people were aware of the issues involved, of TRIPS and generic production. Public awareness increased and this is being reflected in the continuing demand for price reductions both from patent and generic producers and for clarification of the relevant provisions of TRIPS at the WTO.

Despite its victory, the South African government was quick to point out that providing ARVs was not a government priority when the health infrastructure was not yet in place to support that provision. At a meeting held to thank UK NGOs for their support throughout the court case, the Health Minister Manto Tshabalala-Msimang went as far as saying that she felt that the case had been hijacked by AIDS activists and the demand for ARVs overshadowed the purpose of the legislation which was accessibility and affordability of all medicines.[9] Unlike Brazil, therefore, free provision of treatment for people living with HIV and AIDS as a right does not have the same political support in South Africa.

The relationship between the TAC and the South African government has at times been confrontational. TAC's defiance campaign against the government, openly and illegally importing cheap generic ARVs from Thailand in 2000, did much to highlight the government's own inaction and unwillingness and the TAC continues to lobby the government to create a national treatment plan. On August 21, 2001 it filed a suit at the Pretoria High Court against the Minster of Health, Dr Manto Tshabala-Msiang and nine provincial health ministers, citing violations of eight sections of the Constitution around the rights of women and children to access healthcare. The violations stem from the government's failure to provide nevirapine, an ARV that prevents the vertical transmission of HIV from an HIV-positive mother to her child. Despite the TAC once again being successful in the courts, the government refused to make nevirapine available to the women who need it. In July 2002, the Constitutional Court denied the government's right to appeal the Pretoria High Court's earlier ruling that the government must provide nevirapine to HIV-positive pregnant women in state hospitals. Political will was still lacking on the part of the government and in December 2002 the TAC submitted a complaint to the South African Human Rights Commission against the Member of the Executive Committee (MEC) for Health in Mpumalanga province, Ms Sibongile Manana, for contempt of the Constitutional Court order, since she had done little at that stage to implement the order.

However, in a major turnaround in August 2003, the South African government announced that it would develop a national HIV/AIDS treatment program by October 2003. Whilst the move was welcomed by activists, with the TAC announcing they would end their civil disobedience campaign, the government did not explicitly promise ARV provision to all those who need it and there was both skepticism as to how effectively the program would be implemented once it has been developed and cynicism that the announcement was timed to coincide with forthcoming elections (Kaiser Report, August 11, 2003).

The TAC was founded on Human Rights Day, December 10, 1998. The campaign has grown so rapidly that the TAC held its first congress and adopted a constitution in March 2001. Its emergence changed HIV and AIDS politics in South Africa. Until then the civil society HIV and AIDS lobby had been weak: it was isolated from the government's program of health reform; its level of understanding of the HIV and AIDS pandemic was minimal and it did not keep up to date with developments elsewhere; activists relied on access to government ministers and failed to mobilize mass support for an excellent 1994 National AIDS Program, the main demands of which were subsequently not implemented (Achmat 1999). The founding of the TAC was also a major turning point since prior to this AIDS NGOs had concentrated on providing care and support. Treatment was considered something that was only feasible overseas. The TAC raised awareness that treatment was possible in South Africa and that treatment and prevention must both be part of a response to HIV and AIDS if it is to be effective. The campaign emphasis has been on constructive reform, not eradication, of TRIPS or the WTO, with a legal strategy as well as mass mobilization and support from community level.

Mass support is essential to ensure that national legislation and policies are enacted by the government, and sensitizing the population is one of TAC's key objectives. The TAC does this by engaging groups from many different sectors of civil society: community-based organizations, faith-based organizations, trade unions, youth groups, labor organizations and those dealing with children's rights. This broad spectrum not only increases the reach of AIDS NGOs and builds on an already existing civil society but also benefits the other organizations. COSATU, for example, can now have access to rural areas, which it didn't before, through its membership in the TAC.[10] Since 1994 civil society has been weakened by former activists

joining the government and with funds being challenged through government departments that previously went to NGOs.[11] Nevertheless, the TAC's
success is attributed in part to its leadership's knowledge and experience,
much of which was gained during the struggle against apartheid. Significantly, the TAC is seen to be the first successful social movement of its kind
in the post-apartheid era.

The TAC was awarded the Kaiser Family Foundation Nelson Mandela
Award for Health and Human Rights for its contribution to improving
access for treatment for people living with HIV and AIDS in South Africa
in February 2003. However, access to ARVs for the people who need them
is still a long way off. Other initiatives are developing rapidly – mining
companies have considered providing ARVs to their workforce; Bristol
Meyers Squib stated that they will not sue Aspen Pharmacare, a South
African generic manufacturer, if it chose to produce copies of the ARVs
Videx and Zerit; the government accepted a free offer of two years' supply
of Diflucan (fluconazole) from Pfizer; and, in December 2002 the South
African Medical Association and the Nelson Mandela Foundation launched
a treatment program designed to give free ARV therapy to 9,000 people.
These initiatives, however, are not long-term policies, can be withdrawn
and as such are no substitute for a systematic government policy of treatment provision.

Whilst the TAC has greatly influenced campaigning for access to HIV
and AIDS treatment beyond South Africa, including the launch of the 21-
country strong Pan-African HIV/AIDS Treatment Access Movement in
August 2002, it has also had an influence beyond the field of HIV in South
Africa itself. The TAC has led and focused the first real criticism of the
post-apartheid administration and in doing so, has opened the way of
other legitimate criticism of ANC's policies, including policies on land and
the economy. The TAC has allowed civil society to move beyond the sense
that any criticism of the ANC was a betrayal of the liberation movement to
legitimize calls for the government to uphold the rights enshrined in the
new constitution.

Kenya

Although not all of the 2.5 million adults living with HIV and AIDS in
Kenya would require ARV treatment at the same time, at the end of 2002
not more than 2,000 people were estimated to be receiving ARV treatment.[12]
Compared to Brazil and South Africa, civil society mobilization around
access to treatment in Kenya is in its early stages. But as in Brazil and
South Africa, NGOs have taken on a major role of HIV and AIDS service
provision, in terms of care and prevention.

The focus of the Kenyan Coalition on Access to Essential Medicines
(hereafter the Coalition) has been on ensuring that domestic legislation

contains provisions that will make access to treatment more likely for those who need it. The bill in question is the Industrial Property Act 2001, which was passed in the Kenyan parliament on June 12, 2001. It makes Kenyan law TRIPS-compliant by increasing patent protection to 20 years and by allowing the Kenyan government to grant compulsory licenses to generic manufacturers, giving patent pharmaceutical companies six months' notice before it grants the license. It also allowed for generic importing but an amendment made in June 2002 requires importers to seek the express permission of the patent holders. Pressure from the Coalition and other stakeholders brought about the re-amendment of the Act in August 2002, allowing for generic importation. However, a Bolar provision, although available under TRIPS, is missing from the Act and needs to be in domestic legislation to be legally utilized.

The Coalition has used a number of tactics to influence government policy. It has approached policy-makers individually to educate them on the issues involved. Parliamentary Committees have been lobbied by both legal experts and people living with HIV. The Coalition has provided legal advice on the individual clauses of the bill. The Coalition lobbied the government not to accept price reductions offered by the major pharmaceuticals as an alternative to ensuring long-term rights with their domestic legislation. However, observers suggest that the government's real aim was in fact to bring down drug prices, with the Kenyan Public Health Minister Sam Ongeri quoted as saying that they are pushing the drug companies into creating competition (*The Guardian* 2001). The Coalition has also used the media to raise public awareness on the issue, including a media blitz the week before parliamentary debate of the bill which resulted in a petition of 50,000 signatures being solicited from all over the country in just one week and being presented to parliament. Local and international press conferences were held whenever it was felt that pharmaceutical companies were putting up resistance to the bill.

A non-confrontational approach to policy-makers has been considered as central to their success.[13] Success of the Coalition is also attributed to its wide-ranging composition of members, as with the TAC in South Africa. They come from all sectors of civil society: professional associations, community-based groups, faith-based groups, organizations of people living with HIV and AIDS, pharmacists, generic manufacturers, lawyers, doctors, AIDS activist and journalists. However, ARVs are still out of the reach of the majority of Kenyans who need them. In April 2002 the Coalition accused the pharmaceutical Bristol Meyers Squibb of failing to provide a constant supply of its cut-price Videx and Zerit. Patients were forced to switch to alternatives, which is dangerous in combination therapy, or to interrupt treatment. Nairobi's Mbagathi hospital was at times obliged to hand out 100 mg tablets with a razor blade so that patients could cut the pills to get the right dosage (Panos 2002: 34). Other obstacles exist, including the fact that only three generic ARVs are presently registered with the Kenya Pharmacy and Poisons Board, but these are drugs which cannot be combined into one triple therapy.

Conclusion

Whilst Kenya is clearly at a different stage in securing access to treatment to both Brazil and South Africa, the three different experiences suggest that there are certain prerequisites for the success of a civil society campaign around these issues. These include a strong leadership of people with expertise and experience; a degree of partnership with the government, particularly in terms of uniting against the pressures from Western pharmaceuticals and governments protecting their trade interests; mass support of the population who are aware of their rights and what treatment is available; active involvement of all sectors of civil society, not only HIV and AIDS organizations; and a legal strategy.

The very nature of the right to equal access to healthcare is also significant. It is a right firmly in the public sphere, and one which does not question existing social norms, gender relations or perceptions of traditional behavior and morality around sex. It is a right that many different sectors of civil society and the general population can comfortably unite behind since it poses no threat to a patriarchal system, within which constructs of masculinity and sexual behavior are proving so hard to change.

Price reductions, decisions to unite to take advantage of pooled procurement discounts, discount price offers from generic producers to NGOs and governments, and deals between developing governments and pharmaceuticals are taking place on an increasingly regular basis, including the launch by WHO of a new treatment advocacy network, the International Treatment Access Coalition, made up of NGOs, international organizations, donors, developing country governments and research institutions, in December 2002. However, since Brazil, closely followed by Costa Rica, is at present the only less developed country that has come close to providing universal free access, these measures and a strong civil society movement alone are not enough. Genuine political will is essential. There needs to be a collective consciousness that access to treatment is a right, that it is not only for the rich or well-connected and this right needs to be not only enshrined in domestic legislation but also enforced. Financial commitments from both national governments and the international community have got to increase dramatically to provide a response on the scale that is necessary. Generic production has to be expanded and those with the capacity to manufacture generics be allowed to export them to countries without their own pharmaceutical industry. And finally, stigma and discrimination against people living with or affected by HIV and AIDS has to be eliminated in order for people to be willing to access the services that exist, or may exist in the future, to save their lives.

Notes

1 Quoted in the Congress of South African Trade Union's (COSATU's) "Submission on HIV/AIDS Treatment, Care and Support," to the Health Portfolio Committee in South Africa, May 10, 2000, www.cosatu.org.za/docs/2000/hivaids.htm

2 These include Article 12(1) of the International Covenant on Economic, Social and Cultural Rights; Article 24(1) of the Convention on the Rights of the Child; and Article 16 of the African Charter on Human and Peoples' Rights. The 1978 WHO and UNICEF Declaration of Alma Ata declares that the highest possible level of health is not only a worldwide goal but also a fundamental right, as does the WHO Constitution. The Convention on the Elimination of All Forms of Racial Discrimination calls on state parties to prohibit and eliminate discrimination in the enjoyment of the right to public health and medical care (Article 5(e)(iv)) and the Convention on the Elimination of All Forms of Discrimination Against Women requires state parties to eliminate discrimination against women in the right to protection of health (Article 11(l)(f)).

3 Personal communication with Sophia Mukaso, then Director of the AIDS Support Organization (TASO), Uganda, March 27, 2001.

4 Whilst TRIPS applies to all medicines, activists campaigning for access to antiretrovirals have led the civil society movement on access to treatment. Those who campaign for more money to be spent on the development of drugs for TB and malaria may fear that HIV and AIDS is detracting from their cause, but highlighting the inequities in health provision for people with HIV and AIDS could have a beneficial knock-on effect for other diseases affecting less developed countries.

5 In direct contrast to attempts to restrict access to cheaper drugs in developing countries, within the United States there is a growing concern over the high prices of medicines for the elderly. In July 2001 the US House of Representatives voted overwhelmingly in favor of importing prescription drugs sold more cheaply overseas for personal use. The Pharmaceutical Research and Manufacturers of America (PhRMA) opposed the legislation and says that it will continue to do so in the Senate. "Measure easing drug imports passes in House," *New York Times*, July 12, 2001.

6 Personal communication with Ezio Tavora dos Santos Filho, July 9, 2001.

7 Personal communications with Jorge Beloqui, Grupo de Incentivio de Vida and São Paulo University, July 5, 2001.

8 Personal communication with Theodore Steele, June 20, 2001.

9 Meeting at South Africa House, London, May 11, 2001.

10 Steele, personal communication, op cit.

11 Personal communication with T. A. Bolani, National Consumer Forum, July 18, 2001.

12 Personal communication with Caroline Sande, Campaign for an AIDS Free Society, November 29, 2002.

13 Personal communication with Pauline Ngungiri, Society for Women Against AIDS in Kenya, June 16, 2001.

Bibliography

Achmat, Z. (1999) "We can use compulsory licensing and parallel imports: a South African case study," AIDS Law Project, at www.hri.ca/partners/alp/tac/license. shtml (visited July 2001).

Carrusco, E. (2000) "Presentation made to the 13th International Conference on HIV and AIDS in Durban, July 2000," *Session Report*, at www.aids2000.org, July (visited August 2001).

Families USA (2002), "New 2001 data show big drug companies spent almost two and one half times as much on marketing, advertising and administration as they spent on research and development," at www.familiesusa.org/ new2001data.htm, 17 July (visited December 13, 2002).

Garrett, L. (2001) "Officials' dilemma in AIDS fight," at www.aegis.com, 17 August (visited December 2001).

The Guardian (2001) "Battle over cheap drugs goes to WTO," June 16.

Heywood, M. (2001) "Pharmaceuticals case ends . . . not with a bang but a whimper," *AIDS Analysis Africa* 12 (1) (June/July).

IMS Health (2002) "World pharma sales 2001: US still driving growth," at www. ims-global.com/insight/report/global/report.htm, April 30 (visited December 2002).

International HIV Treatment Access Coalition (ITAC) (2002) "Coverage of antiretroviral treatment in developing countries," at www.itacoalition.org, December (visited December 2002).

Kaiser Daily HIV and AIDS reports (August 23, September 4, 2001; August 11, 2003).

Love, J. (1999) "Notes on the United States Trade Representative watch list and reports," at www.cptech.org/ip/health/whatrlists.html, July 15 (visited August 2001).

Matoros, A. (1999) "Access to treatment: AIDS-affected population in Costa Rica wins constitutional challenge," *Canadian HIV/AIDS Policy and Law Newsletter* 4 (2/3), at www.aidslaw.ca/Maincontent/. . . Newsletter/spring99/geneva98–6. htm (visited August 2001).

Médecins Sans Frontières, Campaign for Access to Essential Medicines (2003) "IPS: WTO-CANCUN: cheap medicine agreement under fire from NGOs' www. accessmed-msf.org/prod/publications.asp?scntid=12920031041437& contenttype=PARA, September 11 (visited November 11, 2003).

Ministry of Health of Brazil (2001) *National AIDS Drug Policy*, May 2001.

Oxfam (2001a) *Formula for Fairness: patient rights before patent rights*, Oxfam Company Briefing Paper on Pfizer, July.

—— (2001b) *Dare to Lead: public health and company wealth*, Oxfam Briefing Paper on GlaxoSmithKline, February.

Panos (2002) *Patents, Pills and Public Health,* Panos: London, December.

Partnerships for Health Reform (2000) "Brazil contracts NGOs to fight HIV and AIDS," at www.phrproject.com/publicat/inbriefs/ib48fin.htm, June (visited December 2001).

The Philadelphia Inquirer (2001) "Brazil battles AIDS and US resistance," at http://inq.philly.com, June 24 (visited August 2001).

TAC (2001) "An explanation of the Medicines Act and the implications of the court victory," TAC Statement on the Court Case, www.Hivnet.ch:8000/topics/treatment-access/viewR?990, April 24 (visited July 2001).

Vitoria, M. (2002) "Model of success. Universal access to treatment in Brazil," *Insights Health*, ID21, Institute of Development, University of Sussex, March.

Wellmann, C. (1999) *The Proliferation of Rights: moral progress or empty rhetoric?* Boulder, CO: Westview Press.

World Health Organization (2002) "Coverage of selected health services for HIV/AIDS prevention and care in less developed countries in 2001," WHO, at www.itacoalition.org (visited December 12, 2002).

8 Climb every mountain

Civil society and the conflict diamonds campaign

Ian Smillie

Introduction

On a cold, rainy November day in 2002, in the small Swiss resort town of Interlaken, something remarkable happened. The world's diamond industry, along with the governments of 52 countries, plus another 15 represented by the European Union, put their seal of approval on an agreement to end the trade in conflict diamonds. Without non-governmental organizations (NGOs), which were also at the meeting, it would never have happened. High on the Jungfrau overlooking the town, it had snowed, and for a few moments the clouds broke to reveal the mountain, looming over the town in its brilliant cloak of new white snow. It seemed like a metaphor for what had happened in the meeting rooms of the Victoria–Jungfrau Hotel, a brief opening and small step towards the solution to a problem that a group of NGOs had been battling for more than four years to secure.

Four years. It seemed like an eternity in NGO time. For the diamond industry it also seemed like an eternity: four years of accusation, demonstrations, fear that a powerful consumer boycott might suddenly erupt into a diamond world that had been badly hit by the 1997 Asian economic meltdown, and then again by a market downturn after September 11, 2001. For the governments that gathered at Interlaken, however, four years was nothing. It was, in fact, something of a record in reaching a complicated international agreement on anything, much less an issue that transcended the political and trading interests of countries on every continent, which cut across evolving political and economic sensitivities in the European Union, which cut into perceived World Trade Organization (WTO) obligations, which drew strength from still smoldering Cold War embers, which had engaged the United Nations Security Council in a dozen detailed investigations, and which lay at the center of debates about African development, underdevelopment, sanctions-busting, resource exploitation, mercenaries, theft, murder, state collapse and war.

NGOs and agenda-setting

Conflict diamonds were first brought to the world's attention late in 1998 by a small British NGO called Global Witness. Global Witness had been started only five years earlier by three dropouts from the environmental movement who had previously been working on issues such as banning the ivory trade in order to protect elephants in Africa. They had seen that environmental and human rights problems were complex and interrelated, and in order to solve them, the source of the problem – rather than public exhortation – needed to be addressed. They began to look at the role of resources in conflicts, which at that time very few people had examined. The first issue they tackled was timber exploitation in Cambodia. Their concern was not timber or forests but what the exploitation of forests by unscrupulous logging firms was doing to Cambodia and Cambodians. The firms, mostly Thai, were in the thrall of the Khmer Rouge, and the funds – as much as $20 million a month at its height – were being used to buy weapons and to fuel a brutal, rear-guard Khmer Rouge struggle, long after it had disappeared from the CNN radar. The evidence of commercial and official cupidity exposed by Global Witness was irrefutable. It forced both governments and aid agencies, in particular the World Bank, to take action, which in due course cut off the Khmer Rouge money machine and helped in its final demise.

In 1998, Global Witness turned its attention to the war in Angola, and found that diamonds were fueling the União para la Indepêndencia Total de Angola (UNITA) war machine. UNITA, which had long before lost any moral or political justification for its 20-year war effort, and which had lost the Cold War rationale needed for its American backing, was funded now almost exclusively through the sale of diamonds. In a December 1998 report entitled *A Rough Trade*, Global Witness reported that between 1992 and 1998, UNITA controlled between 60 and 70 per cent of Angola's diamond production, generating $3.7 billion to pay for its war effort (Global Witness 1998: 3). Half a million Angolans died, and many more were displaced, their lives ruined.

A year later, in January 2000, a small Canadian NGO, Partnership Africa Canada (PAC), released its own report on diamonds, *The Heart of the Matter: Sierra Leone, diamonds and human security* (Smillie et al. 2000). That report told the story of Sierra Leone's Revolutionary United Front (RUF), a rebel movement devoid of ideology, without ethnic backing or claims to territory. Charles Taylor, the Liberian warlord, had financed the early stages of his rampage to power by selling timber. As Global Witness had shown in Cambodia, the market for tropical hardwood is lucrative, and once Taylor secured the Port of Buchanan, he had both the supply and the means to export. But diamonds would prove to be even more lucrative. Taylor backed Sierra Leone's fledgling RUF, giving it a Liberian base, weapons and an outlet for whatever it could steal in Sierra

Leone. The RUF trademark was grisly: they chopped the hands and feet off civilians, often small children. As a terror technique, it was extremely effective in clearing the country's alluvial diamond fields, providing the RUF and Taylor with a highly rewarding money machine.

Explaining conflicts

Apart from an unbridled quest for power, these "revolutionary" movements in Angola, Sierra Leone and Liberia were baffling to journalists, diplomats and academics alike, unfamiliar with Africa and grappling with a change in the way wars were being fought. No longer something that took place mainly between nations and between formal armies fighting pitched battles, conflict was now something that occurred mainly within countries, often between inchoate groups with unclear ambitions and ideologies. Robert Kaplan, a widely read American journalist, attempted an explanation. In "The coming anarchy," an article that appeared in the *Atlantic Monthly* in February 1994, Kaplan described West Africa in general, and Sierra Leone in particular, as symbols of

> [W]orldwide demographic, environmental and societal stress, in which criminal anarchy emerges as the real 'strategic' danger. Disease, overpopulation, unprovoked crime, scarcity of resources, refugee migrations, the increasing erosion of nation–states and international borders, and the empowerment of private armies, security firms, and international drug cartels are now most tellingly demonstrated through a West African prism.

Kaplan's "anarchy" thesis was underpinned by an influential article published in *Foreign Affairs* the summer before. In "The clash of civilizations?," Samuel P. Huntington wrote,

> [T]he fundamental source of conflict in this new world will not be primarily ideological or primarily economic. The great divisions among humankind and the dominating source of conflict will be cultural. Nation states will remain the most powerful actors in world affairs, but the principal conflicts of global politics will occur between nations and groups of different civilizations. The clash of civilizations will dominate global politics. The fault lines between civilizations will be the battle lines of the future.
>
> (1993: 22)

Kaplan accepted the Huntington thesis, but where Sierra Leone was concerned, it was a clash between civilization and a lack thereof. In a later book, *The Ends of the Earth* (1996), he expanded on his original thesis about Sierra Leone as a non-country, confirming a description of Freetown airport and its immigration officials as "a junkyard guarded by junkyard dogs" (1996: 41). Huntington too turned his "Clash of civilizations?" into a 1996 book, but removed the question mark in a spirit of newfound assertiveness that gained special resonance after September 11, 2001.

Meanwhile, in another part of the academic forest, there was a different school of thought, expounded most vocally by Paul Richards. Richards, an anthropologist with many years of experience in Sierra Leone, saw the RUF rebellion as a combination of two things. The first, set out in *Fighting for the Rainforest* (1996), was a deep primordial sentiment, in which modern times clashed with ancient beliefs about land, the 'dramaturgy' of the rainforest and the patrimony of a preliterate people. Richards' second thesis was that young Sierra Leonean males had overdosed on Rambo films, shown for years throughout Sierra Leone on generator-powered VCRs and well known throughout the country. It will be recalled that in *First Blood*, John Rambo returns home after serving his country in Vietnam to find a town in the grip of corrupt politicians and law enforcement officials. After being abused by a corrupt sheriff, he takes to the woods to fight back against the forces of evil, becoming the subject of a manhunt in the process. The analogy between Rambo and the RUF is interesting, although it wobbles in the translation when – as was the case in Sierra Leone – the Rambo wannabes consume lashings of marijuana and cocaine, and then rape, plunder and murder at will.

The Rambo thesis (fighting for justice and democracy) does have appeal, but without the "rainforest" overlay, the reality is not far removed from Kaplan's "coming anarchy." Combined with the rainforest idea, however, it fades into a fog of cultural anthropology that is not very helpful in the search for clear explanations and, more importantly, practical solutions. Richards did view the RUF, however, as a "coherent movement" whose "political project cannot be ignored" (Richards 1996: 33). Neither Kaplan nor Richards gave diamonds more than a passing glance.

A third school of thought emerged at the same time from a group of young Sierra Leonean academics, who saw the political roots of the RUF in the inherent gangsterism of what they called a "lumpen youth" – uneducated, disaffected dead-enders, chaperoned into violence by a demagogic leader, drugs, chips on their shoulders worthy of any tropical rainforest, Libyan finance, and conveniently vague ideas about ending military rule and corruption.[1]

Establishing the link: diamonds and war

Whatever ideology (or rather "idea") RUF leader Foday Sankoh started out with when he first attacked Sierra Leone government positions in 1991, he soon turned his attention to ways in which the fight could be sustained financially. The key lay in the diamond fields of Kono District, which the RUF took, and retook as the war progressed. *The Heart of the*

Matter (Smillie *et al.* 2000) traced Sierra Leone's diamond story from its decline into corruption in the 1970s through to 1999, when formal diamond mining had come to an almost complete halt. By then, there were no government-supervised diamond exports, while across the border in Liberia, diamond exports were thriving. Between 1994 and 1999, more than $2 *billion* worth of diamonds were imported into Belgium from Liberia. Liberia, however, is a country with almost no diamond production of its own. At the very best of times it never surpassed $10 million in exports a year. This report, published by PAC, exposed diamond fraud of massive proportions. It accused the diamond industry at large of complicity, and the Belgian authorities in particular of closing their eyes to massive corruption, in part to protect the Antwerp diamond trade which had been diminished in recent years by competition from Israel and India.

Between them, Global Witness and Partnership Africa Canada had put the diamond industry on notice, and they also singled out the giant De Beers conglomerate for special attention. De Beers has traditionally controlled about 80 percent of the world's trade in rough diamonds.[2] In its annual reports in the mid-1990s, it had crowed about its ability to keep mopping up diamonds from Angola, despite the unsettling business of war. In addition to diamonds from its own mines in Southern Africa, De Beers bought diamonds on the "open market" and maintained offices in Guinea, the Democratic Republic of Congo (DRC) and elsewhere, taking whatever was on offer, no questions asked. Control over supply was key to sustaining the high price of diamonds in a world where more and more gem-quality finds were occurring. Antwerp and De Beers were the largest entrepôts for diamonds, but they were not alone in failing to see the damage that their product was doing in Africa. Russia produces about 20 percent by value of all the world's rough diamonds while more than 25 percent are produced in Botswana. Australia, Namibia and South Africa are also significant producers. Israel accounts for about 26 percent by value of all the rough diamonds that are cut and polished in a year. The equivalent Indian figure is more than 40 percent. The United States consumes more than 40 percent of all diamond jewelry sold in a year. None of these countries or their diamond industries had anything to say about conflict diamonds until the issue was exposed by NGOs.

The problems of Sierra Leone and Angola were not unique. Under the helmsmanship of Mobutu Sese Seko, formal diamond production in Zaire (now the Democratic Republic of the Congo) apparently fell from 18 million carats in 1961, to 12 million in 1970 and only eight million in 1980, finally leveling off at about 6.5 million carats in the 1990s. Production "apparently" fell to these levels, because these are the figures that were recorded. But Mobutu "informalized" much of the diamond industry, bringing it and its profits under his own control and that of his cronies. Miners, middlemen and *diamantaires* devised a simple way to avoid his rapacious appetite and a heavy system of informal taxation (otherwise known as "bribery"). They simply smuggled their product across the river to Brazzaville. The ups and downs of Belgian diamond imports from Brazzaville, in the Republic of Congo, are, in fact, a relatively good barometer of war and corruption in the DRC. In 1997, when the DRC was undergoing the chaotic transfer of power from Mobutu to Kabila, Belgium imported $454.6 million worth of diamonds from Brazzaville. By 1999, however, when things had settled down, and when it looked as though Kabila might actually be a new wind sweeping away the corruption and cronyism of the past, Belgium imported only $14.4 million worth of diamonds from Brazzaville, and there was growth in imports from the DRC. By 2000, however, the blush was off the Kabila rose, and the volume from Brazzaville soared to $116.6 million, almost doubling again in 2001 to $223.8 million.[3] The human cost of this level of corruption, and of the resource-based war that followed Kabila's takeover, was enormous. In 2001, the International Rescue Committee, an American NGO, issued a report showing that 2.5 million more people had died in the DRC during the second half of the 1990s than would otherwise have died, had the resource wars not occurred.[4] In April 2003 they issued a new report, boosting the number to 3.3 million – the worst human calamity since World War II (Roberts *et al.* 2003).

It is probably safe to say, therefore, that some 3 million people died during the 1990s as a result of wars fueled in part, or in whole, by diamonds. These diamonds came to be known as *conflict diamonds*, or *blood diamonds*.

The Kimberley Process

The United Nations Security Council finally withdrew its UN peacekeeping force from Angola in 1998. There was no peace to keep, and the rebel UNITA movement had repeatedly broken UN arms embargoes with impunity, paying for light weapons, tanks, rocket launchers and ground-to-air missiles with the millions it derived from diamonds. In 1999, the Security Council Sanctions Committee on Angola, chaired by Canada's UN ambassador Robert Fowler, fielded an "expert panel" to examine the connection between diamonds and weapons, first exposed several months earlier by Global Witness. The Security Council had banned UNITA from receiving weapons, but they were still getting through. The expert panel sought to discover how the sanctions were being broken. When they reported to the Security Council in March 2000, they also had the advantage of the PAC report which had been released a short time earlier. Unable to ignore what the NGOs had already shown, for the first time a UN report named sitting heads of government as accomplices in the breaking of UN sanctions. The Presidents of Togo and Burkina Faso were named as both diamond and weapons traffickers.

A Security Council ban was placed on any Angolan diamonds not certified as clean by the Angolan government, although as subsequent reports would show, very little changed. During the first half of 2000, however, something did change: the attitude of the diamond industry. De Beers, spooked by the Global Witness report, had closed all of its buying offices in Africa in 1999, now taking diamonds only from its own mines and from known companies with which it had a formal mining arrangement. Worried that growing NGO awareness and publicity might spiral out of control, the government of South Africa called a meeting of interested governments, NGOs and the diamond industry in May 2000. The meeting, held in the town of Kimberley, where South African diamonds had been discovered 135 years before, was ground-breaking, not least because of the eclectic mix of people. NGOs were able to talk for the first time directly with the Belgian Foreign Minister; De Beers was able to have a direct conversation with its accusers. Many diamond officials had their first encounters with NGOs. The meeting reached no conclusions, but the participants did decide to hold another meeting at which the issues could be explored further.

This was the beginning of what became known as the "Kimberley Process," and it eventually culminated, a dozen meetings and 30 months later, at Interlaken. But the story is getting ahead of itself. The road from Kimberley to Interlaken was a bumpy one, with detours, accidents and more than a few false starts. To its credit, the diamond industry had realized by the summer of 2000 that if it didn't take the NGO charges seriously, it faced a public relations disaster that could turn into a devastating commercial problem. It was not just NGO lobbying and a UN report that alarmed them. In May 2000, a peace deal in Sierra Leone fell apart. With its back to the wall militarily, the government of Sierra Leone had accepted an arrangement brokered by the United Nations and the United States. Rebel leader Foday Sankoh had been brought into the government as head of a mineral resources commission and given the status of Vice-President. A UN peace-keeping force was then sent to Sierra Leone, but the RUF resisted its attempts to move peacekeepers into rebel-held diamond areas. Then, in an accidental/on-purpose confrontation, more than 500 United Nations peacekeepers were kidnapped by the RUF. Some were killed and the rest were held for ransom.

The UN operation went into a tailspin. Such a thing had never happened before. There was talk of withdrawal, which panicked Sierra Leoneans, fearful of being left to the devices of the RUF. A massive public demonstration outside Foday Sankoh's house in Freetown turned violent when his armed guards shot and killed 17 civilians, and it was soon discovered that an RUF *coup* had been narrowly avoided. The bigger geopolitical issue, however, was the potential collapse of the UN peacekeeping mission, the first since the UN disasters in Somalia, Rwanda and Angola. In fact the entire concept of UN peacekeeping was now thrown into question, and active thought was given to abandoning Sierra Leone to its fate. Journalists flocked to Freetown, and for a moment, the "CNN Factor" – so long absent from this brutal and forgotten war – kicked in.

In the end, the UN hostages were released, and the UN was given a stronger mandate. But in the process, Partnership Africa Canada's report, *The Heart of the Matter*, now five months old, found a new audience, and journalists had something other than Robert Kaplan's "The coming anarchy" to explain events. Sebastian Junger, author of the novel *The Perfect Storm*, understood the issue, and his story – a lengthy feature for *Vanity Fair* (2000) – highlighted RUF thuggery and the diamond issue. The August 2000 issue of *Vanity Fair*, with Junger's story, appeared in July, on the eve of the Antwerp World Diamond Congress. The Congress, a bi-annual gathering of the most important companies and individuals in the diamond world, was given over almost completely to the issue of conflict diamonds. There was concern that the conflict diamond issue now airing in the diamond heartland was getting completely out of control. The only thing worse would be a *60 Minutes* exposé. The NGO antagonists were invited to the World Diamond Congress, as was Robert Fowler. It was an interesting gathering, not least because NGOs were allowed into most of the meetings and were, despite the danger they represented, treated cordially. The diamond industry was moving rapidly from a position of denial to one of engagement. One of the outcomes of the congress was the creation of a World Diamond Council, representing a range of companies and nationalities, and designed to get a grip on the issue before it went any further.

By now, other NGOs had become involved. Fatal Transactions, based in the Netherlands, was formed by a coalition of five European NGOs to act as a focal point on the conflict diamond issue. Oxfam International had become involved and participated in the Antwerp meeting, as did Amnesty International and World Vision. Global Witness and PAC had done the research, understood the details and led in the discussions, but they were small organizations and didn't have name brand recognition. Oxfam, Amnesty and World Vision did, and their US representatives came with the backing of a growing coalition of European and American NGOs, including several church organizations. The head of one had suggested that if a boycott was wanted, he could activate the 30,000 ministers in his church – all of whom officiated over at least one wedding a week if not many more. They could discuss diamonds every Sunday until the industry did the right thing.

A boycott was what the industry feared most. Images of the earlier fur boycott loomed large in their thinking, and it was mentioned over and over during the World Diamond Congress. De Beers Chairman, Nicky Oppenheimer, spoke about how destructive a boycott would be, not just to a legitimate industry, but to an industry that provided jobs and income in countries untainted by conflict diamonds. Diamonds are a major part of the economies of South Africa, Namibia and Botswana. They are important to the economies of Russia and Australia; they are the largest economic force in Canada's Northwest Territories. And in India almost a million people work in the diamond cutting and polishing business. Nelson

Mandela made a speech in South Africa denouncing irresponsible talk about a boycott.

The boycott discussion was interesting, because it was only industry leaders and their surrogates who talked about it. NGOs rarely mentioned a boycott. First, they didn't have to; the industry was doing all the talking. Second, and more importantly, NGOs did understand the economic importance of diamonds, beyond the wars they fueled. The purpose of the growing campaign was never to hurt the industry: it was to stop conflict diamonds. That said, there would be several occasions in the long months ahead when NGOs would ask themselves whether negotiation was the right approach. They could not make an equation between Sierra Leonean lives and jobs in Namibia. For all NGOs, the industry could go straight to hell if, in the final analysis, the diamond wars did not stop. In an attempt to assess the developmental value of the diamond industry, Partnership Africa Canada released a report in 2002 entitled *Diamonds Forever or For Good?* (Hazleton 2002). The report was an investigation into the economic benefits of diamonds to the countries of Southern Africa. It found, in fact, that diamonds do not create more than about 30,000 jobs in the entire region, and that while they have been of special benefit to the economy of Botswana, 60 percent of that country's population still live on less than two dollars a day.

The key to the Kimberley Process, however, was not the diamond industry. A blanket intergovernmental agreement was the only real answer, backed by national legislation in the countries that produce and trade rough diamonds. Through the last half of 2000 and in 2001, the Kimberley Process gathered steam. It gathered steam, but the train did not leave the station. More and more governments joined the debate, realizing that their mining industry, or their processing or trade in diamonds, would be affected as the discussions focused more and more on a possible agreement aimed at solving the problem. As new governments arrived, the basic concept became more complicated. The core idea was that there should and could be a global certification system for all rough diamonds.[5] Under such a system, each diamond-producing country would undertake to ensure that no conflict diamonds entered the pipeline between the mine and the point of export. In other words, the government of producing countries would guarantee that its diamonds were conflict-free.

The second part of the emerging system related to the transportation of diamonds from one country to another. If an agreement could be reached, it would include provisions for standardized, tamper-proof parcels, to be accompanied by forgery-proof certificates. Advance information with all the details of each shipment would be transmitted from the exporter to the importer, and confirmation of receipt would be acknowledged by the importer back to the exporter. The third part of the system concerned countries like Belgium, Britain and Israel, where rough diamonds are sorted and many, if not most, are re-exported. How could there be any assurance that the re-exports were clean, when it was commonplace every year for smugglers to unload millions of dollars' worth of undeclared goods on Pelikanstraat or 47th Street with impunity?

Essential to a comprehensive agreement would be an undertaking by the governments of these countries to issue a re-export certificate ensuring that the diamonds were clean. The more difficult problem would be to ensure that the diamonds actually *would* be clean. A partial solution was offered by the diamond industry. The World Diamond Council offered to develop what it called a "chain of warranties" within the industry, which would require diamonds to be tracked, by value and weight, as they moved from one dealer to another. This would give the exporting authority the assurance that conflict diamonds had not entered and contaminated the system.

Many issues, of course, arose. Kimberley meetings were held in London, Brussels, Luanda, Pretoria, Moscow and Gaborone. They were two-day affairs which got bigger as time passed, losing the informality of the early events. Governments arrived with official statements professing gratitude at the wonderful hospitality of the host country and a determination to end the scourge of conflict diamonds forthwith. And then they would raise objections at virtually every turn. The conformity of the plan with WTO obligations became a major issue. The shape of the actual Kimberley Certificate and the font to be used in printing it occupied several hours during various plenaries. At one meeting there was a 90-minute debate on the wording of the final communiqué: had there been "significant progress" in the meeting, or just "an emerging consensus" about the design of the certificate? It turned out to be the latter.

In Gaborone, one session went on until after one in the morning, debating membership requirements. The United States and others wanted the system to be open to all countries that would comply with the minimum standards being developed. This would help to sidestep any WTO challenge that might use the restriction of trade as an argument. China said that it made no sense, given the history of diamonds, to allow any and all countries into the system without a discussion of their credentials. NGOs took the side of China, but understood that China was not talking about diamonds, it was talking about Taiwan. For almost a year thereafter, the Taiwan debate simmered, although the word Taiwan was never spoken in plenary. Taiwanese trade offices in London, Ottawa and Geneva lobbied NGOs, asking a pertinent question: if Taiwan – which has a small trade in rough diamonds – was kept out of the system, would a parallel and potentially counterproductive underground trade develop, defeating the purpose of the whole exercise? Taiwanese delegations traveled to the Ottawa meeting in March 2002 and the Interlaken meeting in November that year, but they were not seated because China threatened to walk out. Burkina Faso, however, which has no diamond trade beyond its sanctions-busting noted in the UN Security Council Report, was permitted to attend all meetings and to sign up to the Interlaken declaration. Liberia, whose diamonds had been banned by the Security Council after May 2001, was invited to send its Minister of Mines to the London meeting of September 2001 and to the Interlaken meeting. But Taiwan, a member of the WTO, was not permitted to participate.

NGO tactics and allies

The NGOs tried to steer clear of the Taiwan issue, but their role in other matters was critical. NGOs insisted that the issue of conflict diamonds was a security issue, not a trade issue, and that the 1994 General Agreement on Tariffs and Trade (GATT) contained appropriate human security provisions which supported the Kimberley Process. A lawyer hired by ActionAid to study GATT was the first to recognize this provision as a way forward, although some governments, notably Canada, the United States and Japan kept ringing the WTO bell throughout the process. Statistics were another stumbling block. Diamond production and trade statistics were notoriously unreliable, or simply non-existent. Without good statistics, however, a certification system could never hope to function effectively. At the Kimberley meeting in Moscow in July 2001, PAC presented a paper on the need for reliable diamond production and trade statistics, and this particular logjam finally started to break. But the greatest NGO contribution, perhaps, was the continuing pressure on governments and the industry to act quickly and decisively.

At the September 2001 meeting in London, NGOs presented a petition signed by over 200 civil society organizations in North America, Europe and Asia, demanding more decisive action. The document – first distributed in photocopy form because a printed version had not arrived – was quickly dismissed. When the final version arrived from the printers, however, in bright red with a 300 point headline – STOP BLOOD DIAMONDS NOW! – it created a considerable stir. Amnesty International mimicked a De Beers television advertisement, and placed a dramatic action cartoon on its website showing rebels hacking the hand off a civilian in order to get at diamonds. American NGOs worked with two dedicated Congressmen, Tony Hall, a Democrat, and Frank Wolf, a Republican, in sponsoring a congressional "Clean Diamond Bill" that would ban conflict diamonds from the United States. The US diamond jewelry industry, worried about the provisions of the bill but understanding the demand for better regulation, worked with a Senator, Judd Gregg, on softer legislation. In June 2001, World Vision bought some time as the credits were rolling on the last episode of the popular television program, *The West Wing*. In the program, Martin Sheen plays a likeable American President. The World Vision promo showed film of Sierra Leonean children without hands. The voice of Martin Sheen told viewers that diamonds were contributing to such atrocities, and if they wanted to stop them, they should ask their congressman to support the Hall/Wolf bill.

Within days the Gregg bill had disappeared, and the US industry made peace with the NGOs and the Clean Diamond Bill. NGOs worked the media. They worked closely with all the major international television networks; with national and international radio; with print journalists and the Internet. Feature articles appeared in *Esquire, National Geographic, USA Today,* the *New York Times, Der Spiegel* and *Jornal do Brazil.* Feature programs were shown on television in Britain, Canada, Japan and in the United States. *60 Minutes* (and *60 Minutes II*) finally did the story, working closely with NGOs on background material and giving them access to the cameras.

In addition to material about conflict diamonds produced for their supporters and the general public, NGOs also produced policy-related documents, opinion pieces and background research. Early in the debate Global Witness produced a detailed description of what a certification system might look like (Global Witness 2000). Partnership Africa Canada produced research papers on diamonds in Guinea, Canada and India. It produced a follow-up report on Sierra Leone which examined the role of the Lebanese diaspora in the illicit diamond trade, and it reviewed other international agreements for their provisions on monitoring.[6]

The NGO coalition was an interesting one. It was never a formal grouping; there were no regular meetings; no chair; no "members." There was no "leadership" as such, although because Global Witness and Partnership Africa Canada had dedicated resources and people for the issue, they tended to be more active and informed on day-to-day issues. Other key players were the British NGO ActionAid, Oxfam International, the Amsterdam-based Fatal Transactions, World Vision and Amnesty International. Important participants also included two African NGOs representing broad coalitions in their own countries: the Network Movement for Justice and Development in Sierra Leone, and CENADEP in the Democratic Republic of the Congo. This coalition was supported and backed by a loose grouping of 200 other NGOs around the world, including an important coalition of American NGOs. Altogether, it was an eclectic grouping: development and human rights NGOs; NGOs in the North and the South; very big NGOs and very small NGOs; faith-based NGOs and activist campaigning NGOs. While there were occasional disagreements over tactics, there was never anything like a dispute. Each organization carried out its own activities, but there was regular sharing of information by e-mail, frequent telephone conference calls, and meetings before and after each Kimberley session. The coalition's strength appeared to derive from its informality and the broad range of interests, and from a willingness to share, to listen and to cooperate when common stands were required.

The NGOs had four sets of allies through the Kimberley Process. The first was the diamond industry. The relationship was frequently adversarial, and the industry essentially wanted the NGOs to go away. But for this to happen, the NGOs would need to be satisfied that an effective agreement was in place. Although the industry balked and kicked at each NGO demand, there was little disagreement by the time of the Interlaken meeting. This, however, would not have been obvious to the casual observer. Only a week before Interlaken the diamond industry had held its second World Diamond Congress since the issue had emerged, this time in London. But this time the NGOs were not inside, they were outside demonstrating. A bomb threat cleared the building at one stage, and among the demonstrators was a remarkably good Marilyn Monroe lookalike and four actors in top hats and tails, acting out scenes from *Gentlemen Prefer Blondes*. A year earlier, NGOs had pressed the industry to ensure that its proposed "chain of warranties" would be open to public scrutiny, in the form of government-supervised audits. An initial refusal had given way to an agreement. But by the time of the London meeting, no details of this chain of warranties had been released. The Marilyn Monroe lookalike, in a tight red dress and long white gloves, was not demanding diamonds, she was demanding commercial transparency. A week later at Interlaken, outside the main Kimberley Process meeting, the NGOs and industry representatives had a private discussion, marked at first by shouting and recrimination, and then by a more reasoned discussion about how to carry remaining issues forward into 2003. The dynamic was an interesting one, because by then all the industry and NGO participants had struggled through a dozen Kimberley meetings together; all were on a first-name basis; and there were regular personal, phone and e-mail contacts between meetings. Although they were often at each others' throats, they shared a common interest: stopping conflict diamonds. And they shared common frustrations as well: government delegations at Kimberley meetings worrying tiny issues like terriers with bones, refusing to come to grips with substantive issues.

The second NGO ally was the United Nations. The first UN Expert Panel report on Angola in March 2000 had changed the nature of the debate. It was no longer "just" an NGO campaign; the Security Council itself now had its own study confirming what NGOs had said. Sanctions-busting governments were "named and shamed" (well, maybe not shamed, but at least embarrassed and annoyed). Other Expert Panels followed: Sierra Leone, the Democratic Republic of Congo, Liberia. These, and a continuing Angola panel issued several reports between 2000 and the end of 2002, confirming and reconfirming the connection between war, weapons and diamonds. Interestingly, all the panels took advice and information from NGOs, and NGO personnel were seconded to serve on some of them.[7] In December 2000 the UN General Assembly passed a unanimous resolution endorsing the Kimberley Process, urging it to reach an effective conclusion, and asking it to report back in a year. Once this happened, the Kimberley Process had a new form of legitimacy, and a time frame. This helped many of the participating delegations explain the urgency and the importance of the issue to their governments.

The third ally in the process, and perhaps the most important, was the government of South Africa. Without a governmental champion for the process, it would certainly have taken a very different turn in its early stages. In fact the thing most feared by the industry and South Africa – an NGO boycott – might well have come to pass, in the absence of any alternative. South Africa called the first Kimberley meeting, and it chaired the process throughout the following months. It gathered and disseminated information, it did the background preparations for all the meetings and hosted three itself. It was instrumental in getting the UN General Assembly Resolution drafted and passed, and when all about them were losing their heads – which happened on more than one occasion – the four South Africans, who had stayed with the process from its beginning, never once appeared to lose patience, interest or heart.

A fourth ally was a community of academics and research institutions that began to take an interest in the economics of civil war, just as the NGO campaign was gathering strength. The World Bank began a program to study the economics of civil wars, crime and violence in 1999. In 2000, the International Peace Academy published an edited volume on economic agendas in civil wars – *Greed and Grievance* (Berdal and Malone 2000) – drawing attention to the work of several academics on the generic issue. Informed by the NGO work on diamonds, these institutions and others helped to publicize the issue in new ways, and to new audiences. Throughout 2001 and 2002, across Europe, North America and Africa, there was a spate of academic conferences on the subject, at which NGO campaigners were invited to speak and present papers.

The agreement

In March 2002, a make-or-break Kimberley Meeting was held in Ottawa. Depending on who was counting, it was either the twelfth or thirteenth meeting in the series. Appropriately for the train station metaphor, the meeting was held in the Ottawa Congress Center, a converted railway station. As the hours passed most of the insoluble problems melted away, and by the end only one remained. NGOs had insisted from the outset that the system would only be credible and effective if there was regular, independent inspection of all national control systems. If all countries were eligible to join, there was an obligation that all be subject to regular inspection. Why would more rules be any more effective than the laws already in place against theft, murder, sanctions-busting and human rights abuse? The draft Kimberley agreement, however, left monitoring vaguely to decisions that would be made at annual plenary meetings, and then to take place only in cases of "indications of significant non-compliance."

For NGOs, regular independent monitoring was a fundamental requirement if the system was to be effective. And those NGOs present at the Ottawa meeting had to decide at the eleventh hour whether they would endorse the agreement as far as it had gone, or dig in. If they dug in, they feared that several delegations would withdraw from the process and the Kimberley Process might very well collapse. India, China, Russia and Israel had all spoken against regular monitoring. While some governments were favorably inclined, at least privately, none spoke in favor of the NGO position in the plenary discussions. The issue threatened to turn septic. NGOs held their ground against a withering attack from several governments. They were said to be bargaining in bad faith; they were called "deplorable" by one government delegation – oddly harsh language in a diplomatic forum where tempers never flared in public. The World Diamond Council pleaded for reconsideration. In the end, and without enthusiasm or even full agreement among themselves, the NGOs agreed to endorse the Kimberley system as developed to that point. They reserved the right to speak publicly about the monitoring issue, however, and they said that they would not let their concern drop as the system moved forward.

Between March and November 2002, governments worked to ensure that the required regulations, and, if necessary, legislation, would be in place to enable a launch of the Kimberley Process in January 2003. And they came together at Interlaken to review progress and tie up whatever loose ends might remain. On the opening day, the South African Chair asked each delegation whether or not it would be ready to implement on 1 January. There were more professions of gratitude for the wonderful hospitality offered by the host country, and more professions of concern that the scourge of conflict diamonds end once and for all. But there were also strong statements of readiness from most countries. There were a few holdouts – Japan and Thailand said they might be ready "later," not seeming to understand that if they were not in the system, their diamonds would be banned from world trade. Cyprus, Malta and Ukraine said they were working towards compliance as quickly as possible. Most of the others were, they said, ready, willing and able.

A few glitches remained. The system for gathering and monitoring statistics had still not been worked out, although this was expected to be in place before the end of the first quarter of 2003. Interestingly, NGOs present at the Interlaken meeting suggested that the responsibility be farmed out to the private sector through a public tender, as governments had proven incapable of coming to grips with the issue in more than a year. Some governments continued to mewl about the WTO and their desire to be in full compliance with GATT obligations, as though they had considered the GATT just as religiously when it came to steel, softwood lumber or farm subsidies (in the end, the WTO did give the Kimberley scheme an exemption, based on human security considerations). And of course, the major NGO concern remained regarding the lack of regular independent monitoring of all national control mechanisms.

These issues notwithstanding, several important changes took place in the diamond world on January 1, 2003. First, several countries that had been laundering diamonds were to be forced to stop immediately. These included Gambia, Zambia, Rwanda, Uganda and others. These countries, all entrepôts for conflict diamonds as well as the wider trade in illicit goods, represent more than a quarter of a billion dollars' worth of rough diamonds, if not more. Second, all Kimberley Process participating governments had to issue certificates of legitimacy for rough diamonds leaving their borders. Even if there was no clear monitoring process, they were now on record as authenticating their exports. In due course, inspection will come. If it is not formally agreed in the Kimberley Process, it will be done by NGOs, by journalists and by the Security Council in the form of continued Expert Panels. One way or the other, governments will be obliged to deal with the demand for public scrutiny on their diamond control systems. And third, diamond shipments that are not accompanied by the proper, standardized Kimberley Process documentation will be refused entry or seized. There is an old Mafia expression: "Punish one, teach many." This is not a million miles removed from standard judiciary-based ideas of crime and punishment. The diamond industry is relatively small; word travels fast. Many of those who bought conflict diamonds in the past did so out of ignorance or greed. Ignorance will no longer be an excuse. And greed will have to be weighed against possible consequences. Before 2003, there were none. After January 1, the possibility of losing a million dollar shipment entirely would have to be weighed against the $20,000 or $30,000 that might be gained by taking the risk.

For NGOs, the proof of the pudding will be in the tasting. They expected more bumps in the road as the agreement came on stream. They intended to participate actively in the Kimberley Process meetings as the system was rolled out. They intended to keep pressing for an appropriate monitoring system, and in its absence, Global Witness and Partnership Africa Canada planned a jointly operated pilot monitoring scheme of their own.

Senior industry representatives had said at the World Diamond Congress in October 2002 that the issue was an "extraneous" one. Several pointed to the end of the wars in Sierra Leone and Angola and asked why so many rules had to be developed for such a small and diminishing problem. The NGO response was loud and clear: the wars were not over. War continued in West Africa, lapping over the borders of Liberia, Guinea, Sierra Leone and Côte d'Ivoire, and diamonds continued to play a role. Conflict and resource plunder continued in the DRC. And while Angola had no war, equally there was no peace, and there would be none until the corruption of the diamond and oil industries was diminished in favor of investments to halt the starvation and underdevelopment that plagued so many hundreds of thousands of Angolans. This, in the end, will be the continuing challenge for the diamond industry, and for the governments that benefit from it: to ensure not only that conflict diamonds are halted, but that this enormous resource, which has caused so much death and destruction, is now used not just to enrich companies and government officials, but as a real resource for development.

This will be the enduring legacy of the conflict diamond debate: an insistence not just that diamonds do no harm, but that they actually do some good as well.

Notes

1 See *Afrique et Développement/Africa Development* (1997) XXII (3/4). The volume contains nine articles by Sierra Leonean scholars on the subject of "Lumpen culture and political violence: the Sierra Leone civil war."
2 The figure has dropped to approximately 60 percent in recent years.
3 Figures compiled from various reports of the Diamond High Council, Antwerp, and *Diamond Intelligence Briefs*, Tel Aviv.
4 The story of conflict diamonds in the DRC is detailed in Dietrich 2002.
5 Discussions about marking diamonds or in some way identifying their physical characteristics arose, but made little headway. Markings can be changed, copied or cut off a diamond, and the technology for physical 'fingerprinting' has not yet developed to a practical stage.
6 These reports are available from the Partnership Africa Canada website at http://www.pacweb.org/e/index.php?option=displaypage&Itemid=65&op=page&SubMenu=Conflict%20Diamonds
7 The author left his work with Partnership Africa Canada to serve for six months on the Sierra Leone Expert Panel in 2000. Other panels included individuals seconded from Human Rights Watch in London and the International Peace Information Service in Belgium.

Bibliography

Afrique et Développement/Africa Development (1997) "Lumpen culture and political violence: the Sierra Leone civil war," XXII (3/4).

Berdal, M. and Malone, D. (eds) (2000) *Greed and Grievance: economic agendas in civil wars*, Boulder, CO: Lynne Rienner.

Dietrich, C. (2002) *Hard Currency: the criminalized diamond economy of the Democratic Republic of the Congo and its neighbours*, Ottawa: Partnership Africa Canada.

Global Witness (2000) *Possibilities for the Identification, Certification and Control of Diamonds,* London: Global Witness.

—— (1998) *A Rough Trade*, London: Global Witness.

Hazleton, R. (2002) *Diamonds Forever or For Good? The economic impact of diamonds in Southern Africa*, Ottawa: Partnership Africa Canada.

Huntington, Samuel P. (1996) *The Clash of Civilizations: remaking the world order*, New York: Simon and Schuster.

—— (1993) "The clash of civilizations?" *Foreign Affairs* 72 (3): 22–49.

International Rescue Committee (2001) *Mortality in Eastern DRC: results from five mortality surveys*, Bukavu: IRC, May.

Junger, S. (2000) "The terror of Sierra Leone," *Vanity Fair*, August.

Kaplan, R. (1996) *The Ends of the Earth: a journey at the dawn of the 21st century,* New York: Random House.

—— (1994) "The coming anarchy," *Atlantic Monthly*, February.

Richards, P. (1996) *Fighting for the Rainforest: war, youth and resources in Sierra Leone*, Oxford and Portsmouth, NH: The International African Institute in Association with James Currey and Heinemann.

Roberts, L. *et al.* (2003) *Mortality in the DRC: results from a nationwide survey*, New York: International Rescue Committee, April.

Smillie, I., Gberie, L. and Hazleton, R. (2000) *The Heart of the Matter: Sierra Leone, diamonds and human security*, Ottawa: Partnership Africa Canada.

United Nations Security Council (2000) *Report of the Panel of Experts on Violations of Security Council Sanctions against UNITA,* March 10.

Index